Iraq's Armed Forces

This book provides the first comprehensive study of the evolution of the Iraqi military from the British mandate era to post-Baathist Iraq.

Ethnic and sectarian turmoil is endemic to Iraq, and its armed forces have been intertwined with its political affairs since their creation. This study illustrates how the relationship between the military and the political center in Iraq has evolved, with the military bringing about three regime changes in Iraq's history before being brought under control by Saddam Hussein, up until the 2003 war. The instability that followed is partly due to the failure to create a new military that does not threaten the region, yet is still strong enough to deter rival factions from armed conflict. The reconstitution of the armed forces will be a prerequisite for an American withdrawal from Iraq, but this book argues that immense challenges lie ahead, despite the praise from the Bush administration for the progress of the new Iraqi Army.

This book will be of great interest to students of Middle East studies, military and strategic studies, and contemporary history.

Ibrahim Al-Marashi is a visiting scholar at the Annenberg School for Communication at the University of Pennsylvania. **Sammy Salama** is a Middle East expert with the Monterey Institute of International Studies, California.

Series: Middle Eastern military studies
Series editor: Barry Rubin
Interdisciplinary Center Herzliya, Israel

Iraq's Armed Forces

An analytical history

Ibrahim Al-Marashi and Sammy Salama

Routledge
Taylor & Francis Group

LONDON AND NEW YORK

First published 2008
by Routledge
2 Park Square, Milton Park, Abingdon, Oxon OX14 4RN

Simultaneously published in the USA and Canada
by Routledge
270 Madison Ave, New York, NY 10016

Routledge is an imprint of the Taylor & Francis Group, an informa business

Transferred to Digital Printing 2009

© 2008 Ibrahim Al-Marashi and Sammy Salama

Typeset in Sabon by Wearset Ltd, Boldon, Tyne and Wear

British Library Cataloguing in Publication Data
A catalogue record for this book is available from the British Library

Library of Congress Cataloging in Publication Data
A catalog record for this book has been requested

ISBN10: 0-415-40078-3 (hbk)
ISBN10: 0-415-56023-3 (pbk)
ISBN10: 0-203-92876-8 (ebk)

ISBN13: 978-0-415-40078-7 (hbk)
ISBN13: 978-0-415-56023-8 (pbk)
ISBN13: 978-0-203-92876-9 (ebk)

Contents

Illustrations

Maps

Tables

Preface

As an Iraqi-American my relationship with the Iraqi military was an unconventional one. I grew up with stories of my mother's uncle who served in the Iraqi military of the 1960s. She would proudly remember his arrival to her home upon taking leave from his post at the Habbaniyya air base near Falluja. She would recall the way his crisp pale green military uniform made him seem even taller, the way he would turn on the radio and dance for her and her sisters in spite of his snug-fitting jacket. The Iraqi military of Baathist Iraq was a different story however. It was this military that some of my relatives fled Iraq to escape military service and others were compelled to join only never to return from the front. It was a military I grew up learning about as a young child, piecing together an image of the Iraqi armed forces from the news coverage of the Iran–Iraq War that my father watched on our wooden paneled TV. It was a military I watched as a teenager during the 1991 Gulf War on the same outdated wooden paneled TV.

It was not until I became a Ph.D. student, that my relationship with the Iraqi military changed. When part of my research on Iraq's security forces was plagiarized by the British government prior to the 2003 Iraq War, I went from watching the news on military affairs on Iraq to being part of this news. As the story about my article circulated, I joined the throngs of news pundits commenting on the Iraqi military. Looking back at those transcripts of my media appearances, where I discussed topics such as the "elite Republican Guards," I wondered if I really contributed to the public's knowledge of the Iraqi military, or just added to the sound bites that made up the terminological fog that pundits and government officials alike produce during war time.

During my first trip to Iraq in 2004, I first came face-to-face with the final remains of Iraq's armed forces. In my unpublished memoir of growing up as an Iraqi-American I describe my first experience of meeting unemployed officers from the former Iraqi military struggling to survive in the "new Iraq," or passing by a row of destroyed tanks on the way to Basra. Years after the 2003 Iraq War, I still have an attachment to the Iraqi military, but not as a confused child, nor as a media pundit, but merely as a concerned Iraqi who wonders if the new Iraqi Army can keep my ancestral home together.

For the last five years my co-author Sammy Salama and I have been scouring through literally thousands of documents produced by the Iraqi military dating back to the Iran–Iraq War. These files have emerged from a variety of sources. Some were given to us directly by acquaintances who served in the Iraqi military. These documents ranged from the books they used in military school to their discharge papers. Some of the Iraqi military documents were also made public by an archive at Harvard University. Those documents provided an unprecedented insight into the internal workings of Saddam Hussein's Iraq, and a window into the machinations of how the Baath Party managed the Iraqi military. When compiling the research for this history, I hoped to use this material, interspersed with oral histories of former Iraqi soldiers and officers. The study of the Iraqi documents and the interviews yielded enough material to serve as their own work, which will be published in the future. Nevertheless, having examined these sources, they helped us gain a perspective of what it would have been like to be a soldier on the front lines or one of the privileged elite officers in the Republican Guards.

As a historian of Iraq, I had hoped that after the 2003 Iraq War I would be able to conduct archival research in Baghdad for this book. Unfortunately most of Iraq's archives were damaged after the war, denying me opportunity of delving into my country's past. Researching the Iraqi military was also hampered by more mundane constraints, such as border crossings. My efforts during a visit to Iraq to take a suitcase filled with books by Iraqi authors on the military were thwarted as some of the material was considered sensitive to the country I was entering and was confiscated at the border post. Thus, the history of the Iraqi military now lies in London. Most of the material on the Iraqi military during the mandate era and the 1950s and 1960s can be found in the libraries of the School of Oriental and African Studies and Oxford's Middle East Centre and in Kew's Public Record Office. Fortunately, other British archives can be also accessed via electronic data bases made available by the UPA Collections offered through Lexis Nexis and Thomson Gale Middle East Online Series, ensuring that at least some parts of Iraq's history cannot be damaged by the ravages of war.

We hope that this volume will contribute to a greater understanding of the military that endured the longest war of the twentieth century (the Iran–Iraq War) and fought the world's superpower on two separate occasions, and whose future survival in the twenty-first century remains in question.

Ibrahim Al-Marashi

Acknowledgments

Our thanks are due to many people who helped us prepare this book. Ali Allawi, a former fellow at Oxford University and the interim Defense Minister in Iraq in 2004 also provided us with research advice on the Iraqi military. Foulath Hadid, a Fellow at St. Antony's College in Oxford recommended to us valuable primary material for this study. Eugene Rogan, Director of the Middle East Centre at Oxford has always been a valuable mentor and the Centre's library, with its archives of primary material on Iraq, proved invaluable for the research.

Charles Tripp of the Politics Department of the School for Oriental and African Studies (SOAS) in London gave me valuable advice on this topic, and his research into Iraq provided the foundations for our study. He also helped us to access the SOAS Library, which has a vast store of memoirs from prominent military personalities in Iraq.

We would like to thank Toby Dodge who introduced us to the valuable documents dealing with Iraq in the Public Records Office (PRO). Brandon Wolfe-Hunnicut, a history Ph.D. student at Stanford University, aided us with the research of the British archives dealing with Iraq. An Elie Kedourie Grant from the British Academy supported our research in the PRO. We hope that this book will honor the memory of Kedourie who also worked on Iraq.

Anthony Cordesman of the Center for Strategic and International Studies has analyzed the Iraqi military in detail since the Iran–Iraq War and was kind enough to regularly e-mail us his ongoing research into the new Iraqi Army. Ahmad Hashim also shared his research with the authors and advised us on finding primary and secondary materials for the book. Hala Al-Fatah, Peter Sluglett, Faleh Abd Al-Jabar and Sami Zubaida gave us valuable critiques when I began writing this book three years ago.

The daring journalist Nir Rosen gathered documents and books for the authors during his many visits to Iraq. We are also grateful to Zeyad Kasim, the dedicated Iraqi blogger, who allowed us to use his maps.

We are also indebted to the research assistants who helped us collect documents for this study. In Istanbul, my students Berk Esen and Gonca Alp at Sabanci University, and Senay Yegin and Asena Yavuz at Koc

University provided their time to help with conducting research errands for this book. Cameron Hunter, at the Monterey Institute of International Studies, also helped with the research and editing. We would also like to thank the series editor, Barry Rubin, and the editors at Routledge and Wearset, Andrew Humphrys, Kelly Alderson and Sally Quinn, for their patience during the writing and editing process.

Ibrahim Al-Marashi is indebted to his sister for reading over the text. As a creative writer she helped massaging the passages into a language that could be made accessible for those who do not have a military background. He is grateful to Dean Ahmet Alkan of Sabanci University in Istanbul for arranging a post-doctoral fellowship to allow time for the research and writing of the book. He would also like to thank his parents, who arranged interview opportunities with former members of the Iraqi military in the US and UK. To those soldiers who served in the former and current Iraqi armed forces, I would like to thank them for their time to meet me in Baghdad to discuss their often painful and sometimes proud moments in the military. Most of you that I interviewed were engineers, medical doctors or logistic managers, who were never comfortable holding a rifle. Your services could have been a great value to Iraq had you not been made redundant after 2003. The last time I spoke to you was three years ago. For those of you still in Iraq, we pray that you remain safe.

Istanbul and Monterey, California
August 2007

Notes on transliteration

In our transliteration of Arabic terms and names we tried to maintain faithful to the system used by the *International Journal of Middle East Studies* and the *Encyclopedia of Islam*, with a few modifications.

For the few Persian and Turkish names, we have used the transliteration system according to those languages, so that names such as "Rida" in Arabic become "Reza" in Persian or "Kamal" becomes "Kemal" in Turkish.

Instead of using the diacritical marks to represent the letter *'ayn* we have used a double "a." For example, Ja'far al-'Askari would be written as Jaafar Al-Askari. Only when providing direct Arabic transliterations have we used the diacritical mark for the letter *'ayn*, such as Military Intelligence (*Al-Istikhbarat Al-'Askariyya*).

For other names such as "Faisal" or spelled "Feisal," we used the spelling "Faysal." For the sake of conformity with the mainstream media we have spelled the former Iraqi leader as "Saddam Hussein" although the transliteration "Husayn" is used for other figures with this name.

Abbreviations

AMS	Association of Muslim Scholars
AWAC	Airborne Warning And Control
CPA	Coalition Provisional Authority
DBE	Department of Border Enforcement
FPS	Facilities Protection Service
ICDC	Iraqi Civil Defense Corps
IGC	Iraqi Governing Council
KDP	Kurdish Democratic Party
KRG	Kurdistan Regional Government
MNTSC	Multi National Transitional Security Command
NDP	National Democratic Party
ORHA	Office of Reconstruction and Humanitarian Assistance
PUK	Patriotic Union of Kurdistan
RAF	Royal Air Force
RCC	Revolutionary Command Council
RIAF	Royal Iraqi Air Force
SCIRI	Supreme Council for the Islamic Revolution in Iraq
UAR	United Arab Republic

1   Introduction

"We could not withdraw at once and leave chaos. There we were, and there we had to remain and to administer, for the time being at any rate."

Those words may sound like a Bush administration official discussing the situation in Iraq in 2007, as the debate for an American troop withdrawal increased with intensity. However they were uttered in 1924 by B.H. Bourdillon, a counselor and advisor to the office of the British High Commissioner in Iraq (Bourdillon 1924: 277). The British High Commissioner was analogous to the US Coalition Provisional Authority (CPA), both institutions designed to rule Iraq after a war and both having veto powers in regards to Iraqi political affairs. While the old adage that those who cannot learn from history are doomed to repeat it may be trite, in the case of the US and the new Iraqi military, it is also startlingly accurate. The United States' hopes that the Iraqi military would be the savior of the "new Iraq" were the same hopes that the British had for the Iraqi military they created in 1921 during the mandate. Just as the American and the Iraqi security forces had met with resistance, the British presence in Iraq was also troubled by a similar insurgency. In fact, the term "insurgent" was also used in the 1920s to describe those who opposed the political center in Baghdad with violence. The British and the Iraqi military dealt with such insurgencies on and off for fifteen years. At the time of this publication, US and Iraqi forces had been dealing with an insurgency that began just four years ago and whose duration is still unknown. The ethnic and sectarian divisions between Shia, Sunnis and Kurds plaguing the American trained Iraqi military are by no means new. British officials dealing with Iraq complained about this very same phenomenon in the Iraqi military of the 1920s and 1930s in their correspondence with the Colonial Office and then Foreign Office in London. Years ago in Britain, the taxpayer public was concerned about the growing costs of suppressing an insurgency, or as Bourdillon stated, money "pouring into the sands of Iraq," just as there were similar concerns expressed domestically in the US after 2003. The hope in 1924, as it was after the 2003 Iraq War was that their troops could leave, and their role be replaced by an expanding Iraqi military. However, the formation of an Iraqi military was a daunting task in the 1920s, as it proved to be at the turn of the twenty-first century.

Introducing the Iraqi military

This work gives a military-centric view of Iraq's history. Despite the importance of the military in Iraq, there is not a single book in the literature that covers the Iraqi military from its creation to its demise and ultimately, its painful rebirth. The Iraqi military has been perhaps the most scrutinized armed force in the world. With the invasion of Kuwait in 1991, it came to the attention of the international community that the Iraqi military numbered close to one million men under arms, making it the largest conventional armed force in the Middle East. During the 1991 Gulf Crisis, the mainstream media depicted the Iraqi military as a leviathan threatening the region with its vast forces capable of overrunning the oil resources in neighboring Saudi Arabia. The Iraqi military was trumpeted during the Iran–Iraq War as well as the Kuwait crisis as a "Sword of the Arabs," poised to defend the Arab nation from the threats emanating from an anomalous alliance between Iran, Israel and the US. During the 2003 war, the international media continued to frame the Iraqi military as a formidable foe highlighting the threat posed by elite Republican Guards and the emergence of a new tenacious fighting force, the Fidayin Saddam. However, within the span of three weeks, "The Arab Sword" collapsed in the face of a military invasion, demonstrating for the second time that the Iraqi military was essentially a paper tiger.

As the US and UK became mired in the reconstruction of post-Baathist Iraq, the reconstitution of the Iraqi armed forces seemed a prerequisite for an American withdrawal from Iraq. After the 2003 Iraq War, Bush administration officials, as well as the international media cast the military as Iraq's savior; as the sole force that could secure the nation's future in the shadow of a growing insurgent threat. While this administration praised the progress of the new Iraqi Army, immense challenges lay ahead, as these forces were being built essentially from "scratch," and at the same time were divided by ethnic and sectarian identities within themselves.

The Iraqi military was one of the first institutions created in Iraq, and its importance for comprehending the development and current dynamics of the Iraqi state must be stressed. Created in 1921, the military served Iraq uninterrupted for eighty-two years until its disbandment by the CPA after the 2003 Iraq War. All of Iraq's governments had sought to use the military as a means to buttress their own legitimacy. At the same time the military clashed with governments as it would often have differing visions of their nation, its corporate future and the role Iraq itself should play in the Arab world. There emerged a symbiotic relationship between the Iraqi government and the military. They both used each other and needed each other. Since the creation of Iraq, a dominant feature of its political process has been the military's attempts to control the fate and identity of the nation. While the military was one of Iraq's oldest institutions, it hardly contributed to its stability, interfering in its political development on numerous occasions by either dictating the formation of a government or overthrowing it all together.

Iraq's military was not a monolithic entity. The reasons for the omnipresent threat of military intervention and unstable civil–military dynamics in Iraq were related to the politicized officers in the armed forces, the first being ex-Ottoman officers. They were followed by junior officers and soldiers within the Iraqi military, a body that was by no means impervious to various ideological currents coursing through Europe, the Arab world and Iraq itself. The military was never unified ideologically, but rather was divided by nodes of power based on personal ambition, ideological or ethno-sectarian interests. Any government in Baghdad had to be weary of the ideological currents and socio-economic cleavages running through the military, particularly the officer corps. The divisions were based on generations, class, religious and ethnic differences in the Iraqi military, a reflection of Iraq's society itself. In spite of these differences, throughout Iraq's political development, the Iraqi military prided itself on being a pillar of national security and unity, albeit at the helm of a predominantly Sunni Arab officer corps. Nevertheless, even the Sunni dominated officer corps was riddled with factions maneuvering to seize power for themselves, hence the constant regime changes in Iraq's history.

Despite the tumultuous military history of Iraq, there are some consistent trends in the relationship between the Iraqi armed forces and the political center. Historically, the Iraqi military maintained internal security in Iraq, policing the threats posed by tribal uprisings, sectarian revolts and Kurdish militias. Unlike conventional militaries confined to barracks and prepared to defend their nation's interest in the face of external threats, the Iraqi military served as an institution of domestic security, helping the state secure legitimacy through a gun barrel. In this capacity, the military became a central institution in domestic politics and instrument of repression that increased with intensity the accession of power of Saddam Hussein.

Even as the military maintained internal security, it was also a persistent threat to the governments of Iraq, whether it was the monarchy, the officers ruling Iraq from 1958 to 1968 or the civilian rule of the Baath party. The Iraqi military has always constituted a double-edged sword: the government ensured that the priority of the military was to protect the regime in power, but at the same time the military was a threat to that very power itself. Military intervention, until 1968 when the Baathists took and held power, was the ultimate arbiter of Iraq's divisive politics.

Analyzing militaries

The typologies of civil–military relations are categorically based on Eric Nordlinger's *Soldiers in Politics, Military Coups and Governments* (1977: 10–18) and Morris Janowitz's *Military Institutions and Coercion in the Developing Nations* (1977: 79–80). Models of civil–military relations are usually divided into two categories: non-praetorian and praetorian systems. In non-praetorian regimes, civilians control the military and the military does not have absolute independent political power from the civilian government. According to William Hale's work on the Turkish military, praetorianism can be defined as "situations in which the military, specifically, exercises independent political power, either by using force or by threatening to do so" (Hale 1994: 305). Samuel Huntington in his early work on civil–military relations described praetorianism as a system that allows for the dominant role of the military as a political institution. The military assumes a dominant role in a political system that is characterized by weak civilian institutions, which lack a developed level of political institutionalization that can manage political action in a stable process (1968: 194–5). Nordlinger defined the praetorians as "interventionist officers," who are the "major or predominant political actors by virtue of their actual or threatened use of force" (1977: 2). Without a system that can manage political action in a stable process, the military thrives as the arbiter of the political process. The process of praetorianism changes governments by coups rather than through elections or other standard procedures: "They intervene in politics when relying upon their control over the enlisted men who actually wield the guns, tanks, and planes in order to influence governmental decisions or occupy the seat of government themselves" (ibid.: 3).

Praetorianism in the military emerges when elements among the officer corps have certain demands and threaten to carry out a coup if they are not met. If a coup is carried out, the officers have the option of replacing civilian government with other civilians. These coups have been referred to as "displacement coups" or "palace revolutions," changing the civilian make-up of the government. After a coup praetorians can take direct control of the government, transforming a civilian government into a military one. Even though civilians may make up part of the military government, the officers or an officer hold most of the power. At this point, the praetorians return to the barracks once they have rearranged the political system to their liking, or continue to rule indefinitely. Before discussing these various types of praetorian systems, we will define non-praetorianism to demonstrate the differences between the two.

Non-praetorian systems

The colonial army

Janowitz describes the "colonial army" role in maintaining domestic order and internal security in various European colonies (1965: 10). The colonial army contrasts with a "liberation army" and a "post-independence army." For example, France developed a military in its Algeria colony, led by French officers but manned by Algerians, which ultimately came in conflict with an Algerian liberation army, the National Front for Liberation (FLN). After Algeria's independence, this liberation army then evolved into a post-independence army. The Indian military was a colonial army that emerged under a long British colonial tradition, while the Iraqi Army developed out of a short indirect colonial experience that lasted more than ten years under the British mandate. However, the experiences of the Indian and Iraqi militaries were quite different and hence the need for a hybrid model, which we refer to as a "mandate army."

The liberal-democratic army

A "liberal-democratic army" model describes civil–military relations in liberal democracies where civilians are in control of a de-politicized military, particularly in determining its budget and internal structure. A civilian ethic is a crucial component of this relationship where the military customarily acquiesces to civilian government policies even if the military leadership may disagree with those policies (Nordlinger 1977: 10).

The totalitarian-penetration army

Unlike the liberal-democratic model, the "totalitarian-penetration army" describes a relationship where a single ruling party has indoctrinated the military to a point where it becomes an ideological military or a military of the ruling party. In this case the party controls the armed forces and not vice versa. Political conformity is rewarded and regarded as the basis for promotions rather than military acumen in the field. Party members are assigned to various military units as a way to monitor the armed forces. The ruling party often establishes paramilitary forces loyal to the party, or elite military units to rival and check the regular army. Then, secret police and military intelligence agencies monitor these various factions of the armed forces. This relationship existed in Communist USSR and China, and as we will argue, Baathist Iraq.

Praetorian systems

The moderator/veto army

Three types of militaries are identified in praetorian systems, based on their aims in the political process and how they legitimize their right to intervene in politics. The first typology, the "moderator," "arbiter" or "veto army regime," occurs when the military does not seize power directly, but rather has the power to veto actions, policies and decisions taken by the incumbent government. Civilian politicians remain in power and civil executive and legislative institutions continue to exist, however their actions have to meet the approval of the military, or in some cases the military dictates their policies. Moderator regimes are usually conservative and challenge any governmental decision that may threaten the military's interests or what it deems the status quo. In this case the military carries out "displacement coups," used to describe civilian governments being removed and replaced by governments friendlier to the military establishment.

The guardian army

In a "guardian army regime," military officers take power for themselves, but only for a limited period of time, usually a couple of years, such as those that emerged in Turkey from 1960 to 1961, 1971 to 1973 and 1980 to 1983. In these cases the military seeks to re-establish "order" out of the "chaos" civilian politicians have created, and it usually promises to return to the barracks once they have created the conditions that would prevent a return to the prior instability. As in the Turkish case, the military supervises the creation of a new constitution that seeks to remedy what it perceives as the "mistakes" of the past, and once it is confident that the political process has been stabilized, the military hands over power to a civilian government.

The ruler army

In "ruler army regimes," the military seeks to exercise direct power for an indefinite period of time. Unlike the moderator army or the guardian army, the officers in such regimes have wide ranging ambitions, and rule in the name of a revolution or radical modernization. These regimes usually seek authoritarian control over the political system. As Hale wrote, "They thus try to achieve not just control of the government, but complete regime dominance, including a high degree of penetration and mobilization of the society from above" (Hale 1994: 310). A military leader or leaders control the executive and seek revolutionary changes in the political system by overthrowing a monarchy, a civilian prime minister or president, or another general for that matter. The ruler regimes usually initiate sweeping economic and social changes that can include nationalization programs and land reform.

Analyzing the Iraqi military

As this book is a history of the Iraqi armed forces, it delineates the turning points in its development from a military-centric point of view. The typologies to analyze the development of the Iraqi military and its role in Iraqi politics come from a combination of these models.

The Iraqi military was created in 1921 during the British mandate of Iraq, hence the title of Part I, "The mandate army." Rather than using Janowitz's term the "colonial army," the mandate was a system of indirect control, where the British had the ultimate say in how the Iraqi military developed. This Part includes the chapter entitled, "Creation, conscription, and cohesion" that describes this period from 1921 to 1936. It deals with the creation of the Iraqi military during the British mandate, the subsequent Iraqi government policy of nationwide conscription and the Iraqi political elite's efforts to use the armed forces as a tool of national cohesion. The military, it was hoped, would incorporate Iraq's various communities into a single, national institution that would transcend ethnic, religious and sectarian differences, albeit with a Sunni dominated officer corps.

From 1936 to 1968, the Iraqi military's role in politics falls under the rubric of praetorian regimes. Praetorianism is crucial for Iraq as it would prove to be an enduring symptom of Iraqi politics from 1936 to 1941 and from 1958 to 1968. During these years Iraqi civilian institutions were weak and the armed forces played a prominent role in the political process. Hence Part II is entitled "Praetorian Iraq." This Part includes Chapter 3, "The military moderator regimes," which discusses the period from 1936 to the 1941 Anglo-Iraqi War. The Iraqi military after the nation's independence in 1932 emerged strong enough to dictate government affairs. As the military began to expand, so did the number of factions within it. The military's foray into politics began with the rise of General Bakr Sidqi, who launched a coup in 1936. Rather than dismantling the monarchy, a clique of pan-Arabist officers from 1936 to 1941 was involved in politics behind the scenes, vetoing threatening policies made by civilian leaders. This trend was reversed after the British military intervened to overthrow a pro-German premier who had the backing of various elements in Iraq's armed forces. Chapter 4, "Dismantling the military moderator regime," deals with the dynamics of removing the military from politics, or the de-praetorianization of the Iraqi Army. After the British intervention in 1941, the military factions dictating politics were purged from the armed forces. Despite these purges, elements opposed to the monarchy continued to thrive in Iraq's military and society as a whole and would re-emerge in 1958 when a military coup cum revolution ended the monarchy. Chapter 5, "military coups and the ruler regimes" deals with praetorian ruler regimes that ruled Iraq directly. It covers the period from 1958 to 1968 and three military-led coups that caused abrupt changes in Iraqi leadership. These changes included the 1958 coup that brought to power General Abd Al-Karim Qasim and led to the formation of the Republic of Iraq, the coup of 1963 that brought down his administration and the military coup of 1968 that witnessed the rise of the Baath Party.

From 1968 to 2003 the Iraqi military was subordinated under the Baath Party and followed the totalitarian regime model. Part III, "The totalitarian military," analyzes the Baath Party's indoctrination and subordination of the Iraqi armed forces. Chapter 6 covers the period of 1968 to 1980, "The Baathification of the military." The Baath Party came to power in 1968, but it took several years to gain control over the military. As of 1973, the Baathists were in firm control of the Ministry of Defense and the Republican Guards brigade. By 1975 the Baath under General Hasan Al-Bakr and Saddam Hussein deemed the process of Baathifying the military a success and began a massive increase in troop size and acquisition of foreign military equipment. By this juncture the Iraqi leadership felt confident it could strengthen the armed forces that in turn would not threaten the regime as long as the government was constantly vigilant of the Iraqi Army. The growth of the military would give Iraq enough strength to conduct an offensive operation in 1980 against the Islamic Republic of Iran, a country Hussein considered a threat to his rule after he assumed the presidency in 1979. Chapter 7, "The totalitarian military and the Iran–Iraq War 1980–1984" describes the strategies of the Iraqi leadership that sought to control the military during the first four years of the war. Chapter 8, "The reassertion of the Iraqi officers 1984–1988," analyzes a parallel trend where the Iraqi officers sought to limit the political interference of the leadership in the conduct of the war. While Hussein eventually refrained from personally managing the war, he still maintained the totalitarian structures that prevented a coup from emerging within the armed forces. Chapter 9, "Wars, coups, sanctions, and collapse," covers the period from 1988 to 2003 and the slow demise of the totalitarian military. From 1988 to 1991 the Iraqi leadership feared that the military might emerge during the post-war peace as a threat to the government. Hussein's deployment of the military in another foreign campaign has been analyzed as a means to defuse such a threat and one of his reasons for invading Kuwait in August 1990. The ensuing Gulf War proved to be a disaster for the Iraqi military, although elements like the Republican Guard emerged relatively unscathed. From 1991 to 2003 the military was reorganized and witnessed the rise of new institutions created within the armed forces, such as the Special Republican Guards and Fidayin Saddam and how they thwarted attempted coups during this period. The chapter concludes with an assessment of the performance of the Iraqi military in the 2003 Iraq War.

The formation of a new Iraqi military under Coalition, and more accurately American auspices, closely resembled that of the creation of the Iraqi military under the British mandate. After its creation in 1921, and its disbandment and recreation in 2003, the Iraqi military was hardly a sovereign institution. At both times, this institution was created by foreign powers. In both periods, its arms and training came from these foreign powers, and they, not the Iraqis in power, decided the scope, size and mission of the Iraqi military. In both cases, the growing Iraqi military worked in conjunction with these foreign militaries. Thus, Part IV is entitled "The mandate army redux," and Chapter 10, "The US and the Iraqi Army" examines the aftermath of the 2003 Iraq War, and how the disbandment of the Iraqi military resulted in Iraq's loss of the institution that symbolized its national unity, which further emboldened a growing insurgency. The post-war insecurity in Iraq can be attributed to the failure to create a new military that does not serve as a threat to a future government or the region but is strong enough to deter rival internal factions in Iraq.

The aforementioned models support the argument that the history of the Iraqi military has come full circle. In 1921 the Army was established in a state with weak democratic institutions during a period of civil internal conflict. The destiny of the nation, as well as the Army, was deemed by the Iraqi public as being controlled by a foreign power that sought to exploit its natural resources. As a nationalist backlash, the public projected its aspirations for complete independence on the Army. In order to achieve this independence, that military revolted, and decided to run government affairs, and discovered that control of the state allowed the Army to strengthen its size, armaments and rent seeking abilities within the nation. Eventually the Army became the government itself. Other military men, jealous of the ruling officers, realized that their ambitions for wealth and power could also be achieved if they launched a coup. Thus the military regime became a contested military regime, with officers constantly jostling for power. In this chaos of constant military turnovers, only an authoritarian party that established a totalitarian system was able to bring stability to civil–military relations. A coup-proof system was gradually created preventing the possibility of a military coup. All military coups against this regime failed and it was the Anglo-American invasion of 2003 that finally undermined the totalitarian system. After 2003 an army was re-established in a state with weak democratic institutions during a period of civil internal conflict, and a foreign power controlled its destiny.

The personalities involved in this cyclical history of Iraq's military are numerous and their names often resemble each other, especially when Saddam Hussein Al-Takriti came to power, and most every officer had the last name "Al-Takriti." Charts of prominent officers as well as an appendix (Table A.1) in the back of this book can help the reader make sense of the various figures in this history, as well as its numerous coups. It is also important to address specific terminology when referring to the Iraqi state and the military. In any conflict, a language of power emerges used to vilify the "enemy." The tendency is by no means new to Iraq. During World War I, the "Ottoman Army" was often referred to in Western media or academia as the "Turkish Army" or just the "Turks," denying that Arabs and other ethnicities filled its ranks. During more recent conflicts "Saddam" has been employed as a menacing single word concept in public discourse and in the media, and even the authors had adopted this terminology in their past works. Granted, Saddam Hussein committed horrific acts against his people and his neighbors. Yet other Middle Eastern leaders, such as Hafiz Al-Asad or Husni Mubarak were never referred to as simply "Hafiz" or "Husni' in the media. Furthermore, "Saddam's regime" is often used to demonize his government, without an explanation of the make-up of such a regime. In this history we use the term as it fits in with the terminology on civil–military relations. The reference to the "Iraqi leadership" in the 1979 to 2003 period includes the Iraqi President Saddam Hussein, the political insiders from his hometown and tribe, the members of the Revolutionary Command Council and the highest echelons of the Baath Party, which also included a select few generals. References to the "armed forces," "security forces" or "the military" in the Baathist era, include all of Iraq's armed services, in addition to the Republican Guard, Saddam's Fidayin, the Special Republican Guards, the Popular Army and the military units attached to the intelligence agencies. However, a reference to the Iraqi "Army," specifically signifies the Army that was founded in 1921. The Army, along with the Navy and Air Force were subordinated under the Iraqi Ministry of Defense, unlike the Republican Guard and other anti-armies, which reported directly to the presidency. After 2003 the failure to differentiate between these terms had drastic consequences for the Iraqi nation.

Part I
The mandate army

2 Creation, conscription and cohesion 1921–1936

Defining the mandate military

Janowitz classified the colonial military according to the history and circumstances in which it emerged. Some militaries emerged in countries that did not experience direct colonial rule where the armed forces evolved out of a process of local elites reforming their traditional armies. The Turkish armed forces, reformed from a defeated Ottoman military, would be classified as a "non-colonial military force." Most of the armies that emerged in the Middle East could either be categorized as "ex-colonial armed forces" or "post-liberation armies" established after a national liberation struggle for independence.

The British policy towards its colonial armies generally consisted of training a group of indigenous officers from the colony in modern military techniques. By the time of independence, these former colonies would have a local officer corps who could assume command of the ex-colonial military. However, in Jordan and Iraq, the British exercised a unique indirect system of rule through the post-World War I mandate system, resulting in ex-colonial armies emerging with a different character. Janowitz wrote: "As a result, the professional standards were often relatively low and the officer corps was often enmeshed in the politics of traditional groups, as in, e.g., Syria and Iraq" (Janowitz 1997: 90). He noted that these types of militaries emerged after their national independence with lesser degrees of professionalism, lacking internal cohesion and slow to adopt "Western military values" such as a tradition of public service. However, Janowitz does not define a specific term to classify this type of army, hence the title that the authors have appropriated, the "mandate army."

In Daniel Yergin's comprehensive work on the oil industry he wrote: "For the British government had a most uneasy relationship with the regime it had recently established in Iraq. The two parties could not even agree on what the word 'mandate' meant" (Yergin 1991: 200). Indeed one of the contentious issues over the terms of the mandate was the scope and mission of the Iraqi military. London had envisioned the Iraqi Army as a small voluntary force built along British lines to secure its strategic interests. The Iraqi government envisioned a large conscripted military uniting the disparate communities in a cohesive national institution. The Iraqi goals for its military did not necessarily conform to British goals, leading to a clash between the two that would continue even after the termination of the mandate and Iraq's subsequent independence.

The Ottoman background of Iraq's first officers

In the Ottoman Empire, most of Iraq's first army officers came from lower-middle class Sunni Arab and Kurdish families. They began their education at the military Rashidiyya school in Baghdad, established by Midhat Pasha, a reformist Ottoman governor, or in Istanbul itself in the Harbiye Military Academy. Studying at the military academies provided the only opportunities for higher education for these students, since the expenses were covered by the Ottoman treasury. The Arab Shia's historic apathy towards the Ottoman military meant that they rarely sent their sons to study at these institutions due to their disdain of Ottoman Sunni education. They tended to become merchants and traders as a means of social mobility (Marr 1970: 289).

These Arab officers in the Ottoman military academies were introduced to German instructors who were teaching in Istanbul due to the Empire's close relations with Germany. The German instructors, coming from a recently formed state with a strong national army, influenced the thinking of military officers in the Ottoman academies, including students from the provinces that would later make up the state of Iraq (Simon 1986: xii). By 1912 there were 1,200 officers from the Iraq provinces in the Ottoman military who had begun imbibing new and radical nationalist ideologies developing in the imperial center of Istanbul (Hashim 2003b: 13).

In response to the Turkification policies taking place in the Empire during the early 1900s, secret Arab nationalist organizations began to emerge, such as Al-Ahd ("The Covenant") formed in 1913, comprised of Ottoman officers from the provinces of modern Iraq, as well as Arab officers from other imperial domains in the Middle East. Al-Ahd was founded by an Egyptian Aziz Ali Al-Misri, but most of its members were Istanbul-based officers from the provinces of Iraq (Simon 1986: 29). Some of these officers included Nuri Al-Said, Jaafar Al-Askari, Jamil Midfai, Naji Shawkat, Mawlud Mukhlis and Ali Jawdat, who would all become prominent figures in the politics, both civilian and military, during the mandate period and Iraqi monarchy (Sluglett and Farouk-Sluglett 1987: 7).

During World War I, some of the Arab officers belonging to Al-Ahd defected from the Ottoman military to join the British-inspired Arab Revolt declared by Sharif Husayn of Mecca. They would form the first camp of Sharifian officers who took part in the Revolt. A second group joined Sharif Husayn's son Faysal when he established himself in Damascus as head of a short-lived post-war Arab kingdom (Batatu 1979: 319). Not all of the Iraqi Arab officers in the Ottoman Army defected. While the British tried to encourage its Arab prisoners of war to join the Arab Revolt, a good number refused. For example in 1916, 102 out of 132 Arab prisoners refused to join the Revolt that would pit them against an Ottoman military in which they had served. Prominent figures in Iraqi politics such as Yasin Al-Hashimi fought for the Ottoman military throughout the duration of the War, staying loyal to the Empire until its demise (Simon 1986: 46–7).

The Genesis of "Iraq"

As the Ottoman Empire sided with Germany during the war, the British had induced the forces of Sharif Husayn in the Hijaz to revolt against the Ottomans in exchange for a promised independent Arab kingdom. In the course of the war, the British invaded the Ottoman provinces of Basra, Baghdad and Mosul, most of which the Sharif had envisioned as the core territories of his future kingdom. However the British were well aware of these provinces' potential oil resources, as well as their strategic location as an overland route to their crown colony India, and later incorporated these provinces into the British administered mandate of Iraq. Rather than direct rule, British advisors were to guide an Iraqi government indirectly, whose "advice" on many issues had to be accepted. On June 20, 1920 two months after the San Remo conference decided on British control over these three former Ottoman provinces, Sir Arnold Wilson, the British Civil Commissioner in Iraq announced the mandate to the Iraqi people where the UK would be responsible "for the maintenance of internal peace and external security" (Bourdillon 1924: 277). Under the mandate, "internal peace" and "external security" would mean for the newly formed Iraqi Army that the British would essentially dictate all military affairs and the High Commissioner could veto any decisions taken by the Iraqi government regarding matters related to the armed forces.

The British occupation of Iraq and the subsequent announcement of the mandate resulted in widespread revolts led by tribes resistant to the prospect of paying future taxes, Shia and Sunni clergymen opposed to rule from a non-Muslim power and Kurdish tribes unwilling to submit to an Anglo-Arab authority ruling from Baghdad. These revolts lasted from July to October 1920, and would later assume the title "The Revolution of the Twenties" (*Thawrat Al-Ishrin*) or "Great Iraqi Revolution" (*Al-Thawra Al-'Iraqiyya Al-Kubra*). The rebellion mobilized close to 131,000 men, 17,000 of them with rifles as accurate as those held in the hands of British troops (Dodge 2003a: 135). The Iraqi Revolt of 1920 communicated to the British that they would need to find an Arab ruler for Iraq who would rule under the mandatory framework and deal with the underlying causes of these tribal, religious and ethnic revolts.

Table 2.1 Notable Iraqi officers during the mandate army eras 1921–1958

Name	Background	Education	World War I
Jaafar Al-Askari	1885 Baghdad Sunni Arab	Ottoman Military Academy (OMA)	ex-Ottoman Col. Sharifian
Husayn Fawzi	1889 Baghdad Sunni Kurd	OMA	Ottoman officer
Taha Al-Hashimi	1887 Baghdad Sunni Arab	OMA	Ottoman officer Sharifian
Yasin Al-Hashimi 1919	1884 Baghdad Sunni Arab	OMA	Ottoman Major General, joined Faysal
Muhammad Jawad	n.a. Baghdad Sunni Arab	OMA	Ottoman officer
Jamil Al-Midfai	1880 Mosul Sunni Kurd/Arab	OMA	Ottoman officer Sharifian
Mawlud Mukhlis	1886 Mosul Sunni Arab	OMA	Ottoman officer Sharifian
Sabih Najib Abd Al-Latif Nuri	1892 1888 Baghdad Sunni Arab	OMA OMA	Ottoman officer Sharifian Ottoman officer joined Faysal 1918

Name	Birth/Origin/Sect	Education	Career
Ibrahim Al-Rawi	Sunni Arab	OMA	Ottoman officer Sharifian
Salah Al-Din Al-Sabbagh	1899 Mosul Sunni Arab	OMA Iraqi Staff College	Ottoman Lt. Col. joined Faysal 1919
Fahmi Said	1898 Sulaymaniyya Sunni Arab/Turk	OMA Iraqi Staff Col.	Ottoman officer joined Faysal after 1918
Nuri Al-Said	1888 Baghdad Sunni Turk/Arab	OMA	Ottoman officer Sharifian
Mahmud Salman	1898 Baghdad Sunni Arab	OMA	Ottoman Lt. joined Faysal after 1918
Kamil Shabib	1895 Baghdad Sunni Arab	OMA Iraqi Staff Col.	Ottoman Lt. joined Faysal after 1918
Sami Shawkat	1893 Baghdad Sunni Arab	Military Medical School – Istanbul	Ottoman officer joined Faysal after 1918
Bakr Sidqi	n.a. Sunni Kurd/Turk	OMA Turkish Staff Col.	Ottoman officer joined Faysal after 1919
Amin al-Umari	1889 Mosul Sunni Arab	OMA Iraqi Staff Col.	Ottoman officer joined Faysal after 1918
Aziz Mustafa Yamulki	1893 Sulaymaniya Sunni Kurd	OMA	Ottoman army
Amin Zaki	1887 Baghdad Sunni	OMA	Ottoman army

Sources: Simon (1986: 179–81) and Tarbush (1982: 82–3).

Map 2.1 The 1920 Iraqi insurgency.

After Faysal was ejected from Damascus by French forces keen to establish their own mandate in Syria, the British chose him to serve as Iraq's first monarch. Once expelled from Syria, the ex-Sharifian officers who had served as Faysal's Damascus entourage moved with him upon assuming the Iraqi throne. After officially becoming the monarch in August 1921, Faysal faced a daunting task. He was placed in the center of a political arena of a new state where establishing his authority and maintaining domestic stability seemed distant prospects in the face of a national insurgency. Faysal was at the helm of a British designed political system, featuring a constitutional parliamentary monarchy with a Prime Minister as the head of government, but with a senate appointed by the King. However, Faysal lacked legitimacy as he did not originate from any of Iraq's provinces, and relied on his descent from the Prophet Muhammad's family to appeal to his Muslim constituents. Faysal's accession to the throne was decided by a referendum, but it was debated in Iraq whether the results were manipulated by the British. While the debate of whether any sense of national belonging existed among the ethnicities and sects in Iraq prior to the mandate is not the scope of this volume, needless to say, Faysal was given a kingdom and would need a reliable military force to establish his rule.

Faysal's credentials to lead Iraq and establish consensus and legitimacy among Iraq's communities was challenged by elements among the Arab Shia Muslims, who as a sectarian group made up close to 50 percent of the population at that time. Various elements amongst the Shia clergy and tribes were opposed to British rule and were equally distrustful of a new Arab Sunni Muslim administration that seemed merely to perpetuate the same policies as the Sunni Ottoman rulers of the Iraqi provinces. For the most part the Kurds, forming close to 20 percent of the mandate's population, were also weary of an administration of predominantly Sunni Arabs and had their own hopes of an independent state. Established Arab Sunni elites who staffed the former Ottoman administration and had traditionally ruled over the Arab Shia and Kurds were also distrustful of Faysal, essentially a "newcomer" who could challenge their established authority.

At the same time Faysal could not even claim that he had a monopoly on the use of force, as that was the domain of the British and an Iraqi military had just been established. To prop up the fledgling monarchy, all matters of defense and internal security were entrusted to British forces, including the formation, training and arming of the Army. King Faysal signed a treaty in October 1922 where the British would be responsible for the defense of Iraq, the beginning of a series of treaties that often led to opposition from Iraqis resistant to British influence in their affairs. The need for British aid with external defense was due to the threats from raiding tribes from Saudi Arabia, and the expanding regional powers Iran and Turkey. The borders with the Republic of Turkey had not been defined, and the British and Iraqis alike felt that the northern province of Mosul could be lost if the Turkish armed forces were to advance. Internal security was threatened by incessant tribal uprisings in the north and south.

Faysal's coterie reached out to their fellow Arab Sunnis who had been in Iraq since the Ottoman era. Along with the ex-Sharifian officers, most of them Arab Sunnis as well, these two groups would fill the higher echelons of the new administration. Second, a strong military was seen as a key pillar for Faysal to maintain both "internal stability" and "national cohesion" in Iraq. The monarchy had to demonstrate its ability to meet those two prerequisites to enter the League of Nations, ending the mandate and achieving independence for Iraq. However, while the King became more dependent on the military to restore order in the country, the Iraqi Army would become more dependent on the British as they supplied it with equipment and training. As the UK became more involved in Iraqi affairs, both military and civil, the more politicized the military would become, eventually emerging as an opposition force to the very British influence on which they depended.

The formation of the Iraqi Army

The Iraqi Army was officially founded in January 1921 and began with a Headquarter Staff of ten Iraqis officers (FO 371/8998: 35). In March 1921, the future of the Iraqi military was decided in a conference in Cairo, in a week-long meeting convened by the newly appointed Colonial Secretary Winston Churchill along with forty British military and civilian experts (Simon 1986: 1). Here the British decided on the future of The Kingdom of Iraq and its first king, Faysal, and how he could remedy the domestic maladies ensuing from the 1920 Revolt. In regards to Iraqi military matters, the dilemma facing the delegates was how to reduce the exorbitant costs of British troop deployments in Iraq, while at the same time not impairing Iraq's ability to defend itself, both externally, and, more crucially, internally. A decision was made to build up an Iraqi military, with air support provided by the Royal Air Force (RAF) (Dodge 2003a: 135–6). This army would be of a size to suppress any anti-government and anti-British activities in the country, yet its strength would not be permitted to exceed a limit beyond which the central government in Baghdad might feel emboldened to turn its back to Britain and contravene the mandate. The Iraqi Army would evolve along British lines, with training and equipment provided by the UK (Tarbush 1982: 76).

While the British were deciding on the fate of the Iraqi Army in Cairo, a select group of ex-Sharifian officers were planning to use the Army for their agendas. These officers included Jaafar Al-Askari, the first Minister of Defense and Nuri Al-Said, who held a variety of executive posts and initially served as Deputy Commander-in-Chief of the Army. King Faysal remained as the highest ranking military authority in Iraq (Batatu 1979: 333). Among the select elite of ex-Sharifian officers there were rival factions. Nuri Al-Said was the brother-in-law of Jaafar Al-Askari, and both had studied at the Istanbul military academy and staff college of the Ottoman military (Dodge 2003a: 138). Both sought to limit the influence of a rival ex-Sharifian soldier-politician Yasin Al-Hashimi. One British diplomat summed up their relationship citing Yasin's view of the Nuri–Jaafar alliance: "He had never felt completely happy with Jaafar as Minister of Defence and had more than once tried to have him out of that post, but Nuri would have none of it" (FO 371/20015, November 30, 1936). Yasin forged his ties with the military through his brother Taha, who would become Chief of the General Staff. Both factions would have supporters in the military and the differences between them would eventually lead to a clash. Ironically both Jaafar and Yasin would be removed from the Iraqi political scene by the military. Yasin's cabinet lasted from March 1935 until its overthrow in the military coup of 1936 and Jaafar was assassinated by the coup plotters.

The challenges of recruitment

A pool of more than 600 former Ottoman officers was available to join the armed forces, the majority of them Arab Sunnis from Baghdad and Mosul. Out of this figure, 190 served in the Sharifian Army and 450 had served in the Ottoman military during the War (CO 730/1, Intelligence Report no. 11, April 15, 1921). These officers were unemployed and influenced by newly emerging nationalist ideas, and with their military experience they constituted a potential threat to the government. It was hoped that these officers could be enticed by a steady salary, co-opting them into the new Army (Tarbush 1982: 77). Of the 600 possible officers, 250 were accepted into the officer corps in 1922, on the condition that they enroll in a British training course (Report by his Britannic Majesty's Government on the Administration of Iraq: 158). Some of these officers joined the military out of economic need, rather than loyalty to the newly formed Iraqi state, and some, who were discontent with their working conditions threatened to quit and join the army of the newly formed Republic of Turkey (CO 730/1, Intelligence Report no. 11, April 15, 1921).

The Iraqi Army was a voluntary organization and in its first months around 2,000 volunteers joined. Despite British efforts encouraging recruitment, they had their reservations as some of the recruits came from "undesirable elements" that joined for the lack of finding better employment. However, the numbers of recruits declined after the first few months, which the British attributed to the absence of a "national spirit" in the newly formed Iraq. Even King Faysal addressed the low number of recruits by bestowing the names of important figures in Arab history upon the Iraqi military units, a trend that would continue in earnest during Saddam Hussein's administration. For example, Faysal named one of the battalions in the first Iraqi Infantry, "the Imam Musa Kadhim Battalion" (FO 371/8998: 36), after a revered Shia figure buried outside of Baghdad, and employed ostensibly to increase the number of volunteers among the Shia.

Promotional campaigns in the Iraqi media of the 1920s encouraged young men to join the newly formed armed forces. An article in an issue of the *Iraq Times* exhorted potential volunteers to leave the complacency of their everyday life and enter the military:

> Younger patriots, why don't you go and form a corps d'elite for the Artillery and other services where intelligence is required? It would be so much more useful than wasting your time in the coffee shops

> abusing the Government and the British and the weather and so forth.
> Moreover, it so urgently necessary for the defence of your country. We
> should sleep so much more soundly, if we thought you had a real force
> capable of standing up to the Turks.
>
> (CO 730/7, Intelligence Report no. 27, December 15, 1921)

UK government circles feared that if a large percentage of British military
forces withdrew, with few local volunteers joining the armed forces, Iraq
could not stand up on its own in the face of a Turkish threat. One report
written in 1923 by a British official in the Colonial Office stated:

> The Iraqis have not come forward as recruits for their army as one
> might have expected. This exemplifies the lack of public spirit and the
> apathy which pervades the whole atmosphere in Iraq. They do not
> care.... Those who have thought about it welcome the date for two
> reasons, the one because they have complete confidence in the army
> and look forward to the time when they can use it as they wish, the
> other because they know the day of our departure spells collapse, the
> fall of Faisal and the return of the Turks.
>
> (CO 730/40 33280, June 20, 1923)

The concern in London about a premature British reduction of forces was
that it would work to the benefit of Turkey, a perceived threat to the
coveted oilfields in the north of Iraq.

By 1922 the Iraqi military had 3,618 men, well below the 6,000 man
strength requested by the Iraqi monarchy. While the British encouraged
recruitment, they had set a limit at 4,500 troops (Batatu 1979: 90). Some
Iraqi politicians blamed Britain for preventing the growth of the Iraqi military. However the Army already faced difficulties in recruitment due to
unattractive salaries, and when the Iraqi government increased salaries the
number of recruits rose (FO 371/8998: 36).

British control over Iraq's mandate army

The UK provided the Army's finances, and had the final say on its arms,
training, size and deployment. The monarchy could only declare martial
law, but it could only deploy military units with the consent of the High
Commissioner (Khadduri 1960: 310). In Heller's words, the Iraqi Army
was essentially "a British appendage" (1977: 80). The British Military
Mission was established under the 1922 Treaty of Alliance, with one
British officer assigned to the Iraqi Ministry of Defense and reaching 46
officers by 1930 (Report by his Britannic Majesty's Government to League
of Nations, 1928: 111). The mission maintained considerable control over
the Iraqi military until 1932, and continued to do so even after Iraq's
independence, stirring resentment among the Iraqi officers. Bourdillon,

when describing the mandate's jurisdiction said, "All Ministers are Iraqis, and each Minister has a British adviser who has literally no executive authority whatever" (Bourdillon 1924: 280). However, this "hands off" approach was not the popular Iraqi perception of the role of the British advisors. One of the stanzas of an Iraqi poem lamented, "He who enters the Ministries will find that they are shackled with the chains of foreign advisers" (Tarbush 1982: 40). The UK maintained the right to levy local forces, such as the rival force to the Iraqi Army, the British-officered Iraqi Levies. The British recruited the Levies from the Christian Assyrian population in Iraq, and with 4,984 men, it outnumbered the Iraqi Army of 4,500 men (FO 371/9004: 69).

Another military agreement signed in 1924 gave the UK operational control over the armed forces through Article 7:

> Full consideration must be given to the desires of the British High Commissioner in matters relating to the operations and distribution of the Iraqi army and vested the British Commander-in-Chief in Iraq with the right of inspecting this army whenever he deemed necessary.
>
> (quoted in Batatu 1979: 89)

According to the agreement, 25 percent of Iraq's annual revenues were to be used to finance its military (Simon 1986: 116). The British decided on how those revenues would be spent on arms and training, and all Army operations had to be approved through joint consultations with the British (Hemphill 1979: 95). Nationalist officers deemed these provisions as British infringement on Iraqi military affairs.

By 1924, the Army increased to 5,772 men and a year later it reached 7,500 men and was kept at the same level until 1933. By 1925 the Army comprised six infantry battalions, three cavalry regiments, two mountain regiments and one field battery (Longrigg 1953: 166). Wright, an academic from the University of Chicago described how he perceived the Army, with slightly higher numbers of troops:

> An Iraqi army of eight thousand has been organized, and under the tutelage of British officers it gives an appearance of considerable efficiency. The barracks and drill grounds are clean and the men appear well selected, alert, and disciplined. In the general slovenliness of the East the writer remembers with pleasure his inspection of the Army Training Center accompanied by Nuri Pasha, the able deputy commander-in-chief. The troops have exhibited military qualities in putting down some Kurdish troubles in Ruwandiz and Sulaimaniga.
>
> (1926: 753)

The "Nuri Pasha" and "Sulaimaniga" in the passage respectively referred to Nuri Al-Said and the northern Iraqi city of Sulaymaniyya. Wright's glowing description was contradicted by reports from the British High Commissioner Henry Dobbs who feared that the Army could easily be defeated by one of the armed Iraqi tribes. He believed that an Iraqi military of 9,000 troops would be adequate in maintaining internal security, but he did not expect the Army to be ready in the near future to defend the state from an external adversary (CO 730/82/24432, April 26, 1925). Eight years later, Dobbs was still pessimistic about the state of the Iraqi military. In a speech delivered to the Royal Empire Society in 1933, he described the Army as one of "the most efficient institutions in Iraq," which was "smart both in appearance and in their work" (quoted in Salih 1996: 47–8). However, he still believed that the Army was incapable of quelling an internal rebellion: "Yet, unless their aspirations are satisfied in some way, the Kurds are sure to rebel and the Iraqi army, in spite of years of British training, seems hardly able to cope with them" (ibid.). At that point, the Iraqi Army had not succeeded in suppressing the Kurdish revolts, in addition to the tribal revolts in the south.

During his tenure as High Commissioner, a struggle ensued between Dobbs and the Iraqi monarch over Iraqi troop deployments. Even though the monarchy depended on the British for protection, it also sought to ingratiate itself with public anti-British feeling by ostensibly challenging the foreign restrictions on the Army (Kedourie 1970: 242–3). Dobbs ultimately vetoed the King's motion to have the final say on Army deployments (Batatu 1979: 327). To make matters worse, the Colonial and Air Ministries proposed that British officers be in executive control over the Iraqi Army units, rather than merely serving as advisors (Dodge 2003a: 139). This proposal was viewed by anti-British circles in Iraq as an alleged scheme to keep the Army powerless and dependent on the UK, while serving as an imperial surrogate to secure the oilfields and the overland route to India.

The debate over conscription

Jaafar Al-Askari, the Minister of Defense, first introduced the motion to form an army based on conscription in 1922. The pro-conscription camp also included the King and Nuri Al-Said, and the latter's political rivals, Yasin Al-Hashimi and another politician Rashid Ali Al-Gaylani. Ayse Gul Altinay, in her study of conscription on Turkey, pointed out that conscription is usually seen from a strategic vantage as a manpower issue. To contravene this point, she quoted the historian Victor Gordon Kiernan who wrote, "to see [conscription] solely as a method of conducting wars is to see very little of it" (Altinay 2004: 7–8). From a strategic viewpoint the monarchy envisioned an expanded Army that could control the turbulent periphery. It also envisioned conscription as a means to cement the public's loyalty to a patriotic, professional army that would incorporate Iraqis of all sects and ethnicities, as well as urban, rural and tribal elements into a cohesive, national institution. The elites believed that the image of a independent Hashimite Iraq would be projected and imbued into the soldier, a new model Iraqi citizen, who after his military service would take those ideals into civilian life. The military sought essentially to mold Iraq's communal, ideological and political cleavages into "a national melting pot of sorts" (Parasiliti and Antoon 2000: 130).

Most importantly the plan would draft tribesmen of fighting age into the military, undermining the tribes' potential to resist the government. The debates among British officials over conscription were divided, with some fearing that an expanded Army could threaten the UK's interests in Iraq (Sluglett and Farouk-Sluglett 1978: 83). At that point, the British had been using certain tribes as a tactic to strengthen them against the urban centers opposed to foreign rule, and these tribes had benefited greatly materially and financially by these ties. Conscription could have given the Iraqi military an advantage over tribal forces, hence some of British officials' opposition to the plan (Batatu 1979: 92). Dobbs also anticipated the protests that would emerge from the Shia tribes if conscription were to be enforced (Report by his Britannic Majesty's Government to League of Nations, 1928: 15). After the border with Turkey had been delineated, he saw little chance of it invading and believed that the Iraqi Army should remain a small and efficient internal security force that would not drain the finances of the state. Dobbs' concerns were not only financial, but he feared that a large military would become the pillar of a clique inclined to despotism (Dodge 2003a: 137). Dobbs described Nuri Al-Said as "the imp of mischief" who was "obsessed with the dream of an absolute monarchy founded upon a praetorian army of which himself is the chief" (FO 371 E4471/86/65, September 27, 1927).

Other British colonial officers however were proponents of the plan. Inspector-General Major-General Daly suggested that the Army be expanded to 19,000 troops, with their own air force rather than depending on the RAF and the Iraqi Levies, which had been the British strategy at that time. Daly argued that an armed force confined to maintaining internal security "would lack the inspiration that a national spirit alone can give, and would merely degenerate into a species of police-force or gendarmerie" (FO 371 E6261/112/65, September 29, 1926). Other cynical officials feared that if London approved the conscription measures, Iraqis would *still* be suspicious of the British motives. An expanded conscript army would become even more dependent on the UK for arms and training, and these Britons assumed that the Iraqis would deduce that the British wanted to expand the Iraqi military to strengthen its hold over Iraq.

Despite the aforementioned advocates of conscription, the High Commissioner was the personification of British power in Iraq and his office was strong enough to serve as a political opposition to Faysal's lobby. Dobbs represented the overwhelming advantage in British military power and could threaten to withhold military assistance to the Iraqi government (Report by his Britannic Majesty's Government to League of Nations 1928: 16). The conscription plan had been delayed temporarily, but would finally be established after Iraq's independence.

Military education

Education was the key to fostering national identity and the Iraqi military emerged as a symbol of adulation in the schools. The military figured prominently in an almost sort of military-education or what the authors have termed "milication." This milication emerged within a context of militarism in Iraqi society, partly inspired by these processes occurring at the same time in Turkey and Iran, and in Italy and Germany.

The Iraqi officers who had studied in the Harbiye military academy of imperial Istanbul were instructed by foreign military teachers from the Germany of Wilhelm II, including texts from von Clausewitz, and they instilled in these Arab officers a notion of cultural nationalism (Simon 1986: xii). This interaction provided the seed of an ideology that would flourish in the public and military education system in a future Iraq. Sati Al-Husri, hailing from Aleppo, Syria was a product of the Ottoman civilian education system, graduating from the school for Ottoman bureaucrats, the *Mulkiye Mektebi* in Istanbul. In 1919, he left Turkey to join the short-lived Arab kingdom in Damascus, and then moved with Faysal, along with the other Iraqi military officers, to the newly founded Kingdom of Iraq (ibid.: 30–1). Sati Al-Husri infused militarism into the Iraqi public education system, when he served as the Director General of Education from 1923 to 1927. He developed curricula that inculcated an Iraqi nationalism within a pan-Arabist glorification of an Arab fatherland, a milication that Elie Kedourie referred to as *husriyya* (Kedourie 1970: 274–5). In Husri's opinion, the Army served as a crucial socializing agent to imbue in a new soldier-citizen a cause greater than advancing the interest of his ethnic or sectarian group:

> He lives with a group of the sons of the country, who are drawn from different towns and who hold various beliefs and positions. He lives with them, subject to a system in which they are all included without exception.
>
> (quoted in Cleveland 1971: 167)

Those students who graduated from the *husriyya* schools and then joined the Army, brought into the institution an identity not solely concerned with the independence of Iraq, but the unity of all Arab states free of the trappings of British and French imperialism. *Husriyyas*' advocated an Arab army emerging in Iraq that would liberate it from the British, and then emerge as a nucleus of a pan-Arab state forged through military conflict.

Sami Shawkat was Husri's successor, serving as Director General of Education from 1931 to 1933 and again in 1939 and 1940, until he was finally promoted to Minister of Education. He continued Husri's legacy of instilling the ideas of anti-Britishism, pan-Arabism and military discipline in the wake of the rise in popularity of the armed forces after their role in the massacre of the Assyrians, who had manned the unpopular Levies. Shawkat had served in the Ottoman military and like Husri then joined Faysal in the Arab kingdom in Syria. Shawkat delivered a speech entitled "The Art of Death" (*Sana'at al-Mawt*) to an audience of students and teachers in Baghdad in the fall of 1933, a few months after the Assyrian incident. In the address, Shawkat advocated a militant form of patriotism where a strong leader would lead a nationalist army in a struggle for independence and progress of a resurgent Arab nation (Hemphill 1979: 102). In the speech he declared:

> If Mustafa Kemal did not have forty thousand soldiers trained in the Art of Death ... would we have seen Turkey restore the glories of Sultan Selim in the Twentieth Century? If Pahlevi had not a thousand officers who had perfected this holy art, would we have seen the restoration of the glories of Darius? And had not Mussolini tens of thousands of Black-Shirts skilled in the profession of death, he would not have been able to place the crown of the Roman Emperors upon Victor Emmanuel.
>
> (Shawkat 1939: 2)

The appreciation of a resurgent Turkey and Iran was a constant theme in Iraq's milication. The legacy of these directors seemed to have an effect on the pupils. School children in this period described Iraq as the Arab Prussia, combining their aspirations of an Arab state created through a strong military.

The Iraqi Military College

With military educations, there was also a divergence between what British instructors thought should be taught to future Iraqi officers, and what Iraqi instructors actually taught their students. An Iraqi Military College was opened in 1921 coinciding with the foundation of the Iraqi military. The director and fifteen out of the twenty instructors at the College were Britons, and the instructional material was British military training manuals translated into Arabic (FO 371/8998: 39). All the officers that served in the Army from the Ottoman or Sharifian militaries had to attend these lessons in order to learn the British military system (ibid.: 52). The College was based on the model of the Royal Military College at Sandhurst and those talented graduates from the Iraqi College were given the opportunity to pursue training in the UK and India (ibid.: 37, 44).

However, the British admitted that the school had been handicapped as they rushed to train the Iraqis often in an improvised way (FO 371/10095: 112). It was closed for financial reasons and reopened in 1924 as the Royal Iraq Military College, and in 1928, the Iraqi Staff College was also founded to provide British military training to senior Iraqi officers for staff employment (Special Report by his Britannic Majesty's Government, 1920–1931: 44).

The Military College was open to all students regardless of ethnic or sectarian affiliation, but few attended from the Kurdish or Shia communities as they deemed it as an academic bastion of *uruba* (Arabness). Members of both groups tended to be reluctant to enter an institution that would provide officers to protect an Arab Sunni dominated government. Therefore most of its cadets were of Arab Sunni origin, as were the Iraqi instructors, whereas only 25 percent of the cadets were of Kurdish origin or from the rural tribal areas (Tarbush 1982: 78). This trend ensured that the Arab Sunnis would feature prominently in the officer corps upon graduation.

These educational institutions were designed to create officers in the British mold, but the Iraqis could not isolate themselves from the ideological currents in society, and unbeknownst to their British supervisors, instructors conveyed to their students Arabism and anti-imperialist ideas. Mahmud Al-Durra, a graduate of the school recalled how his military history professor, Tawfiq Husayn compared Iraq to an Arab Prussia, with an emerging military force that could establish a "great Arab state which would restore to the Arab nation its past glories and forgotten civilizations" (Durra 1969: 14). Tawfiq Husayn was educated in the Ottoman military academy and had served in the Empire's army. He did not believe in an apolitical military, and encouraged his students to adopt the notion of the Iraqi Army as the vanguard of Arab nationalism, which should take a direct role in Iraq's politics. He lectured on modern Turkey and Iran, as Husayn's hero was Mustafa Kemal Ataturk, and his lectures inspired more than one officer to envision himself in the role of the Turkish leader (Simon 1986: 132). Some of Husayn's students included officers such as Bakr Sidqi and Salah Al-Din Al-Sabbagh who applied Husayn's lessons and would initiate a series of military coups from 1936 to 1941 (Parasiliti 2001: 84).

Taha Al-Hashimi, brother of the politician Yasin Al-Hashimi was also a product of the Istanbul Harbiye military academy and had served in the Ottoman military. Like Tawfiq Husayn, Taha also taught military history at the College and authored some of its text books. He would assume Husri's position of Director General of Education in 1935, and would later become Commander-in-Chief of the Iraqi Army. He also tutored Faysal's son Ghazi, Iraq's second king. Ghazi also graduated from the College and would leave this institution with a profound respect for the Army and a sense of anti-imperialism and anti-Britishism.

The military and Iraq's independence

In June 1927, Jaafar Al-Askari introduced the conscription bill to the Iraqi Parliament, the *Majlis*, exhorting its members to accept the importance of a national army, declaring, "The national army in every country symbolizes its life and guards its independence" (Al-Hassani 1940: 22). The argument for conscription was also supported by the examples of national armies in Turkey under Mustafa Kemal Ataturk and Iran under Shah Reza Pahlavi (ibid.)

While Jaafar had envisioned conscription as a tool of national cohesion, the plan alienated the segments of society that were supposed to be incorporated into this institution. Representatives of the Shia and Kurdish tribes in Parliament argued that their authority would be weakened as their most able fighting men would be subsumed into a Sunni Arab controlled military. A Kurdish member of Parliament declared, "All Kurds are against conscription" (Tarbush 1982: 90). A Shia member of the cabinet resigned in protest, and a council of Shia tribes issued a statement stating, "Our sect only is to bear the burden" and referred to conscription as a "catastrophe" (Air 23/384, 1/BD/57, October 18, 1928). The predominantly Shia Al-Nahdha Party regarded the bill as a means to co-opt the Shia into the lower ranks of a military led primarily by Arab Sunni officers and controlled by British officers. The Shia, both tribal and urban, also objected to the scheme as it re-appropriated funds that had been allocated to a dam that would have irrigated the areas in which they resided. The bill was eventually withdrawn due to British objections and a refusal to endorse the motion, further convincing the nationalists of a foreign conspiracy to protect the mandate army structure and thwart the emergence of a patriotic, independent military.

In 1921 there were thirty-three British infantry battalions in Iraq, reduced to three by 1926 and by 1929 most troops had left Iraq (Longrigg 1953: 166). To secure British interests after the troop withdrawal, the Treaty of Preferential Alliance was signed in 1930 between the monarchy and the UK as a precondition for Iraq's independence. Otherwise known as the Anglo-Iraq Treaty of 1930, it went into effect for twenty-five years, allowing Britain to maintain a military mission in Iraq and two air bases, one relocated from Hinaydi to Habbaniyya, eighty kilometers west of Baghdad and the other in Shuayba, in the vicinity of Basra in the south. Finally, London could deploy British troops through Iraq at its discretion (Furtig 2000: 205). According to the Treaty the Iraqi government would have to pay for all British military instruction, including the training of naval and air force officers in the UK without the option of choosing instructors from other countries or receiving this education in any other foreign country. All small arms, ammunition, ships and airplanes could only be purchased from the UK. Iraq was committed to allowing the British military mission in Iraq to function and British officers would continue to serve the Iraqi military in an advisory capacity. While Iraq appeared to be on the path to self-rule, nationalist sentiment questioned the arrangement as a disguise for continued British imperial control over Iraq. While in theory the Iraqi government would gain control over its armed forces after independence, the Treaty signified the continued British interference in the realm of defense. Even in an independent Iraq, its armed forces would essentially serve as a neo-mandate army.

Once Iraq had been granted independence in 1932, the government, at least in theory, had the right to expand the Army without approval from the British (Hemphill 1979: 105). A year after formal independence, the King was able to raise the number of troops to 11,500, from the previous strength of 7,500, which had been constant since 1925 (Batatu 1979: 26). Yet, the Iraqi government still wished for a larger army based on conscription and King Faysal believed that his kingdom could not "stand tall" without a national army that would serve as the "the back bone for the creation of the nation" (quoted in Salih 1996: 53). Jaafar Al-Askari, Iraq's first Minister of Defense, questioned how Iraq could establish stable institutions of a state without a strong military to protect them. In a paper of his on the situation in Iraq in 1932, he wrote:

> It would be utterly foolhardy of us to plan the establishment of government, industrial and agricultural industries without putting in place sufficient security forces to preserve the system. The idea of an independent state with civic institutions but lacking an armed force to preserve its internal order and provide external defence is an impossible one. To that extent I part company with those who prefer to give priority to civic affairs, who seem to believe that the state can survive without the help of an army or other form of security force to protect its institutions.
>
> (quoted in Facey and Shawkat 2003: 243)

Al-Askari stressed that the Iraqi Army's priority should be devoted to dealing with internal security, enforcing the rule of law and collecting weapons owned by civilians, but admitted that in the meantime, Iraq would have to continue to depend on the UK for its protection.

King Faysal wrote a confidential assessment in 1933 that mirrored the themes in Al-Askari's paper. The King made a candid declaration about his feelings towards Iraq:

> My heart is full of sadness and pain, to my mind there is no Iraqi people in Iraq as yet. Rather, there are human masses void of any patriotic idea, imbued with traditions and religious vanities. Having nothing that binds them together and listening to evil, they are prone to anarchy and always ready to rise against the government whenever.
>
> (quoted in Salih 1996: 53)

The King feared that the government was "far weaker than the people," as an estimated 100,000 rifles were dispersed amongst the populace and the armed forces only had 15,000 rifles. He worried that the central government did not have the resources to carry out social, economic and political reforms without a substantial military force to protect the state, nor could it deal with a scenario of multiple armed insurrections particularly in both the south and the north of the country. After his somber assessment he proposed a twelve point program for addressing the weaknesses in forming an Iraqi nation. The first and second priorities dealt with the Army(Jawdat 1976: 362):

1 To increase the numerical force of the army, so that it could suppress at least two simultaneous uprisings, remote from one another.
2 National conscription to be announced after the reformation of the army along those lines indicated above.

However, the King would not live long enough to see his aspirations fulfilled. In 1933 King Faysal died just a year after achieving the independence he strived for and his son Ghazi assumed the throne that year.

The Army and the Assyrians

Ghazi's reign was marked by the Army's rise in popularity and subsequent forays into Iraq's political arena. The inexperienced monarch sought to bolster his position by making inroads into the military, which a concerned British diplomat wrote: "The cabinet has already approached me privately with a view to using my influence to control the young King's military enthusiasm and to prevent him from turning to his old friends in the army for political advice" (FO 371/16889 E5331, September 11, 1935). However, the young King proved inexperienced compared to his father, and the politicians who formed Faysal's closest advisors would turn against each other, using factions in the military for support.

In the summer of 1933, the Iraqi government tried to devise a policy to address the Assyrian Christian community. The Assyrians had been unpopular with the Iraqis for joining the ranks of the Levies, viewed locally as a tool of British domination and part of a community unwilling to support the nation's struggle for independence. As one Iraqi writer at that time observed:

> The swaggering Assyrian levies with their slouch hat and red or white hackles, who stood guard at the Homes of the High Commissioner, and Hinaidi, the British Air Force Headquarters, situated in a suburb of Baghdad, became the symbol of British domination.
> (quoted in Tarbush 1982: 97)

The Iraqi military also resented the Levies, which they deemed as a force that the British still favored. As the numbers of the Iraqi Army increased, the Levies' troop strength was reduced in 1926. Their units were disbanded after Iraq's independence, and upon decommissioning, each Levy was given a rifle and ammunition for self-protection in their homes, another source of resentment amongst Iraqis. Most of the Levies still served as guards at British facilities in a manner analogous to private mercenaries (Longrigg 1953: 197). Army officers argued that the Assyrians, as civilians, should not be allowed to keep their arms after Iraq's independence, as they struggled to disarm the rest of the Iraq's population. The Army also took umbrage at the attitude prevalent among the British and the Levies, where it was said among the latter that one of their soldiers was worth three Arab soldiers. The military was keen to disprove this belief, as well as establish a reputation among the Iraqis as a force capable of dealing with internal dissent, in the face of its failures to suppress decisively the Kurdish rebellions.

The politicians in Baghdad found a key ally in Colonel Bakr Sidqi, who promised to liquidate the "Assyrian problem in five minutes" (Hemphill 1979: 106). His forces deployed to the north without the supervision of British advisors allegedly to deal with a potential insurrection among the Assyrians. The Iraqi Army forces engaged in a relatively minor skirmish with an armed Assyrian force and defeated them, but then went on to massacre 300 Assyrian civilians in the village of Summayl. The Army's actions raised its public stature as well as that of its commander, Bakr Sidqi. It was the first instance where the Army could boast of a success after what amounted to a massacre of the Assyrians who had been deemed too pro-British.

Crowds in Mosul and Baghdad took to the streets to cheer the military's actions. Sidqi had emerged as a popular hero and was promoted to General by the Chief of Staff, Taha Al-Hashimi. An Iraqi observer wrote of the euphoria that filled the streets upon the news of the Iraqi military's actions: "Planes of the Iraqi Air Force flew over the city, raining coloured leaflets that carried the following words.... 'Welcome, Protectors of the Fatherland.... Stand up to Your Enemies the Tools and the Creatures of Imperialism'" (quoted in Makiya 1998: 169). The Army's victory imbued the crowds with pride in the armed forces, and led the officers to believe that they had achieved the first step in carrying out a sacred mission of achieving full independence of Iraq (Al-Samir 1981: 111). Addressing the crowds in Mosul, Rashid Ali Al-Gaylani, Prime Minister at that time, declared: "Yes, the army should be strengthened in order that it should protect our honour" (Hemphill 1979: 108). Sidqi also gave a speech promising a greater role for the Iraqi military in the nation's future:

> I offer as a pledge of what the Army is about to perform in the future,
> in accomplishment of the great duty, which the Army has felt and is

still feeling that it must be prepared to perform. Therefore, let us, with Army and Nation, await that day.

(quoted in Stafford 1935: 204)

Sidqi's invocation of "Army and Nation," with the term "Army" preceding "Nation" signified a rhetorical technique that would be employed throughout Iraq's modern history. Sidqi, as a representative of the armed forces, sought to forge a connection between the military and the people as a single entity, struggling for the defense of the Iraqi nation, from threats internal and external.

In the eyes of the Iraqi street, the military had begun to emerge from the shadow of British domination and to assert its authority in a symbolic throwing off of the shackles of the neo-mandate army. Sidqi had tasted popularity and power, and it would be only a matter of time before he would use the armed forces to intervene in Iraq's political affairs.

The conscription lobby used these events as further justification of the need for an expanded military. The popularity of the armed forces was at an all time high, and the events revealed an increased sense of anti-Britishism. Both trends resulted in an increase in recruitment, and in the ensuing euphoria, pro-military politicians could fulfill their desire of a conscripted Army, symbolizing the nation's unity. The events of 1933 also represented the beginning of the state employing military solutions against Iraqi communities that were deemed as threats to internal security, such as Shia and Kurdish rebels, a trend that would begin in the 1930s and continue well until the end of the twentieth century.

The consequences of conscription

By 1934, the Army's first two divisions were formed (Wagner 1979: 64). Universal conscription filled its ranks in June 1935, with the introduction of the National Defense Law (otherwise known as the National Service Law), which was passed in the Parliament and was issued by a royal decree or *irada*. As Dobbs anticipated, the introduction of conscription aroused objections from Iraq's various communities. Writing in 1936 from Baghdad, David Langley's essay "Iraq and Her Problems" described how the Yazidis, a Kurdish community concentrated around the Jabal Sinjar area, practicing a syncretic faith (which he describes as an "obscure devil-worshipping sect"), had resisted the application of conscription to their tribes. He also questioned how the Mandaeans (also known as Sabians), an Iraqi religious community that stresses the supremacy of John the Baptist over Jesus Christ, would try to escape military service "on the plea that their daily baptismal rites necessitate running water, unobtainable in the desert" (Langley 1936: 55). Shia and Kurdish tribes had expressed their opposition to conscription for fear of losing their men of fighting age. The tensions between these communities and the state, led to the British ambassador to Iraq, Edmonds, describing the situation "drifting into something not far off civil war" (FO 371/20795, December 23, 1936).

While only 25 percent of officers were of tribal origin, the tribesmen would provide up to 75 percent of the rank-and-file of the Army (Hemphill 1979: 99). This proved to be a problem when tribal conscripts were deployed to fight against their fellow tribesmen in the 1935 revolt in the mid-Euphrates area. Their loyalty to the tribe was stronger than their loyalty to an army they were forced to join. A British report described this situation: "Many of the officers are believed to be in sympathy with the Government's opponents, and the majority of the rank and file, being Shi'ah ... some few officers actually refused to proceed to the front" (FO 371/18945, March 21, 1935). These tribal members of the armed forces would often abandon the military, taking their arms and joining sides with the tribes.

During the instability in 1935, Bakr Sidqi, who had established a reputation for his ruthless use of force against the Assyrians, was charged with quelling the revolt in the south. In the 1930s the tribes, with their own arsenals, had been able to carve out para-states in the south and north. Sidqi had heavy artillery and the Royal Iraqi Air Force (RIAF) at his disposal, but during his campaign, the RIAF base was flooded, and deprived of air cover, the Iraqi Army's battle with the tribesmen met with little results. Once the planes were able to take off however, they delivered a crucial blow against the "insurgents," the term British officials used to describe armed opponents to the central government. Langley admitted that the RIAF was more ruthless in putting down these tribal revolts than the Royal Air Force:

> Control of this region is to-day in the hands of the Iraq government, so that when certain elements in Mesopotamia feel the searing touch of a fiery sword, wielded in this case by the air arm of Iraq Defence, they are left with crops and hard-earned wealth in flames and a sense of grievance which, it would seem, is the bane of tribal life in the desert.
>
> (Langley 1936: 52)

Using the RAF for internal repression would become a characteristic of the newly independent Iraqi state. One author described this tactic as follows: "The state through its dependence upon air power not only became detached from society but also hung two hundred feet above it, bombing people when they did not behave in the way the state wanted" (Dodge 2003a: 134). By 1935, the tribal revolts in the south had been temporarily suppressed but would emerge only a year later to be quelled once again by Bakr Sidqi. His role in crushing the tribal uprisings increased Sidqi's popularity further among the officer corps and Arab nationalists (Batatu 1979: 101).

In the north of Iraq, the inexperienced Iraqi Army, despite anti-British positions within the ranks of the military, hated to admit that they were still dependent on support from the Royal Air Force in suppressing the revolts. The Kurdish uprising ostensibly began due to ethnic tensions with the Arabs and the failure of their tribal leaders to accept the legitimacy of what was essentially an Arab Iraqi state. The Kurds felt that a promise of an independent Kurdish state after World War I had been reneged on, as were subsequent British assurances that they would be granted a Kurdish autonomous region and government within an Iraqi state. Their revolt intensified when Kurdish leaders were convinced that the British and Iraqi mandate governments were unwilling to grant them substantial autonomous powers.

In the late 1920s, Iraqi forces with the aid of the Royal Air Force were able to drive the Kurdish Shaykh Mahmud Barazani from his positions in Sulaymaniyya in July 1924, forcing him to flee to Iran (Report by his Britannic Majesty's Government on the Administration of Iraq: 157). This campaign was only a temporary victory as most of the battles against Kurdish rebels would lead to brief halts in the fighting, but the Iraqi military was never able to ensure a decisive victory, a trend that began in the 1920s and continued well into the next century. Since the creation of the Iraqi state, a large part of the Iraqi military would be deployed to the north to suppress the Kurdish uprisings.

Even though Shaykh Mahmud was captured in 1931, his forces would still continue to fight the central government. In another campaign in late 1931, the Iraqi military had to request British air support to counter another uprising led by forces loyal to the Shaykh Ahmad of Barazan. The Shaykh's forces inflicted severe losses on the Iraqi military and in early 1932, the Royal Air Force prevented Iraqi forces from a rout by Kurdish fighters allied to the Barazanis (Hemphill 1979: 105). At the time of the revolt, half of the Iraqi military was stationed in the north, and most of the rest of the military was stationed in the south around the Euphrates region to check the tribal revolts. The forces in the north would eventually be scaled down, but close to a quarter of the Iraqi military would continue to be stationed there to deal with Kurdish unrest (Tarbush 1982: 94).

As Iraq gradually developed its own air force between 1921 and 1932, the RAF came to the Iraqi military's aid 130 times (ibid.: 17). Even after independence, the Iraqi military continued to depend on the RAF. By 1936 the Iraqi air force only had thirty-seven pilots, which would later increase by 127 the following year (FO 371/20796/E 44/14/93, December 22, 1936). The RIAF increased from five British-made planes in 1930 to fifty-five by 1936 (Tarbush 1982: 78). Muhammad Ali Jawad, commander of the RIAF, lobbied a further expansion of the air force however the British were reluctant to acquiesce to his request as it would have made it larger than the Royal Air Force stationed in Iraq (ibid.: 33). Still, the Iraqi government preferred to invest in ground forces as only they could hold territory and demonstrate the government's presence to the population.

As of 1936 the army had increased to 800 officers and 19,500 men and was still organized in two divisions (FO 371/20013/E 6797/1419/93 October 30, 1936). One of the British reports indicated that of this number, "a proportion of those being raw conscripts whose fighting qualities are doubtful if opposed by any resistance" (ibid.). Eventually the military crushed the rebellions in the south or what the British termed the "insurgency." Without the help of the Levies or the Royal Air Force the Army had accomplished a task that was inconceivable years earlier. The state had imposed its dominance over the periphery (Lukitz 1995: 92). The military demonstrated to the Iraqi public that it could discipline traitorous Assyrians, rebellious Shia tribes and secessionist Kurds, bringing order in those areas that rejected the authority of the Hashimite state.

The state had sought to mold a reflection of itself in this conscript army, and it eventually incorporated tribesmen, Shia and Kurdish alike, in a military led by officers who were predominantly Sunni town dwellers. However, the monarchy's desire to create this institution as a means of bringing all communities together would also result in a military that emerged as a reflection of Iraq's society, not necessarily a positive development. The armed forces would also reflect the biases and sectarian and ethnic affiliations of Iraq's political elites, the Sunni Arabs. In the long term, an expanded military did not lead to stability in Iraq's politics. Three years after the death of King Faysal, political factions had differing visions of the ideological evolution of the Iraqi state, and the military found itself caught in this battle, and finally emerging as the referee in this arena. It would be Sunni Arab officers, not politicians, that sought to project their own image of what the Iraqi nation should be on to the monarchy, and those struggles within the military often led to coups against the very government it was designed to strengthen. This relationship would pave the way for the establishment of the military moderator regimes after 1936.

Cleavages within the neo-mandate army

Fissures emerged as the Army increased in size, divided between generational gaps, secret cells and the older generation of Iraqi's first officers. The ex-Sharifians dominated the upper echelons of the military, constituting twelve out of nineteen most senior officers. In this period, the neo-mandate army's officer corps was ideologically apolitical. Their loyalty ultimately lay with the monarchy although factions within the Sharifian dominated officer corps sought to carve out greater power for themselves. The politics of the 1920s featured clusters loyal to political personalities rather than ideological parties, and those politicians would seek to control the Iraqi military to bolster their own power base.

With the expansion of what was supposedly envisioned as a Hashimite army, this institution began to incorporate the ethnic and sectarian cleavages in Iraqi society. As one source wrote: "The Iraqis had in effect constructed a roof without walls in so far as the army had failed to establish itself in the image with which it had been provided by its creators and eulogists" (Hemphill 1979: 105). The failure to establish a military in the image provided by its creators was due to fissures in the military based on regional and class origins, and the ethno-sectarian divide that cut across the armed forces.

The regional and class differences were accentuated by the ex-Sharifians who encouraged younger members from their hometowns or tribes to enter the military. This trend of ex-Sharifian patrons recruiting clients through kinship networks would lead to a new generation who entered the military, connected to the economic changes occurring in Iraq in the 1930s. These men were predominantly Arab Sunnis from cities such as Mosul, or smaller towns like Takrit. The Sunni political elite cultivated poorer Sunni men from towns like Takrit and Rawa, which had suffered from economic decline. Its inhabitants would migrate to the capital, where they were encouraged by wealthy officers from their towns to join the military or its academies, later forming the majority of junior and medium ranking officers in the Army. For example, the Takritis, who were traditionally involved in making the *kalak*, a small boat used to traverse the rivers, found their mainstay obsolete with the introduction of modern boats in Iraq and had to find a new livelihood. One of the prominent ex-Sharifian officers was Mawlud Mukhlis, who served in the Ottoman military and later joined Al-Ahd. Raised in Mosul, he originally came from a large landowning family from Takrit, and during the monarchy he was instrumental in encouraging young Takritis to join the Army. One Takriti who joined the military under Mukhlis' auspices was Ahmad Hasan Al-Bakr (a relative of Saddam Hussein) who would emerge as the figurehead of the 1968 coup (Sakai 2003: 139). Another ex-Sharifian officer, Ibrahim Al-Rawi, who became commander of the Fourth Division in the Iraqi Army during the monarchy, encouraged fellow countrymen from Rawa, an Arab Sunni town on the upper Euphrates, to join the military. Other officers among this stratum of wealthy families included Amin Al-Umari, from a distinguished family from Mosul, while others came from prominent Baghdadi families such as Naji Suwaydi, a former Ottoman turned Sharifian officer (Abbas 1989: 205). The military was divided by these patronage networks of the ex-Sharifian officers, and these informal personal networks within the military inhibited its consolidation of an efficient chain of command (Sakai 2003: 140).

While the aforementioned disadvantaged Arab Sunnis were encouraged by wealthy patrons to join the military academy, the Army also included men who had no choice but to join. Conscription led to an influx of young, untrained men into the military, from predominantly Kurdish and Shia peasant families. The Army drafted men aged nineteen and above who were not enrolled in higher education. While the military was to be inclusive of all segments in society, those who were conscripted came from the lower classes, as the upper classes were able to send their sons for education in Iraq or abroad, or could pay an exemption fee known as the *badal* (Al-Samir 1981: 111–12).

The British had hoped for a unifying political ideology to cement the relationship between the Iraqi military and a pro-British Hashimite monarchy. One of the Colonial Office's reports stated, "Although politics are strictly kept outside the army, a political foundation is necessary for army personnel if they are to rise above the condition of mere mercenaries" (FO 371/10095: 110). More than ten years later, Iraq was in a state of flux, with competing agendas of various politicians as well as Iraqi military leaders. During the 1920s and 1930s, socialism, Marxism and fascism had begun to inspire young Iraqi Army officers (Al-Samir 1981: 109). Pan-Arabism had also taken root in the military, particularly among the Sunni Arabs. Even though they were the minority in Iraq, they were dominant in the government and the military, and some Sunni Arabs believed their position in Iraq would be strengthened if Iraq would assume its role as the Arab Prussia in unifying all the Arab states, most of which happened to be Sunni Arab as well.

As early as 1929, a clandestine cell of young pan-Arabist officers began to coalesce around Salah Al-Din Al-Sabbagh, who hailed from a mercantile family in Mosul. His fellow officers shared a common background, mostly young, coming from modest Sunni Arab middle income families from the northern Arab provinces in the vicinity of Mosul, a region that suffered economically after the creation of Syria. With the imposition of customs barriers and change in currencies, the new border between Iraq and Syria curtailed the historic trade between cities such as Mosul and Aleppo and the rest of the Levant (Davis 2005a: 147). It followed that the primarily Sunni Arab officers advocated pan-Arabism, a movement that would rectify the arbitrary boundaries dividing the Arab nation. These officers also believed that the issue of Palestine was the most pressing danger to a future unified Arab nation and that Iraq should do more to support the Palestinians against foreign plans to create a divided Jewish–Arab state.

During the 1930s, two parallel trends were emerging in Iraq with the growth of ideological cliques within the Iraqi military and the birth of an Iraqi intelligentsia. The two would form a symbiotic relationship with each other. Al-Sabbagh was cultivated by the Arab nationalist Yasin Al-Hashimi, one of the ex-Sharifian officers, who became Prime Minister in 1935. Al-Sabbagh and Al-Hashimi had also gathered the ideological support of the pan-Arabist Muthanna Club (FO 317/23217/E 5661/72/93, August 10, 1939). Al-Husri often spoke at the Club and one of its prominent members included Sami Shawkat, the author of the "Art of Death" and founder of the militaristic youth Futuwwa movement. The Muthanna Club's members were primarily middle class Sunni Arabs, mostly merchants and teachers and actively sought to make inroads into the military by recruiting officers. Al-Hashimi also supported another group called the Palestine Defense Committee, which cooperated with the Muthanna Club to raise funds for the Palestinians. In fact, in Yasin Al-Hashimi's capacity as premier, he allowed Al-Sabbagh to conduct a gun smuggling operation to arm the Palestinians (Simon 1986: 71).

While some Arab Shia also joined these predominantly Arab Sunni pan-Arabist organizations, there were other Arab Sunnis in Iraq who disavowed themselves of pan-Arabism altogether. Opposed to the Arab nationalist Muthanna Club, the "Iraqist" or "Iraq firsters" movement was represented by Jamaat Al-Ahali, a social reformist movement founded by Muhammad Hadid, along with three other like-minded intellectuals who had studied abroad in various schools in Lebanon and Europe. Ahali was later joined by the politician Hikmat Sulayman, a former ally of Al-Hashimi, who later had a falling out with the latter when he became Prime Minister. Some of Ahali's members played a role in the post-coup 1936 government, but its Iraqist ideas did not find a reception among the Arab nationalist officers who would dominate Iraqi political affairs from 1937 to 1941.

Yasin Al-Hashimi combined his connections with Iraq's intelligentsia to his connections with the military, and his political rivals would do the same. By 1930, the British had become aware of a growing trend where politicians began to cultivate support among factions within the military:

> Intrigue is to be found everywhere and is not confined to army matters; officers mix freely with the local politicians and are prepared to follow anyone who they think will benefit them. The men as a whole however are stupid and dull in intellect. At present there is no reason to suppose that they would refuse to do what they were ordered providing it was not dangerous.
>
> (Air 23/120, 1/BD56, July 17, 1930)

While the British had a low opinion of the "stupid and dull" military man, these inroads were a concern to them, as certain politicians tried to increase anti-Britishism to augment their own popularity. Al-Hashimi also believed that a future Iraq would emerge as an Arab Prussia to unite all Arab lands, opposed to his rival Nuri Al-Said who had envisioned a Hashimite federation with Jordan. Al-Hashimi's conclusion of a trade agreement with Germany was popularly received in Iraq. In regards to military affairs he doubled the size of the army, and increased the air force to three squadrons without consulting the British advisors. To aggravate the British further and enhance his own nationalist credentials he failed to renew the contracts of several of the British advisors (Simon 1986: 64–7). With the rise of the paramilitary youth organizations and military training programs in the schools, Al-Hashimi fostered militarism and anti-Britishism, trying to weaken the UK's control over the neo-mandate army.

On the eve of the 1936 coup, the officer corps remained a primarily Sunni Arab body. Out of a sample of sixty-one officers during this period, Tarbush only cited one officer being Shia. The trend that began with the Ottoman military structure, where primarily Sunni Arabs were promoted to high positions in the administration and military, was continued in the Iraqi state. This imbalance can be attributed to several reasons. As the primarily Sunni Ottoman Empire was engaged in a centuries old struggle with its neighbor Shia Iran, there was a tendency by the authorities to view the Shia in Ottoman Iraq as a fifth column, sympathetic to their Persian co-religionists (Deringil 1990: 47–8). At the same time, there was a general disdain in the Shia community for its members to join the Ottoman military, or take part in the Ottoman education system, especially the military academies, where it was feared that they would be inculcated with a Sunni Muslim curricula. The Arab Sunnis who served in the Ottoman military would continue to dominate the officer corps of the new Iraqi state, albeit with a few high-ranking Sunni Muslim Kurdish officers as well (Tarbush 1982: 79).

During the monarchy, tensions ran high between these ethno-sectarian groups in the military. One British account reported how "loyalty within the armed forces was not based on either national or professional grounds, as soldiers and officers continue to carry their class, ethnic, and cultural differences with them in the army" (Air 23/120, 1/BD/56, July 17, 1930). Tensions were also reported between Kurds and Arabs in the military:

> The Arabs consider the Kurds treacherous and say they never know whether they will not be shot in the back by the Kurds in action. They treat the Kurdish soldiers with opprobrium. This the Kurds resent in their turn and the whole force is full of mutual jealousy and hatred and mistrust.
>
> (Ibid.)

For most of Iraq's history, the officer corps would remain primarily Sunni Arab, with a few prominent Shia Arab and Kurdish officers, while the lower echelons of the military would be primarily made up of Shia and Kurdish draftees, particularly during the Iran–Iraq War and the 1991 Gulf War when the government had to draw upon its population to bolster the number of the armed forces.

These ethnic cleavages affected another group of officers who were Kurdish or Turkmen in origin. They resented the pan-Arab nationalists (*qawmiyyun*) both in the military and the government as their control over these institutions would lead to their exclusion from the positions of power. These officers tended to the "Iraq-firsters" (*wataniyyun*) camp, as were a good number of Iraqi politicians, who realized that Iraq was part of the Arab world, but were more concerned with domestic Iraqi affairs rather than entangling Iraq with events occurring in the other Arab states.

The advocates of this trend were primarily concerned with developing Iraq and looked to their non-Arab neighbors as models, trying to imitate what Kemal Atatürk had done in Turkey or Reza Pahlavi in Iran (Hashim 2003b: 14).

On the eve of Iraq's first military coup, the armed forces had been transformed from a strictly volunteer, British controlled mandate army, to a conscript army divided by class, tribal, ideological and ethno-sectarian differences. Nationalist officers who sought to break the British hold over the neo-mandate army could only achieve this aim by taking power for themselves. However these nationalists in the officers corps were hardly unified ideologically, divided between Iraq-firster and pan-Arabist camps, in addition to ambitious officers who simply sought to use these ideologies to further their own personal goals. What united these officers however was their common apathy to foreign control over their Army and the nation as a whole.

Part II
Praetorian Iraq

3 Iraq's military moderator regimes 1936–1941

Defining the military moderator regime

The literature analyzing the moderator (arbitrator/veto regimes) in Iraq is scant, and even Janowitz complained of the difficulty in gathering materials to apply this model to the Middle East (Khuri 1982: 19). Nevertheless, it was in Iraq in 1936 when this model was introduced into the region. The military in the liberal model is de-politicized and subordinated to civilian authority, and has internalized a "civilian ethic" that accepts government decisions, even if the military as an organization disagrees with the civilian authority. Due to the respects for civilian state institutions, officers will refrain from intervening in the political arena (Nordlinger 1977: 12–13).

The liberal model stands in contrast to the praetorian model. When the military serves as a praetorian moderator regime, it has the ability to moderate political disputes and ultimately can exercise a veto power when disputes cannot be resolved. As Nordlinger stated, "It is easier to prevent change than to bring it about, and this may be accomplished from the governmental sidelines with their veto power" (Nordlinger 1977: 22–3). The military employs this veto through implicit or overt threats of a coup. Perlmutter preferred the term "arbitrator" as opposed to veto regime and described this model as the following: "They indirectly control the political and civilian institutions, but they do not dominate the executive, the government or bureaucracy" (Perlmutter 1977: 141). The armed forces exercise their moderating power behind the scenes, without overthrowing or taking direct control over the government itself. The officers in this model can launch a displacement coup preventing their opponents from taking power, or it can replace one civilian government with another that is friendlier, thus maintaining a regime that serves the interest of the armed forces. Moderator military officers essentially act as the strongest politicized pressure group vis-à-vis the government, and can moderate the political system by balancing and playing off other contending pressure groups.

The 1936 coup

The growing Iraqi armed forces in its capacity as a mandate army had emerged as a symbol of national independence. By 1936, officers who had put down a series of crippling tribal revolts realized that the monarchy could not survive without their support. As these officers grew resentful of continued British interference in the affairs of independent Iraq, they felt empowered to dictate political affairs. These officers grew weary of corrupt Iraqi officials and unstable governments whose cabinets could last barely a couple of months, and these officers began conspiring to take matters into their own hands, thus transitioning into the role of praetorians.

After taking power on March 17, 1935 through a series of calculated tribal uprisings, Yasin Al-Hashimi's rule as Prime Minister became more dictatorial by 1936. He cracked down on any criticism of his government in the media, increased the scope of intelligence services to monitor any dissent and was responsible for ordering General Bakr Sidqi to crush the tribal unrest, which Al-Hashimi fomented to gain power in the first place. In his government, Nuri Al-Said became Minister of Foreign Affairs and Rashid Ali Al-Gaylani became Minister of Interior. The premier made an enemy in Hikmat Sulayman, an Iraqi politician who had supported Al-Hashimi in the past, only to be denied the Minister of Interior post in the 1935 government. Sulayman was aware of General Sidqi's disdain of Al-Hashimi and found a powerful ally who could command the support of the military. Sulayman also formed an alliance with the Ahali group, a group of liberal reformers and socialists who advocated social democracy, *sha'abiyya* ("welfare for all the people") and freeing Iraq from dependence on the British. Sulayman assured them they could pursue their reform agenda if he was in power and that the alliance with the Army would not lead to a military dictatorship. An unstable coalition, comprising liberal reformers and nationalist army praetorian officers, had been formed.

Hikmat Sulayman was the younger brother of Mahmud Shevket Pasha, who led units of the Ottoman Army into Istanbul in July 1909, forcing the abdication of Sultan Abd Al-Hamid II (Khadduri 1960: 73). During the Al-Hashimi government, Sulayman had spent a few months in Turkey, where he admired the changes brought about by the Kemalists and upon returning to Iraq in December 1935, he was convinced of the need to carry out similar reforms in Iraq (ibid.: 75). The only obstacle was Al-Hashimi, who had prevented Sulayman's rise to a prominent political post. In this respect, Sulayman tried to repeat his brother's feat in Istanbul, by convincing Sidqi to launch a coup to force the Al-Hashimi cabinet to resign.

Both Sulayman and Sidqi shared a similar view of the role of the military in politics: "Their model, as well as their inspiration, was indeed Kemalist Turkey, because that country, they argued, had been able to maintain her independence only through the reorganization of her army" (ibid.: 79). It would appear that Republican Turkey was an inspiration to

Sulayman due to his ethnic Turkish roots, or other Iraqis like Sidqi who wished to emulate the events that occurred at the core of what was once the former Ottoman Empire. The Ataturk model also offered a schemata for aspiring military officers, such as Sidqi, who sought a role in political affairs:

> And there can be no doubt that the history of Ataturk is not lost on military leaders, as they struggle for new political forms which might permit the military to operate as a political umpire rather than as a ruling oligarchy.
>
> (ibid.: 181)

Indeed in this period, Bakr would establish a military moderator regime that essentially became an "umpire" in the game of Iraqi domestic politics.

By winning disgruntled officers to his side, Sulayman disarmed the government of its only tool to crush political opposition. The folly of Sulayman's plan was that he, as a civilian, had invited the Army into the ruling apparatus. He had allowed the military room to maneuver with the administrative structures of the state, helping the Army to emerge as the ultimate judge of who should have authority to rule. The shift in power from civilian to military hands had been facilitated by a disgruntled politician who merely sought to augment his own power. Sulayman would be the politician who ultimately fostered the emergence of the military moderator regime.

There were elements in the Army at this time that were disillusioned with the instability in the Iraqi government and their recent experience of suppressing tribal revolts only to see the politicians reap the glory from their feats. Some officers wondered if the Army itself could rule, thus bringing stability to their country and eliminating British meddling in Iraqi affairs. Other praetorian officers had goals beyond a local Iraqi agenda, seeing their mission as a greater struggle to liberate and then unite the other Arab domains. The two aforementioned agendas consisted of the more activist views held by younger officers opposed to the old guard of ex-Sharifians. It was Bakr Sidqi who rose to prominence due to his role in suppressing the Assyrians and tribal revolts that could command the respect of this generation of nationalist officers. Sidqi had already hinted at a rally after the Assyrian massacres in 1933 that it was the military that would carry out a "great duty" for the nation.

Yasin Al-Hashimi had already alienated General Sidqi, commander of the Second Division stationed near Kirkuk, who felt that it was the Prime Minister's brother, Taha Al-Hashimi that was preventing his promotion to the post of Chief of the General Staff, a position Taha held and which Sidqi coveted. (Ironically it was Taha Al-Hashimi who had promoted him to General after the Assyrian massacres.) Sidqi was also convinced that Taha was not doing enough to strengthen and reorganize the Army. After Sidqi's successes in quelling the tribal revolts in the middle Euphrates, he felt that he could have done a better job as Chief of Staff and commander of all the Iraqi armed forces. The officers around Sidqi also encouraged him to assert his power, since they could benefit from promotions after a coup.

In October 1936, Bakr Sidqi was left as acting Chief of the General Staff while Taha Al-Hashimi was on a visit to Turkey. After Taha's departure, Sidqi and Sulayman were in a position to execute their coup. On October 25, Sidqi had paid a visit to Abd Al-Latif Nuri, commander of the First Division, and apparently discussed the plans for a coup. Sidqi then left Baghdad for his base at Qaratappa situated in between Baghdad and Kirkuk and revealed his plan to a few trusted officers. Sidqi's Second Division would march from the north on to the capital, while Abd Al-Latif Nuri's First Division stationed north-east of Baghdad would provide support (ibid.: 81).

On the night of October 28, 1936 Sidqi's forces moved on to Baaquba to the north of Baghdad and cut all telephone and telegram connections with the capital, preparing to make their final move the following day. On the morning of October 29, Sidqi and Abd Al-Latif Nuri ordered a fellow conspirator, Muhammad Ali Jawwad, commander of the Royal Iraqi Air Force to be ready for the "eleventh hour" whereupon eleven airplanes would take to the skies over Baghdad dropping leaflets that would demand King Ghazi replace Yasin Al-Hashimi with Hikmat Sulayman as the new Prime Minister. What is significant about the leaflets dropped on Baghdad that day was that they opened in the name of the military: "The army, which is composed of your sons, has lost patience with the present Government, who have been concerned only with their own personal interests, disregarding the public welfare" (Tarbush 1982: 121). This communiqué used a national institution, the Army, which had taken on a status of the patriotic embodiment of the Iraqi nation, to de-legitimize the incumbent cabinet and premier. Similar to Sidqi's triumphant speech after the Assyrian massacres, the invocation of the Army first signaled its supremacy, yet at the same time its ties with the people. The coup planners made it known that they had no wishes to overthrow the monarchy, but rather cause a change in the government. It was the aforementioned goal that demonstrated how a faction in Iraq's army had first exercised its veto power. Sidqi and his allied officers had vetoed the government of Yasin Al-Hashimi and offered a replacement. The Army expressed no desire to rule in its message, but rather to work with its fellow compatriots for the further betterment of the nation:

> The army therefore has appealed to His Majesty the King to dismiss the present cabinet and to replace it by another composed of sincere citizens under the leadership of Sayid Hikmat Sulaiman, who is held in greatest esteem and respect by the public.
>
> (Tarbush 1982: 122)

The text, announced to the Iraqi public, was signed by General Bakr Sidqi, and the points made in the leaflet were also delivered personally to the King at the Royal Palace by Hikmat Sulayman, however with a few additional lines threatening to bombard Baghdad in three hours if the King failed to comply. After the three hours had passed, in a demonstrative show of force, air planes dropped bombs near the Prime Minister's office, sending a message to Yasin of the coup planners' serious intentions. Yasin and his cabinet had no choice but to resign to avoid what they feared would become a civil war (Haddad 1971: 63).

As these events were transpiring inside the capital, Sidqi and his troops approached Baghdad from the north. Jaafar Al-Askari attempted to negotiate with Sidqi to prevent the spectacle of the military entering the city. Carrying a letter from the King, Jaafar approached the military units under Sidqi's command in order to stop their advance onto the capital; however Sidqi believed that Al-Askari was trying to thwart the coup and ordered his men to kill him. Even those men loyal to Sidqi were reluctant to kill a man who was considered "the father of the Iraqi army," but Al-Askari was intercepted, forced to pull over to the side of the road and executed by Sidqi's men. Ironically, Al-Askari, Iraq's first Minister of Defense in 1921 who had labored to create a nationwide army based on conscription became a victim to the very institution when it revolted. Sidqi's role in his murder, as well as in the ouster of Yasin Al-Hashimi, earned him enemies among officers who had supported the assassinated Defense Minister and the pan-Arabist premier.

Fearing that they would meet the same fate as Jaafar, Nuri Al-Said who had been Foreign Minister fled to Cairo. The former's decision was wise given that officers involved in the coup had accused Al-Said of building a palace with funds from the British Oil Development Company in exchange for a concession to extract oil from Iraq. The coup planners also accused Rashid Ali Al-Gaylani, the Minister of Interior and Yasin Al-Hashimi of illegally acquiring land during their tenure in government, and they both fled to Syria (Lukitz 1995: 84). Al-Said and Al-Gaylani would conspire to return to power after fleeing Iraq during the coup, and Al-Hashimi would eventually die in exile a year later from a heart attack.

In November 1936 Sulayman became the new Prime Minister, and formed a government with allies from the social reformist Ahali Group. Sulayman, Sidqi and the Ahali Group needed to justify their use of the military to overthrow the Yasin Al-Hashimi government. The need for legitimacy was highlighted by the fact that their action was the first military coup in Iraq, never mind the Arab world, and thus unprecedented in the politics of the region. In a November radio broadcast, in an almost apologetic tone, the Sulayman government justified its cooperation with the "gallant army officers" promising that they would strengthen the pride of the nation, the Army, in addition to delivering reforms of education, unemployment and land distribution (Haddad 1971: 64).

For the British, the coup represented the usurpation of power by the very Army that they had created. The Foreign Office, however, felt confident that their presence and influence in Iraq would not be challenged by the coup:

> the work of the Embassy at Baghdad differs from that of other posts in that remnants of the High Commission (i.e. mandate) days still remain.... The presence of the Royal Air Force and the British Advisory Military Mission, and the fact that His Majesty's Government have the right to be consulted and are consulted an all majors affecting the foreign policy of Iraq.
>
> (cited in Tarbush 1982: 135)

The British were concerned however with the new government's close ties with Turkey. In one report it was observed: "General Bakir Sidqi was a pure Turk and has always had an unbounded admiration for M. Ataturk. Sayid Hikmat Sulaiman is a Turkish Arab, and had for long held similar views about M. Ataturk" (FO 371/20014, November 16, 1936). While most sources cite Sidqi as being Kurdish, the British believed that he was Turkish, and they feared "a weak Government in Iraq, dependent on a pro-Turkish section of the army" (FO 371/20015, December 30, 1936). This correspondence revealed that even after the demarcation of the Iraqi–Turkish border, guaranteeing that the UK had secured its investment in the northern oilfields, the British still regarded Turkey as a potential threat to its interests in Iraq, and that Ankara could expand its influence in Iraq via sympathetic Iraqis in the military. The trappings of the neo-mandate military, including the Advisory Military Mission to the Iraqi Army, as well as the British Air Force could be threatened by the new government. There was also a concern that Iraq may not honor commercial interests related to the oil facilities. As the British decided not to intervene diplomatically, this gave the impression to the coup planners that the UK was primarily concerned with its bases and Iraq's oil resources. The British thus avoided a clash with Sidqi and the Sulayman government essentially allowing the formation of military moderator regime.

The military moderator regime of 1936–1937

Sidqi's coup had come as a surprise to the other officers in the Army not involved in its planning and were impressed by its execution and complete secrecy. Sidqi had provided those officers an opportunity to assume a direct role in politics and many assumed that Sidqi would allow them to achieve their national objectives. However, there was no agreement among these officers of their national objectives. Military officers had admired events that transpired in Turkey and Iran, and some even cherished the thought of going beyond a veto regime to establishing a military government. Other officers assumed that the coup was the first step in creating a militaristic Iraq that could unite the other Arab countries by force.

Sidqi however did not envision a role beyond influencing politics behind the scenes, evidenced by the fact he did not even assume the position of Minister of Defense that was offered to him. Rather he opted to decline an executive post and assumed the position of Chief of Staff that his rival Taha Al-Hashimi held. Sidqi had no interest in the administrative side of politics, but contented himself with maintaining a veto power over political matters. Nevertheless, officers around him who advocated a military dictatorship often goaded Sidqi into taking a more overt role in political affairs. The Minister of Defense portfolio was granted to Abd Al-Latif Nuri, Sidqi's co-conspirator in the coup. Just after the formation of the government, Abd Al-Latif Nuri gave a letter ordering Prime Minister Sulayman to instruct all government officials to conduct themselves "with fairness and courtesy." This in itself was an indication of the new power of the officers. One of their first orders was the directive to the Prime Minister from the Minister of Defense, representing the Army, an action that demonstrated who was really in charge (Be'eri 1970: 18).

While the British had acquiesced to the coup, it was assumed that the military would return to the barracks and abstain from intervening in political affairs. However, British reports criticized Prime Minister Sulayman for failing to return the army "back into its proper place" (FO 371/20013 E6814/141/91, October 30, 1936). Sidqi as a praetorian still exercised power from behind the scenes, for the most part, promoting the officers who took part in the coup and nominating thirty of his supporters to the cabinet (Haddad 1971: 65). He also ensured that the government provided the resources for strengthening and expanding the Army and supplying it with new arms. The military began to make incessant demands for its expansion, and when the British could not meet its demands for arms, it turned to the German and Czech arms manufacturers, the Krupp and Skoda companies, heralding the first deal where arms were acquired from non-British sources (Longrigg 1953: 253). Furthermore, to defend the interests of the military, Sidqi would often interfere in cabinet meetings, challenging the authority of the premier (FO 371/27095 E1235, February 14, 1937).

Sidqi was keen to eliminate any political rivals and sought a purge of the former government, which put him in conflict with the Ahali reformists who were weary of such extreme measures. In his capacity as the new Prime Minister, Sulayman scheduled new elections to be held for Parliament. He soon discovered the need to balance between the competing demands of Sidqi and the military on the one hand and the reformists on the other in organizing these elections. Sidqi feared that new elections could allow for the return of partisans loyal to the Yasin Al-Hashimi government. In January 1937 Ahali planned to transform its group into a political party for the elections, but Sidqi was concerned that an Ahali

Party could grow too strong in their informal alliance. Sulayman had granted permission for the formation of such a party but Sidqi vetoed Ahali's plan. The elections were finally held in February 1937, but only after Sulayman assured Sidqi and his followers in the military that the candidates running were of no threat (Khadduri 1960: 102, 111). By June 1937, the military had alienated the reformists who began to resign from the cabinet. Reformist programs such as nationalization of industries, distribution of state owned land to the peasants and the formation of trade unions were never realized due to Sidqi's objections and his desire to maintain the status quo (Be'eri 1970: 18). The clash between the liberal reformists and nationalist military officers could not be resolved and their resignations demonstrated that Sulayman, as facilitator of the alliance, was ultimately beholden to the military and would have to take its side. However, Sidqi, while in a position to dominate Iraqi political affairs, did not command complete control over the military, ultimately leading to his downfall.

Divisions in the military following the 1936 coup

Bakr Sidqi's followers in the military, such as the commander of the Air Force Muhammad Ali Jawwad were resistant to pan-Arabism. Sidqi and some of his supporters were not Arab but of Kurdish or Turkish descent. Sidqi had been an Arab nationalist opportunist prior to World War I and invoked Arab nationalism after the Assyrian affair to augment his popularity; but once in power, he and his closest officers believed in strengthening Arab–Kurdish relations inside a bi-national state of Iraq. The pan-Arab struggle beyond Iraq's borders was simply not a priority. What these officers did share in common with the pan-Arabist officers was their criticisms of the British role in Iraqi affairs, but the enmity was unable to unite the two factions (Khadduri 1960: 106).

Colonel Salah Al-Din Al-Sabbagh, the pan-Arabist officer from Mosul, would form a working partnership with three other like-minded colonels. Fahmi Said was from Sulaymaniyya, his father an Arab from the Anbak tribe situated near the Tigris and his mother was of Turkish origin. Mahmud Salman and Kamil Shabib were Arabs from Baghdad. All four had had studied in the Ottoman military education system and served in the Ottoman Army during World War I. What they shared in common with other Arab Ottoman military officers such as Nuri Al-Said or Jaafar Al-Askari was their Sunni backgrounds, a group in Iraq that viewed the Ottoman military system as a means for higher education. However Al-Sabbagh's generation came to the Istanbul military academy later than Al-Said or Al-Askari, and fought in the Ottoman military, rather than in the Sharifian army. Al-Sabbagh, for example, was a veteran of the Ottoman campaigns in Macedonia and Palestine.

After Faysal assumed power in Damascus, these four officers joined the army of the first post-Ottoman Arab state. They were all present in Syria when the French ousted Faysal and this short-lived Arab kingdom came to a violent end. This event hardened their belief that the British had allowed the French to destroy this state. Furthermore, the British reneged on their promise of a future Arab nation that would include Iraq, Syria, Palestine and the Arabian Peninsula. These officers also saw the same officials in London that failed to deliver on their promises determining Iraq's future. They begrudgingly returned to an Iraq that was under British occupation, and joined the Iraqi Army not out of a sense of loyalty to the new state, but out of need of a career. Even though they joined an Iraqi mandate army, they saw this institution as a vehicle to achieve Iraqi independence from Britain, and then to liberate Syria and Lebanon from French mandatory control and the contested Palestine mandate from the British (Simon 1986: 131).

Al-Sabbagh's aspirations for the Iraqi military are documented in his memoirs. He criticized British interference in the expansion of a nationalist Iraqi Army that could serve the cause of Arab unity. He believed that the British conspired to create an Iraqi military to serve as an internal security force to crush the Iraqi people, so that the UK could prevent the public from rallying behind a growing Army. In his opinion, it was not the armed strength of the Army that Britain feared per se, but rather its symbolic value as an institution that could foster solidarity between soldiers and the Iraqi masses under "the flag of Arabism" (Al-Sabbagh 1956: 43). He envisioned the Iraqi military growing into the largest army in the region to reunite the disparate Arab states through force. (Saddam Husayn even admitted that Al-Sabbagh was a personal hero and decades later attempted to fulfill the colonel's desire.) However, the reunification of the Arabs, in Al-Sabbagh's view, ran contrary to British strategic interests in the region, thus their alleged interests in weakening the Iraqi Army.

Like the Director of Education Shawkat, Al-Sabbagh admired the events that had transpired in neighboring Iran and Turkey. After attending Ataturk's funeral in 1939, Al-Sabbagh noted:

> I saw signs of progress which amazed me ... a social revolution in education and economics, and in cultural and spiritual affairs. I saw the pride of the Turks in their fatherland, pride in their nationalism, their self-reliance and their independence.
>
> (Al-Sabbagh 1956: 60–1)

While some Iraqi politicians, such as Hikmat Sulayman were inspired by events in Turkey and thus sought an alliance between Baghdad and Ankara, Al-Sabbagh's inspiration emanated from the Turkish Army's ability to establish its independence, a path he hoped would be emulated in Iraq and the rest of the Arab world. The slogan of the pan-Arab officers was "an Arab Iraq" (Be'eri 1970: 20). On the other hand the Sulayman government's priority was "Iraq for the Iraqis," concentrating on internal reform based on the Turkish model, rather than on pan-Arabism (Eppel 1988: 27). Al-Sabbagh accused Sulayman's loyalties of lying first with Turkey and was critical of Sidqi, of mixed Kurdish-Turkish descent, labeling him a Kurd first rather than a true Iraqi (Al-Sabbagh 1956: 17). The British were also cognizant of these divisions referring to General Amin Al-Umari as the "champion of the Arab element in the army, who had felt themselves slighted by Bakir Sidqi" (FO 371/20795, August 18, 1937). Al-Sabbagh argued that Sidqi was over-reliant on the Kurdish segment of the officer corps, and unfairly used his position as Chief of Staff to promote Kurds over the pan-Arabists in the military. In fact, Al-Sabbagh complained that under Bakr's aegis, Arab nationalist officers made up only 10 percent of the officer corps (Al-Sabbagh 1956: 76).

Just as Iraqi nationalism and pan-Arabism found a breeding ground in the military, the Iraqi Communists also tried to establish a foothold in the military. Communist leader Zaki Khayri placed particular importance in spreading Communist ideology in the military. After the 1936 coup, he assessed that Communism would not gather sympathizers among the upper echelons of the military, but realized that inroads could be made into the body of the lower and middle ranks. In Khayri's opinion, one of the precursors of their revolution was the alienation of these soldiers from their superior officers, assessing that the strength of the officers would be undermined without the non-commissioned officers and lower ranks' acquiescence to their coup plans. An unpublished Communist manuscript entitled *The Iraqi Army*, prepared by Khayri, described how clandestine cells were formed in 1935 in the Second Army Division based at Kirkuk (which had been under the command of General Sidqi at the time). A Communist Military Committee had begun agitation within the lower ranks of the Army, but their underground networks were discovered and dismantled after a 1937 purge of their elements in the military (Batatu 1979: 445–6).

The 1937 coup

In August 1937 Colonel Salah Al-Din Al-Sabbagh would assume his role as a praetorian, along with his other three associates: Kamil Shabib, Mahmud Salman and Fahmi Said. They ensured that their sacred mission of pan-Arabism would be fulfilled and that this trend in the military would remain dominant. They conspired with three other pan-Arabist officers, Aziz Yamulki, Husayn Fawzi and Amin Al-Umari, and were known collectively as the "Seven."

The first priority for these officers was to assassinate Bakr Sidqi, the military anchor of the Sulayman government. The motivations behind the assassination plot were numerous and ostensibly in retaliation for Sidqi's role in the death of Jaafar Al-Askari, the former Defense Minister, and a man beloved by these officers. They also blamed Sulayman and Sidqi for the death of Yasin Al-Hashimi, the popular pan-Arab and pro-Palestinian premier who had worked with Al-Sabbagh in the Muthanna Club and the Palestine Defense Council. Even though Al-Hashimi died of natural causes in Syria, it was the coup that sent him into exile, and the stress of the events that were attributed to precipitating his heart attack in June 1937. It was also believed that Sidqi had a role in a failed assassination of one of his critics, Mawlud Mukhlis, popular among the pan-Arabist officers (Longrigg 1953: 253). Mukhlis had played a prominent role in recruiting Sunni Arabs into the military, including townsmen from Takrit, the generation that would go on to overthrow the government in 1968.

On August 11, 1937 General Sidqi was traveling to Turkey to take part in Saadabad Pact military exercises. (The Saadabad Pact had been signed between Iraq, Turkey, Iran and Afghanistan on July 8, 1937.) During a layover in Mosul he was met by Muhammad Ali Jawwad the commander of the Air Force that had helped him seize power in the 1936 coup. One of the four colonels, Fahmi Said was aware of Sidqi's presence at the Mosul airfield. As Sidqi and Jawwad were resting at the air base, a soldier named Muhammad Ali Tal-Afari shot them both dead. Sidqi's moderator regime had lasted a mere ten months.

With Sidqi's elimination, the link between Sulayman's government and the military was practically crippled. The Prime Minister had tried to prosecute the officers involved in the assassination, such as Fahmi Said, but faced a mutiny when an officer in the Seven group, Amin Al-Umari, commander of the Mosul garrison, openly defied Sulayman's orders and declared his opposition to the current government. The other officers that would make up the Seven clique, as well as army commanders in Sulaymaniyya and Kirkuk, sided with the renegade Al-Umari.

Rumors of civil war abounded in the capital during the standoff between the Army in Baghdad, loyal to the premier, and Al-Umari's forces in Mosul. During the tensions, Said Al-Takriti, commander of the Third Division, declared that his forces in Baghdad were siding with Al-Umari's Mosul rebellion for the sake of preventing a civil war (Be'eri 1970: 21). Feeling increasingly isolated, Sulayman resigned a few days later and his cabinet was dissolved. The first Iraqi government that had been established by a coup d'état was overthrown by another coup d'état, a trend that would continue in the following decades in Iraqi history. The August coup represented the victory of the pan-Arabists over the Iraqi particularists. While the two nationalist and essentially anti-British camps had managed to co-exist in the past, by 1937 they would rival each other within Iraqi society and inside the military.

Al-Umari declared that his forces would stand down and not interfere in political affairs any further. It was an insincere statement on his part. The clique of officers known as the Seven could hardly restrain themselves from interfering in future political matters and followed Sidqi's legacy of influencing internal politics from behind the scenes. The only difference was that their military moderator regime operated under a pan-Arabist guise. The officers did not involve themselves with the daily affairs of the state, but from 1937 onwards they moderated disputes between politicians, vetoed any threatening cabinet decisions and even the cabinet itself if they did not approve of its make-up. They invoked this unofficial veto on several occasions by threatening and carrying out coups within a period of four years.

As Sunni Arabs, the officers sought to enhance their minority status in Iraq by linking their nation's identity with that of the greater Sunni Arab world. The Seven were finally in a position to assume their dream of creating their Arab Prussia to expel imperialist influences in the region, unite the various Arab countries and come to the rescue of Palestine, which seemed to be on the road to partition. In their positions of power, they had the coercive measures to ensure the government did not stray from this path.

On August 17, 1937 Jamil Midfai, a former Ottoman officer and member of the post-World War I Sharifian army in Syria, became the next Prime Minister. The King appointed Midfai due to his assurances that he enjoyed the support of the Seven. However, Midfai had an agenda of ensuring that the Seven refrained from interfering in political affairs (Tarbush 1982: 150). To appease them, Midfai promoted the Seven to prominent positions. Salah Al-Din Al-Sabbagh became Director of Military Operations, Mahmud Salman commander of Mechanized Forces and Kamil Shabib commander of the Infantry (Khadduri 1960: 130). Amin Al-Umari became commander of the First Infantry Division, Aziz Yamulki commander of Mechanical Transport and Husayn Fawzi was appointed to the highest military post, the Chief of Staff (Be'eri 1970: 22).

In January 1938 Midfai appointed Sabih Najib as the new Minister of Defense. Like the premier, Najib was apprehensive of the power of the Seven and attempted to exclude them from the political process. The Seven praetorians feared that their enhanced positions would be lost and challenged Midfai and Najib by asserting their veto power. Midfai had dismissed the Minister of Interior in May 1938 and considered appointing a politician from the former Sulayman cabinet, Muhammad Ali Mahmud. The Seven, opposed to a politician from the government that they deposed returning to power, exercised their veto by placing military units on alert. As a result, Midfai never appointed Mahmud (Tarbush 1982: 155).

Midfai was aware that he could not gain the support of the army officers, and purged politicians from the government who were clients of the Seven. Rumors had emerged that the Minister of Defense was about to retire some of the prominent officers, and to preempt this action, the Seven in December 1938 vetoed Midfai, insisting that he resign. On December 24, the highest ranking officer of the Seven, Husayn Fawzi, Chief of the General Staff, deployed a military detachment outside of Baghdad. Once demonstrating the forces at his disposal, he met with King Ghazi and asked him to dissolve Midfai's cabinet. Aziz Yamulki, commander of Mechanical Transport, approached Prime Minister Midfai in his home and personally demanded his resignation. Midfai had no choice but to give in to the officer's demands. The military had vetoed Midfai's government without firing a shot, marking Iraq's third coup d'état. On December 25 a new government was formed.

The August 1937 coup allowed Nuri Al-Said and Rashid Ali Al-Gaylani, two veteran Iraqi politicians, to return from exile following the 1936 Sidqi putsch. At this point, their previous rivals, Jaafar Al-Askari and Yasin Al-Hashimi had passed on and were no longer actors in the political process, leading to an eventual showdown between Al-Said and Al-Gaylani over who would emerge as Iraq's strongest politician. Taha Al-Hashimi, the former Chief of Staff, had also lost his power as a result of the first coup in 1936. The three were rivals, united by the realization that the Army could serve as the most powerful vehicle to allow them to regain complete control over the government. They believed that the Seven officers had enough support in the military to facilitate their political comeback. The Seven also sought an alliance with these politicians vying to reclaim their lost authority and believed that they could manipulate the three politicians to do their bidding. Midfai's resignation allowed for their return to power.

On December 25, 1938 Nuri Al-Said became the new Prime Minister, however cognizant of the fact that the Seven brought him to power and of the need to control them in the future. According to Al-Sabbagh, the Seven had chosen Al-Said because he promised prior to the coup not to resist the Army's exercise of its veto power. According to Al-Sabbagh, Al-Said said he would "give the army the right to have its say in all that concerned the resignation of any government, the establishment of a new one and the decision as to its premier" (Al-Sabbagh 1956: 133). Al-Gaylani was granted the post of Chief of the Royal Diwan, which gave him influence over the throne, but not enough power to satiate his desires. A conflict emerged between Al-Said and Al-Gaylani in securing the loyalty of the officers to further their own political goals.

Al-Said decided to break the power of the Seven by forming an alliance with the faction of three officers headed by Chief of Staff Husayn Fawzi, which included Al-Umari and Yamulki (FO 406/78 E779/4481/93, February 21, 1940). When they spurned him, Al-Said turned to the faction made up of the four colonels led by Al-Sabbagh. Political power games had pushed these four officers to the forefront, and ironically, Al-Said, who had nurtured the rift within the Seven, would later become its victim in 1941.

The moderator regime of the Four Colonels

By 1939 the Iraqi military had 1,426 officers and 26,345 men (FO
371/23217/E 2372/72.93, February 28, 1939). Iraq's second king, Ghazi
died in 1939, leaving his infant son Faysal II to assume the throne. The
military officers moderated between the political factions as to who would
be appointed to the caretaker position, the Regent. The four colonels, as
well as Prime Minister Nuri Al-Said favored Abd Al-Ilah, a twenty-six year
old relative of Faysal. Due to his young age, they believed he could be
more easily controlled. The other three officers in the Seven group preferred that the forty-one year old brother of Faysal, Prince Zayd, serve as
the Regent (Simon 1986: 129). In this conflict, the four colonels emerged
as the stronger moderators, and Abd Al-Ilah became the Regent.

With the outbreak of World War II in September 1939, the UK asked
Iraq to break diplomatic relations with Germany. The Seven praetorians at
the time were anti-British, but reluctantly gave in to this request, but vetoed
Al-Said's decision to declare war on Germany. In order to support the
British war effort, in February 1940 Al-Said announced his plans to send
Iraqi troops to join the Allied front in the Balkans. Chief of Staff Husayn
Fawzi questioned why an Iraqi Army should fight in a distant conflict in the
Balkans, when Iraqi troops should be dispatched to support the Palestini-
ans. His faction consisting of the three officers asked Al-Said to resign from
the government (ibid.: 136). However the four colonels sought to protect
their client Al-Said and declared their support for the Prime Minister.

Fawzi, Al-Umari and Yamulki as a triumvirate collectively rejected the
four colonels' decision. On February 21, 1940 Al-Umari mobilized the
First Division at the Washshash Camp west of Baghdad. The four colonels
responded by placing the Third Division at the Rashid Camp in the capital
on alert (Longrigg 1953: 281). The colonels also secured the loyalty of the
Second Division in Kirkuk and the Fourth Division in Diwaniyya. The triumvirate had mobilized only one division outside of the capital. The
colonels' forces were inside of Baghdad and were mobilized in the north
and south. With the majority of Iraq's armed forces on the colonels' side,
the Regent decided to ally himself with the latter and the three praetorians
within the Seven were forced to retire (Be'eri 1970: 29).

In the aftermath of this coup, the four colonels became known collectively as the "Four Colonels," or the "Golden Square." The allies of the
Four Colonels were given the posts left by the three opposition military
officers. Amin Zaki, one of the supporters of the Colonels was made Chief
of Staff, and Kamil Shabib relieved Al-Umari of command of the First
Division. The Four commanded the key divisions of the Army, and thus no
internal force, be it a tribal revolt or dissident factions in the military,
could have dislodged them from power. Salah Al-Din Al-Sabbagh, as their
leader, controlled the most important positions in the military and the
Colonels' veto in government affairs could not be ignored. They were in de

facto control over Iraq. In his memoirs Al-Sabbagh described the extent of new powers of the Four Colonels, where politicians would compete seeking the patronage of the officers, so that they could overthrow "so and so's cabinet because it is so and so ... Rustam Haidar because he is a Shi'a ... the other because he is a traitor ... and the other because he is a communist, etc." (Al-Sabbagh 1956: 71).

The fourth coup d'état had successfully led to the consolidation of power of the Four Colonels and these praetorians demonstrated that they were the power brokers keeping Al-Said in power. A British article in *The Times* quoted how Nuri Al-Said still expressed the belief that after this coup, the military would refrain from political affairs: "Nury Pasha nevertheless believes that the chiefs of the Army will in future restrict their activities and ambitions to purely military aims" (*The Times*, March 19, 1940: 9). Ironically, as they acquired the exclusive veto power of the military, the Four Colonels would be in a position to bring down Al-Said's government a year later.

The Colonels moderated a political crisis once again during a standoff between Nuri Al-Said and Rashid Ali Al-Gaylani. In order to moderate between the two, the Four Colonels enlisted an outsider, the Mufti of Jerusalem Hajj Amin al-Husayni. The Mufti had been residing in Baghdad since October 1939 and was respected by the Four. The Mufti was not only a religious figure, but an officer who had studied in the Ottoman military academy and served in the Ottoman military with one of the Four Colonels, Mahmud Salman, in Izmir during World War I (Simon 1986: 139). During the crisis between Al-Said and Al-Gaylani, the Mufti had brokered a compromise between the two where as of March 31, 1940 Al-Gaylani would become Prime Minister and Al-Said Minister of Foreign Affairs. Al-Said was willing to let Al-Gaylani assume the highest executive post, leaving him with the difficulty of balancing Iraqi affairs between the British and pro-Axis sentiment in the country.

Al-Sabbagh's coterie had cooperated with Al-Said until they deemed his pro-British loyalties were a liability after the defeat of France in June 1940. On the other hand, the Four Colonels found in Rashid Ali a political client who supported their ideological platform. Unlike Iraq's other politicians, Al-Gaylani was not an Ottoman military officer, but rather a lawyer and an active member in the Ottoman-era Committee of Union and Progress. In fact, he did not join any of the secret Arab societies such as Al-Ahd. It did not appear that he espoused Arab nationalism prior to World War I unlike many of his Arab contemporaries, but by 1939 Al-Gaylani had espoused a world view similar to the Four Colonels' anti-British Iraqi nationalism and vision of Iraq as the core of a future unified Arab nation. Both the Colonels and Al-Gaylani operated in an educational and militaristic milieu that harkened back to a golden Arab past and for them the Iraqi Army was a vehicle to restore these former glories. Therefore, the Four Colonels supported Al-Gaylani's espousal of neutrality during the

War, his willingness to challenge the 1930 Treaty and the British role in Iraqi affairs, and his secret contacts with the Axis. While Al-Gaylani and his supporters have been described as Nazis or Nazi sympathizers, their approaches to the Axis powers were out of pragmatism and not ideological affinity to a system of beliefs that considered Semitic Arabs as a category just above Semitic Jews. A German victory against the UK would end British interference in Iraq's political destiny. Naturally, the British deemed Al-Gaylani as a threat to their interests in Iraq and called for his removal (Batatu 1979: 208).

Towards the end of the summer of 1940, Al-Said in his capacity as Foreign Minister invited the Four Colonels for a meeting to discuss the possibility of Al-Sabbagh, commander of the Third Division, leading an Iraqi expeditionary force to fight the Italians in Libya. Unbeknownst to Al-Said, the Four Colonels' true loyalties rested with the Premier Al-Gaylani, who opposed the Libya plan, as well as another plan for a contingent of British troops to arrive in Basra. The Four Colonels' were also devoted to the Mufti Al-Husayni, who along with Al-Gaylani believed that Iraqi troops should be fighting for the Palestinian cause and not that of the Allies. Al-Sabbagh invoked his veto against the Libya motion, and the plan was dropped (Khadduri 1960: 193). The rift between the Colonels and Nuri Al-Said was never healed after that confrontation (Al-Sabbagh 1956: 143).

By December 1940, the British continued to pressure Prime Minister Al-Gaylani to resign, and Nuri Al-Said was keen to remove a political opponent. Al-Gaylani resisted their demands and in late January 1941 called upon his patrons, the Four Colonels to intervene on his behalf. The Colonels approached the Regent Abd Al-Ilah, asking him to allow Al-Gaylani to keep his office. The Regent decided to challenge the Colonels declaring that the military should stay out of politics. The Four Colonels implied that they could use their veto power by placing the Army on high alert, and the Regent reluctantly gave in to the officers' demands.

However on January 30, the Regent was faced with another dilemma when Al-Gaylani asked for royal permission to dissolve a Parliament hostile to the Prime Minister. The Regent, cognizant of the Four Colonels' patronage of Al-Gaylani, asked the Prime Minister for time to mull over the decision. Abd Al-Ilah thereupon fled Baghdad and proceeded to Diwaniyya in the south, where he sought protection from General Ibrahim Al-Rawi, commander of the Fourth Division. Al-Rawi belonged to the generation of ex-Sharifians who fought in the Arab Revolt and felt inclined to protect a member of the Hashimite family. Thus, while Al-Gaylani sought the patronage of the Four Colonels, the Regent had to counter that patronage network by becoming a client of General Al-Rawi. Having done so, the Regent was in a position of balancing the Fourth Division against the military units under the Four Colonels in case they would use the Army to enforce their veto (Longrigg 1953: 286).

Upon hearing the news, one of the Colonels, Fahmi Said encouraged Al-

Gaylani to resist pressures to resign. In a meeting with the members of the Four Colonels during this standoff, Al-Sabbagh stated his opposition to the Anglo-Iraqi Treaty, which would have given the right for British troops to transit through Iraq: "The army cannot permit foreign troops, armed to the teeth, to roam the country, while it stands by without reacting" (Be'eri 1970: 30). It was a strong worded statement indicating that the officers would veto the British troop motion. As to the resignation of Al-Gaylani, he declared, "Nothing of the sort must take place. Iraq is blessed with a stout-hearted army" (ibid.). However, with the prospect of civil war looming, Al-Sabbagh eventually gave in and advised Al-Gaylani to resign, which he did on January 31, 1941. The Regent had successfully managed to cancel out the veto power of the Four Colonels but only by seeking patronage from General Al-Rawi. The fifth coup attempt since 1936 had failed, but the Regent's actions did not mean that the Colonels had lost their say over government affairs, since the Four Colonels pressured the Regent to allow another one of their preferred candidates, Taha Al-Hashimi become the new Prime Minister. Although the Regent had another candidate in mind, he gave in to the Colonels' wishes when they threatened again to use their military might. While Al-Rawi had protected him during the first crisis, the Regent doubted that the General, as an army officer would protect him again from fellow military officers. The sixth coup launched by Iraqi praetorians since 1936 had succeeded.

Taha Al-Hashimi became Prime Minster the following day on February 1, 1941. The Regent had hoped that Al-Hashimi would retire the Colonels upon becoming premier, but the new Prime Minister was reluctant of clashing with the praetorians who brought him to power and that had so much influence in the Army. He had maintained cordial relations with them in the past and felt that he could foster reconciliation between the officers and the Regent. The Four Colonels on the other hand saw in Al-Hashimi a client they could control for their own ends. They would continue to moderate the policy of the government, refusing to allow relations to be broken off with Mussolini's Italy after Iraq had already given in to British demands to break off relations with Germany. Even though the Colonels brought Al-Hashimi to power in 1941, as the Prime Minister he realized that he would have to check their power eventually. He politely tried to encourage Al-Sabbagh to accept a transfer from commander of the Third Division to commander of the Second Division in Kirkuk, and have Shabib give up his command of the First Division to accept the command of the Fourth Division in Diwaniyya. The transfers would result in two of the Four Colonels accepting posts that would station them outside of Baghdad, the political center. Both of the Colonels simply vetoed the request of the Prime Minister. Al-Hashimi then accepted their refusal but asked for their assurance that they would refrain from intervening in political matters. The Four Colonels began to resent what they perceived as Al-Hashimi's interference, in addition to his pro-British attitude. In

February 1941 a meeting chaired by the Mufti, in which Al-Gaylani and the Colonels were present decided that Taha had to be removed in favor of returning the post of Prime Minister to Rashid Ali Al-Gaylani (Khadduri 1960: 208). The plan for another coup was set in motion.

In March, the conflict between the Regent and the Four had reached a crisis point. Al-Hashimi, under orders from the Regent, attempted to transfer Shabib out of Baghdad once again, which he refused a second time. In a British report it was agreed "that a forward policy in Iraq was now desirable, with the object of causing a rupture with Italy and of upsetting the extremist clique, which included the Mufti and the 'Golden Square' [The Four]" (quoted in Tarbush 1982: 174). However, on March 21, when Abd Al-Ilah informed the British ambassador of his plans to remove the Colonels, he was discouraged as it might lead to "violent reactions" from "the military clique" and their ally the Mufti (FO 371/270162, March 24, 1941).

During the impasse, the Chief of Staff Amin Zaki and the Four Colonels met on April 1, 1941 and placed the Army on alert. Army formations then marched into Baghdad taking over key installations, such as the telegraph office, telephone exchange and broadcasting stations announcing their call for the resignation of Taha Al-Hashimi's government (Tarbush 1982: 174). The praetorians decided that Zaki and one of the other Colonels, Fahmi Said, commander of the Armored Forces, would deliver an ultimatum to Taha demanding he resign. Taha refused to resign where upon Zaki and Said insisted. At that point Taha did resign, and then the Army surrounded the Regent's house and tried to compel the Regent to reappoint Al-Gaylani as Prime Minister. But Abd Al-Ilah had escaped, as he had done in the past when he fled to Diwaniyya, now seeking refuge in Jordan, and was later joined by his ally Nuri Al-Said. Al-Hashimi's government had lasted a mere two months from February to April 1941. Al-Gaylani worried how his new government would have any legitimacy as the Regent was not present and could not declare a royal decree bestowing power upon him, making his premiership unconstitutional. The Colonels assumed their moderator powers in direct contradiction of the constitution by ordering Al-Gaylani to summon a session of Parliament, where the Iraqi Senate and Chamber of Deputies would appoint a new Regent. Al-Gaylani formed a new government on April 12, 1941 ushering in the events known as the April 1941 "Rashid Ali coup."

The April 1941 coup

While the 1941 events have been referred to as the "Rashid Ali coup," it was launched by the Army under the aegis of the Four Colonels, with support from pan-Arabists among the Sunni middle class. According to Batatu, "At no point in 1941 did Rashid Ali rise to a decisive political role. The Four Colonels had the higher hand from the first to last" (1979: 205). The two organizations in which Al-Sabbagh and Sami Shawkat had a strong influence, the pan-Arabist Muthanna Club and the paramilitary youth organization, the *Futuwwa* praised the actions of the Four Colonels (Longrigg, 1953: 288). The Youth Cadets or the *Futuwwa* had been established in 1939 by Shawkat, in his capacity as Director General of Education, as a system of paramilitary education at the secondary school level "to create in the youths a military spirit and love of discipline" (Salih 1996: 57). One of the *Futuwwa*'s instructors included Al-Sabbagh himself. The emergence of the *Futuwwa* served a vivid reflection of the martial symbolism in education and the militarization of Iraqi politics at these times (Al-Musawi 2006: 21).

The 1941 coup was also congratulated by the Axis powers. The Four Colonels were convinced that the Axis would win the war after their victory in Greece and contacted Germany for arms (Simon 1986: 147). Al-Gaylani, fearful of an armed British intervention, wanted to at least seek recognition from the UK for his new government, but the Colonels vetoed his decision. The Colonels also pressured the cabinet to forbid a British contingent to land at Basra. The British had already been stationed in Iraq at the two RAF bases, but the officers were opposed to additional land forces arriving.

Invoking the 1930 Anglo-Iraqi Treaty, on April 28 the British ambassador to Iraq informed the Iraqi government that 2,000 British troops would ignore its decision and land in Basra. On the following day, the troops disembarked in Basra, and one of the Colonels, Fahmi Said deployed troops under his command from the Rashid camp, eleven kilometers south of Baghdad, towards positions overlooking Habbaniyya, the British base. By April 30, the troops were given orders to shoot down any plane that took off from that facility. On May 2, all British planes at the base took off attacking the Iraqi positions, and on the following day ironically attacked the British-supplied Iraqi planes stationed at the Rashid air base. Thus began the Thirty Day War with Britain. The Germans who had been preparing for an invasion of the Soviet Union were too preoccupied to offer substantial support to the Iraqis. After the British attack, the Prime Minister sought to compromise with the British, but the Colonels threatened to shoot Al-Gaylani if he attempted to do so (Haddad 1971: 72).

The Iraqi military proved incapable of offering sustained resistance to the British forces, suffering from low morale, desertions and confusion in the higher ranks. Since 1936, the military's attention had been consumed by political affairs to the neglect of strengthening the armed forces. Among the Four Colonels during the fighting, Fahmi Said suffered a nervous breakdown, Kamil Shabib deserted and Al-Sabbagh was "losing his nerve" (Tarbush 1982: 180). By May 6, the Iraqi forces began withdrawing as British forces from Jordan attacked, taking Falluja on May 19 and routing the Iraqi troops there. In the south, British forces made a rapid two pronged advance from Basra on to Baghdad. By May 29, British forces were on the outskirts of Baghdad, bringing an end to the reign of the Four Colonels and the collapse of Iraq's military moderator regime.

4 Dismantling the military moderator regime 1941–1958

The military after 1941

After the Thirty Day War of 1941, the Regent Abd Al-Ilah and Nuri Al-Said returned to power by October 1941 and reasserted their strength by eliminating the moderator potential and veto power of the military. Their task was facilitated by the Army's already weakened status due to a reduction in numbers from desertions. According to the British Colonel Gerald de Gaury, the British chargé d'affaires appointed to the Regent, prior to the 1941 conflict the Army had four divisions and 44,217 men (De Gaury 1961: 146). After the war, the army was in a pitiful state:

> Its boots were (at the end of the Second World War) mostly unfit for wear in marching, its supply of clothes short, its leave long overdue, it pay meagre, and its rations had been reduced to a figure of a thousand calories below the minimum considered necessary by European medical men for Eastern troops. Money for repair of barracks and camps has been stopped. The Police were forbidden to assist in tracing or arresting deserters and by the summer of 1943, out of an established strength of thirty thousand men, twenty thousand were deserters.
>
> (ibid.)

De Gaury, while not stating the obvious, had pointed out in his report that the operational units in the military were approximately 50 percent below strength. The Head of the British Military Mission in Iraq, Major General Renton was tasked with reorganizing the Army and wrote:

> If special attention is paid to training and morale of officers and the elimination of political influence, [the] Army should be able to regain the standard reached in 1927–33 when successful operations [were] undertaken against the Euphrates Arabs, Sulaimani, and [the] Barzan Kurds. . . . Consider therefore we should try to sugar the pill as much as possible by accepting the inclusion of light tanks in the mobile troops and some medium and anti-tank artillery, purely as token forces. This may have the effect of keeping Iraqis happy.
>
> (FO 371/40044/E700/42/93, January 6, 1944)

Major General Renton found every unit "under strength-untrained-immobile-and quite unfit to take the field" (FO 371/40044/E6246/42/93, September 27, 1944). Renton regrouped the army by reducing its strength from four to three divisions. Those officers with anti-British tendencies who did not flee Iraq were either purged or retired (De Gaury 1961: 30). The older generation of Ottoman-trained officers was taken out of their retirements and resumed their posts as they were considered politically more reliable (Longrigg 1953: 311). From these two reports, the British sought to re-establish the mandate army model, so that it would not be allowed to interfere in politics, making the Army still dependent on the UK for arms.

The British also realized their mistake in neglecting the symbiotic relationship between the military and public education and sought to undo the work of Husri and Shawkat. British advisors would remain in the Iraqi Ministry of Education and in the Army to ensure these trends did not re-emerge, and nationalist and militaristic themes in Iraqi textbooks were deleted (Simon 1986: 161–2).

Three of the Four Colonels, Fahmi Said, Mahmud Salman and Kamil Shabib, were eventually arrested and hanged. Salah Al-Din al-Sabbagh, by dressing as a dervish, wandered into Turkey, where he was interned and had the chance to write his memoirs. He too was eventually extradited to Iraq and hanged on orders of the Iraqi government (ibid.: 165).

By 1943, Al-Said declared his confidence that the purges had succeeded. The British had reoccupied Iraq, and controlled the size, scope and retraining of the Iraqi military. The neo-mandate army had indeed been re-established. However, the British were still wary of anti-British tendencies among the younger officers, but there was a limit as to how many officers they could purge. While the British advisors in the government along with Al-Said implemented these purges, they ultimately deprived it of talented officers who could protect the monarchy from internal threats, particularly a Kurdish rebellion that would flare up in the north in September 1943 (Salih 1996: 80). The revolt, led by a prominent tribal leader, Mulla Mustafa Barazani, exacerbated Kurdish–Arab tensions in the military and posed an imminent threat for an Iraqi administration attempting to reform this institution (Longrigg 1953: 325). Apparently some Kurdish officers were removed from the military according to a British report detailing a conversation between Al-Said and Majid Mustafa, a Kurdish minister. During a heated exchange, Mustafa said, "you have just removed 30 or 40 Kurdish officers for no other reason that they were Kurds" (FO 371/40028/E3302/26, May 23, 1944).

The Iraqi Army advanced in Kurdish held areas in August and September 1945, with the Royal Iraqi Air Force bombing areas where the Barazani rebellion had taken root (Salih 1996: 95). The military faced difficulties in fighting the forces loyal to Barazani, and sought to enlist the support of irregular Kurdish tribal forces opposed to Mulla Mustafa. Barazani's troops retreated into Iran, were they found refuge in a Soviet sponsored breakaway state centered in the town of Mahabad; a state similar in scope to a Soviet backed Azerbaijan Republic based in the Iranian city of Tabriz. The leader of the Iranian Kurdish movement, Qadhi Muhammad would form a Kurdish Democratic Party with Barazani that would later play a pivotal role in Kurdish military relations in Iraq. However, for the time being, the Army had dealt with a Kurdish threat and the Regent rewarded the armed forces for their efforts (Longrigg 1953: 327). In December 1945, the Regent delivered a speech where he declared, "The Army's efficiency came to light in the punitive operations carried out by the Government against the Barzanis" (Salih 1996: 100). The use of the term "punitive" demonstrated how the state legitimized the Army as a tool to deal with Iraq's internal "problems," or communities merely resistant to the monarchy's authority.

The military in 1948

The year 1948 would prove to be a tumultuous year for the monarchy. Iraqi nationalists began to demand the revision of the Anglo-Iraqi Treaty of 1930, whereupon Prime Minister Salih Jabr negotiated a revised version treaty in Portsmouth in the UK on January 15, 1948, which became effective for twenty-five years. According to the Treaty, the British air bases would be evacuated, but it allowed for British troops to return in the case of war. The surviving nationalist officers were particularly resentful of a Joint Defense Board with the UK as they felt such an institution would challenge their authority. They also objected to an article of the Treaty that stipulated that the Iraqi Army could be used to protect British interests outside of Iraq (ibid.: 117). The officers were unwilling to protect British interests in Iraq, never mind those interests outside of the state. Finally, the Treaty allowed the British to maintain their bases in Habbaniyya and Shuayba in a time of war, and nationalist officers remembered how their heroes, the Four Colonels, were first attacked by British airplanes stationed in Habbaniyya. The Treaty signaled to the officers that the UK presence in Iraq would continue indefinitely.

The Treaty symbolized continued British domination over Iraqi affairs, and provided a pretext for opposition parties to agitate. Iraqi Communists began to demonstrate against the Treaty, and their protests were joined by students and widespread riots ensued. The events, known as the *Wathba* or "The Leap" posed a serious challenge for civil–military relations in Iraq. The government, cognizant of past military coups during periods of instability, hesitated to deploy the armed forces against the rioters. The Army had not yet been deployed in Iraq's capital as a tool of internal coercion, and had only seen action in the peripheral areas of Iraq, the tribal south and north. Despite the purges of nationalist officers from the military, there was a fear that some of the officers were sympathetic to the protestors' opposition to the new Treaty.

From a military viewpoint the riots in themselves were insignificant. The Regent at the end rejected the Treaty and dismissed the premier Salih Jabr who was responsible for the negotiations. However, the fact that an episode of domestic instability passed without military interference demonstrated that the military moderator regime of the 1930s, which intervened during political crises, had been dismantled.

While it survived one test, the 1948 Arab–Israeli War could be considered the catalyst that planted the seeds of the monarchy's ultimate demise. Iraq, along with other Arab states, denounced the creation of Israel and dispatched military forces to aid the Palestinians in May 1948. When the Arab–Israeli War of 1948 broke out, Iraq had 21,000 men organized into twelve brigades. Iraq deployed one Iraqi armored battalion and four infantry brigades, close to 5,000 men to take part in the fighting (Pollack 2002: 150). The 1948 war represented the first deployment of Iraqi troops outside of its borders, as the armed forces had been primarily involved in maintaining internal security while partaking in coups on the side. For some of the officers, particularly the pan-Arabists, the war proved an opportunity to take an active role in aiding the Palestinians, assuming their role as an Arab Prussia.

Towards the end of May 1948, Iraqi Army units held a strategic triangle of towns running from Nablus to Janin to Tulkarim. However, there were problems facing the Iraqi troops from the outset of the conflict. They had to depend on a long line of logistics and communications that ran from Baghdad through Jordan. The other Arab states taking part in the conflict, Jordan, Syria, Lebanon and Egypt did not have a unified command due to the political divisions among them. Furthermore, the Iraqi military was for the most part inactive during the conflict, sitting in the "triangle," even to the point where the phrase in the Iraqi dialect *maku awamir* ("there are no orders") took a life of its own, associated with the passivity of Iraqi forces during the war (Heller 1994: 39). Nevertheless, the Iraqi forces did secure the town of Janin from Israeli forces, affecting the demarcation of what would later emerge as the West Bank.

According to Batatu, the Army lacked preparation, leadership and sufficient arms as a result of the monarchy's desire to weaken the military following the events of 1941 (1979: 31). The Army's legacy of internal coercion resulted in unpreparedness to deal with a foreign engagement, particularly in a theater that did not border Iraq. Iraq's military had been restructured after World War II with British assistance for maintaining internal security. The greatest threat to internal security after the war was a Kurdish separatist movement that could come under Communist influence from the Soviet Union. While the British helped train the Iraqi military to fight in the mountainous north to defeat the Kurdish rebels, there were no British efforts to help the Iraqi military fight a war well outside its borders. The officers deployed to the Palestine front were resentful of the Iraqi leadership and the British, and believed that their forces were dispatched by the monarchy merely for a symbolic show of Arab solidarity. In the memoirs of Ismail Al-Arif, he described the officers' resentment to the government after the 1948 debacle: "The officers perceived clearly that the pro-British Iraqi politicians had bound the army's hands in the war in order to conspire with foreign powers in establishing the state of Israel" (Al-Arif 1982: 40). Salih also pointed out that besides the monarchy's lack of enthusiasm for the war, these pan-Arab officers were also commanding Kurdish and Shia Arab infantry men, who as non-Sunni Arabs were unenthusiastic about fighting for predominantly Sunni Arab Palestine (Salih 1996: 105). After returning from the front lines in 1949, some of the officers considered bringing the Iraqi military back into the political process after the leadership humiliated them in Palestine. It was this war and later events in Egypt that would spark the imagination of a younger generation of officers in Iraq.

The 1952 Egyptian Free Officers' coup

In 1952, a group of Egyptian officers known as the Free Officers overthrew the Egyptian monarch. One of the Free Officers, Jamal Abd al-Nasir (also written as Gamal Abd Al-Nasser) emerged as the new Egyptian leader and would develop a creed known as Nasirism stressing neutralism and non-alignment during the Cold War, Arab unity and socialist reform. The pillars of his platform were not necessarily new to the Arab world, and another organization, the Arab Baath Party (later known as the Arab Socialist Baath Party), founded by the Syrian Michel Aflaq, espoused similar principles. However the military tended not to be inspired by the Baath as they saw it as a party for the young, educated civilian elite (Helms 1984: 68). Nasir, on the other hand, was an officer, and Nasirism offered a model for military officers to seize power.

Nasirism sought to project Egypt and its leader as a nucleus that would unify the foreign, military and social policies of all the Arab states, including a future Palestinian state to be liberated as a result of this cooperation. Second, Nasirism entailed an activist policy of exporting its ideals, including the incitement of violence in countries that were deemed anti-Nasirist. Nasir exhorted the masses and the armies in these countries to overthrow their governments, particularly in Iraq and Jordan. The two Hashimite states that refused to align themselves with Nasir were deemed as "traitors" and "slaves of imperialism" by the Egyptian radio program, "Voice of the Arabs." Nasir's communicative policy sought to alienate the armies from the rulers, in conjunction with attempts to forge connections with the Iraqi Army directly. Nasirist Egypt attacked the Iraqi monarchy, and particularly its most prominent politician, Nuri Al-Said. The monarchy was cognizant of the Army's potential of repeating what had happened in Egypt. As a precaution, units of the Iraqi military were denied access to ammunition and large Army movements were not allowed inside of

Baghdad in order to prevent a coup. At the same time, the leadership made efforts to regain the trust of the armed forces, by distributing housing stipends and plots of land to the officers (Batatu 1979: 31).

Despite the leadership's lack of faith in the Army, it was deployed as an instrument of internal control during an uprising in Baghdad in 1952, the second period of prolonged domestic instability after the *Wathba* of 1948. The protests called for the nationalization of Iraq's oil in response to the recently signed Iraqi–British Oil Agreement (Al-Arif 1982: 42). Soon, political parties began to call for direct elections to the Iraqi Parliament. The military did not intervene during the massive protests that broke out on November 22, 1952, known as the *Intifadha* or "Uprising," but the younger generation of officers originated from the same class that took part in the popular disturbance (Troutbeck 1959: 85). Officers sympathized with the protestors' demands and the protestors also sympathized with the military, shouting "long live the Army" (*The Times*, November 24, 1952: 6). An emergency cabinet was formed under the Chief of Staff, General Nur Al-Din Mahmud. However, this military Prime Minister did not take the opportunity to form a moderator regime, proving that he was not an ambitious officer who wanted to usurp civilian power. He gave in to some of the protesters' demands by holding new elections, and when they took place on January 17, 1953, the General resigned (Salih 1996: 120).

With the rise of Nasirism, the military served as a reflection of the ideologies prevalent in the Iraqi public. The bulk of the officer corps was drawn from predominantly Sunni Arabs, mostly from the lower middle classes. By 1953 most of the Iraqi officers above the rank of brigadier were Sunnis (FO 371/110991, May 29, 1953). Despite the homogeneity in ethno-sectarian terms, officers were divided ideologically, subscribing to Communism, pan-Arabism and its new variant Nasirism. Some of the pan-Arabists were loyal to the right-wing Arab nationalist Iraqi Istiqlal Party, and others were beginning to join the pan-Arabist, but Shia dominated Baath Party. Others were Iraqi nationalists or "Iraq firsters" who were opposed to the role of the British in Iraqi affairs and wanted greater social change. Some of these officers supported the left leaning National Democratic Party (NDP) (the successor to Ahali), which was distrustful of Nasir's politics. What united these officers is their continued resentment of the pro-British monarchy, and a political process dominated by exclusive elites.

Groupings of these Iraqi nationalist officers began to coalesce in the 1950s, inspired by the Egyptian officers who overthrew the pro-British monarch Faruq and then the Syrian officers who overturned the pro-French government in Syria. The Iraqis sought to follow these Egyptian and Syrian military men who assumed power as officer politicians, establishing military ruler regimes in their countries. One of the Iraqi officers, Rifat Al-Hajj Sirri began to recruit similar minded colleagues into a secret organization. These officers believed that General Nur Al-Din Mahmud's appointment to Prime Minister during the 1952 *Intifadha* signified the return of the military to the political forefront and the Army's role as the only force that stood between the political opposition and the monarchy. The government's reliance on the military demonstrated the King's weakness and an opportunity for an organized officers' movement to seize power for themselves.

The officers that began to join these secret organizations represented a generational shift from the officers of the veto regimes or the pro-monarch ex-Sharifians. The new generation of protestors, opposition politicians and officers and troops emerged from a nationalist milieu cultivated by Al-Husri and Shawkat. The soldiers were exposed to intense nationalism and pride in the military in primary and secondary school, and continued to receive lessons in Iraqi and Arab nationalism at the military academies. General Najib Al-Rubayi was one of the nationalist officers who survived the purges, and as an instructor at the Staff College, he criticized the monarchy and instilled nationalist sentiments in the young officers studying under him. Al-Rubayi had served as a brigadier in the 1948 War and was critical of the lack of support the monarchy gave the military. The officers who made up this younger generation generally ranged in rank from first lieutenant and no higher than colonel. They tended to have a greater interest in politics, as opposed to the older surviving generals (with the exception of Al-Rubayi who expressed strong political views). The young officers believed that most of the generals were supporters of the monarchy, as they benefited materially from the leadership's patronage, and hence supported the status quo. The younger officers did not envision a role for them in their future struggle (Khadduri 1969a: 20).

The officers involved in the military moderator regimes from 1936 to 1941 had been trained in the Ottoman military academies, and were of senior rank when they had intervened in Iraq's political affairs. The younger generation consisted of officers who were mainly battalion and brigade commanders who joined the military after Iraq's independence in 1932. These officers were younger soldiers during the days of Bakr Sidqi and the Four Colonels, and had taken part in the military coups, or at least sympathized with them.

Abd Al-Karim Qasim illustrated the gap between Iraq's first officers and this new generation. Qasim was born in Baghdad on December 21, 1914, at a time when many of Iraq's first officers were still in the Ottoman military or joining the secret Arab officers' society Al-Ahd. His father owned a small farm in Baghdad and realized that the military offered his son a free education. In 1932, the year of Iraq's independence, Qasim entered the military academy at the age of seventeen, becoming a second lieutenant two years later, and took part in Bakr Sidqi's suppression of the 1935 Euphrates tribal revolt. Qasim was also believed to have been involved in the Sidqi coup. Qasim's relations with Muhammad Ali Jawwad, the commander of the Air Force that took part in the 1936 coup, was a revealing portrait of patronage networks in the Iraqi military that across these two generations. Qasim, a lieutenant at that time, was Jawwad's cousin, and after Jawwad and Sidqi were assassinated at the Mosul airfield leading to the subsequent coup of 1937, Qasim was transferred to the Fourth Division in Diwaniyya in the south, far enough from the capital not to cause any trouble (Be'eri 1970: 174). Qasim took part in the conflict with the British in 1941, supporting the actions of the Four Colonels, who represented the first generation of Ottoman trained officers. He was not singled out during the post-1941 purges and was promoted to major in 1945 during the campaign against the Kurdish tribes. He took part in the fighting in the first Arab–Israeli War, where he became a battalion commander with the rank of lieutenant colonel and served under Najib Al-Rubayi. Qasim was described as a silent and secretive person. His cousin, Colonel Fadhil Abbas Al-Mahdawi reported how Qasim's parents were anxious that their son had not married and asked Al-Mahdawi to intervene on their behalf. However Qasim was devoted to a secret cause to rid the country of imperialism and did not want any distractions until he achieved that goal (Shwadran 1960: 15). Apparently the Free Officers offered him the opportunity to realize his aspirations.

By 1955 Qasim had risen to the rank of brigadier (ibid.: 16). In that same year Iraq had signed the Baghdad Pact and Qasim and Al-Rubayi served together again in an Iraqi military mission in Turkey. They were impressed by the strength of the Turkish armed forces and Qasim became an admirer of the reforms that had been carried out by Mustafa Kemal Ataturk (Khadduri 1969a: 78). The "Ataturk model" took on a new life after the death of the Turkish leader due to the stability of its reforms. Janowitz argued that the appeal of this model to officers in other developing countries, ranging from Iraq to South Korea, was that it demonstrated how a military in government transformed itself into a political party and implemented social and economic progress (Janowitz 1977: 64).

Bearing in mind Qasim's experiences during the defeat of the Iraqi military in 1948, the Ataturk model must have seemed even more appealing to him. The defeat in Iraq's first war abroad had a significant impact on the solidarity of the officer corps. It would lead to the crystallization of disaffected officers into clandestine cells of which Qasim would join. Military defeats tend to politicize the military establishment, and thus Janowitz wrote that the case of Ataturk emerged as a classic inspiration for officers who had undergone such humiliation. Ataturk himself was a successful military commander, who had repulsed the invasion at Gallipoli. He emerged from World War I as a popular hero with "an image of invincibility" and became even more popular with his campaign that expelled Allied occupying forces from what would later become the Republic of Turkey. Having led a successful campaign, Ataturk assumed a position of confidence where he and the revamped Turkish armed forces had forged a professional military identity and gained legitimacy to drive the political process (ibid.: 112). For officers in Iraq, there was a similar desire to expel what was perceived as an occupying power, the UK, forge a professional identity among its armed forces and take an active part in domestic Iraqi politics. Furthermore, the Ataturk model offered a program beyond a means for the military merely to conserve its power: "In the recent past, Turkey, under Ataturk, represented the one case in which a military oligarchy, under an enlightened leader, made fundamental contributions to social and economic modernization" (ibid.: 180–1). The Iraqi officers had a successful example in Turkey of a model of political development and sought to replicate it in Iraq.

Tensions in Iraq increased as Nasir rallied against the Baghdad Pact signed between Iraq, Turkey, Iran, Pakistan, the US and the UK on February 24, 1955 as an alliance to contain Soviet influence in the region. For Prime Minister Al-Said, the Pact offered the advantage of the transfer of the two British bases to Iraqi control, and the Anglo-Iraqi Treaty of 1930 would no longer be in effect, thus avoiding the chaos caused in 1948. However, it was not enough to appease some of the Iraqi officers who resented their country joining the Pact as they felt they were serving an imperialist agenda. According to Ismail Arif, some officers considered the Pact subversive and antipatriotic. He wrote:

> The principal affronting alliance was the one with the West and the Muslim, but *non*-Arab Middle Eastern countries of Iran, Turkey, and Pakistan, which was later known as the Baghdad Pact. The conclusion of the officers was that this agreement did nothing more than push the British out the window in order to invite them to enter the front door.
>
> (Al-Arif 1982: 40)

The Pact resulted in more advanced arms from the UK. Al-Said and the leadership hoped this rearmament of the Iraqi armed forces would counter their hostility to the alliance. They were mistaken.

In 1954 the underground Iraqi Free Officers movements began to expand. Qasim joined in August of that year when he was still a colonel. Colonel Ahmad Hasan al-Bakr and Major Salih Mahdi Ammash, two officers loyal to the Baath Party, also joined. (The two would play a critical role in helping the Baath come to power in 1968.) Ammash served as the Free Officers' link to the Baath Party. Qasim, through his friend Muhammad Haddid, was in contact with the National Democratic Party, Colonel Salih Abd Al-Majid Samarrai with the Istiqlal Party and Colonel Wasfi Tahir maintained contacts with his cousin Zaki Khayri of the Communist Party (ibid.: 47–8). These links demonstrated that informal networks not only existed within the military, but between the armed forces and political parties. These connections cemented the Free Officers' ties with the groups that formed the political opposition to the monarchy.

The Iraqi Communist Party (ICP) had been working to address the ethno-sectarian inequalities in the Army. As its primary members and constituents were the deprived segments of the Kurdish and Shia communities, its communications often sought to address the disadvantages they faced rising through the ranks. Mahdi Hashim, one of the founders of the Party wrote "of the eighty staff officers of the Iraqi army only three come from Shi'i families, while 90% of the soldiers are sons of the Shi'i community" (Al-Musawi 2006: 57). In 1955, the Communists formed an organization to coordinate its activities with the military, the Union of Soldiers and Officers. Unlike the Free Officers, which only accepted officers, the Communist outfit accepted soldiers of all ranks. Among its goals was an Iraqi withdrawal from the Baghdad Pact, the expulsion of all foreign military advisors who were primarily British and raising the living standards of the troops. Among its most powerful adherents were two Sunni Arabs from the Jubur tribe, Staff Brigadier Ismail Ali, commander of the artillery of the First Division, and Colonel Ibrahim Husayn, a battalion commander (Batatu 1979: 792–3).

A meeting of the Free Officers is said to have taken place in a house in the summer of 1956 convened by Ismail Arif. Qasim was not present at this meeting, but was most likely aware of it, as when word of the meeting was discovered by the authorities Qasim was called in for a talk with Nuri Al-Said. Qasim, despite his antipathies to the British, had a close relationship with Al-Said, who affectionately called him "Karumi," the Arabic diminutive of Karim. It is even reported that during this meeting, Al-Said affectionately asked him, "Is it true, Karrumi, that you are plotting against us?" (Haddad 1971: 93). Qasim obviously denied such conspiracies were taking place. Al-Said had also called in Rifat Al-Hajj Sirri, one of the founders of the Free Officers and asked if he was plotting against the monarchy. When Sirri denied this charge, Al-Said responded, "Look, if your plot ever succeeds, you and the other officers will be engaged in a struggle among yourselves which will not end until each of you hangs the other" (Khadduri 1969a: 87). Al-Said words predicted a stark reality. Sirri would be one of the first victims of these intra-military rivalries once the officers seized power in 1958.

Rather than executing these officers in the summer of 1956, a number of them who were suspected of intrigue were transferred as military attachés abroad (Farouk-Sluglett and Sluglett 1987: 48). A Supreme Committee of the Free Officers, otherwise known as the Central Organization of the Baghdad Organization, was formed during this period, made up of Army and Air Force officers with the rank of major and above. This cell was headed by Brigadier Muhyi Al-Din Abd Al-Hamid, who was sympathetic to the opposition National Democratic Party (Khadduri 1969a: 23). Another prominent figure in this cell was Brigadier Naji Talib, a Shia pan-Arabist, who was at that time the military attaché in the UK (ibid.). However, Abd Al-Hamid's cell was independent of the other group of Free

Officers, made up of Abd Al-Karim Qasim who was stationed in Jordan as of November 1956. Both Talib and Qasim had been sent out of Iraq due to the monarchy's suspicions of these officers. The intermediary between the two cells was Colonel Wasfi Tahir, a Communist sympathizer and a member of Abd Al-Hamid's group (Be'eri 1970: 173). In the spring of 1957 the two factions merged into a Central Organization (Farouk-Sluglett and Sluglett 1987: 48). The Central Organization was primarily made up of fourteen officers, most of whom were Arab Sunnis. Some Kurdish officers supported the Free Officers with the hope that once in power they would be more willing to grant concessions on Kurdish autonomy. The Free Officers also tried to recruit Shia officers under the banner of Iraqi nationalism (Khadduri 1969a: 19).

Abd Al-Salam Arif was another representative of this new generation of younger officers, born in Baghdad on March 21, 1921, the son of a tribal shaykh from the town of Ana. He was related to another tribal leader Shaykh Dari, imprisoned for the assassination of a British official, and Arif was inspired by his relative's actions as part of Iraq's nationalist struggle (Khadduri 1969a: 89). Arif had taken part in the 1948 Arab–Israeli War during the battle of Janin, and the friendship between him and Qasim was formed in 1956 while they were deployed with the Iraqi Army in Jordan. In April 1957 Qasim suggested that he be admitted to the Free Officers (Al-Arif 1982: 54).

By 1957 the monarchy was unaware of the strength of these secret cells and still perceived the Army as politically unmotivated and content with the incentives it was being offered. Batatu quoted a Western diplomat in Baghdad at the time, who said prior to the 1958 Revolution that, "The army officers, are far better paid than in Iran or Turkey. The crown prince keeps well in touch with them and on Army Day gave out from his own land for the building of their homes." The diplomat did mention that, "there is some nationalism among junior officer, but no real gripes." Referring to the Free Officers in the Egyptian Army who overthrew the monarchy, he said, "They are not heavily infiltrated by political parties nor are there any cliques as in Faruq's army" (quoted in Batatu 1979: 764). Both foreign diplomats and the civilians in the monarchy alike failed to appreciate implications of a national army, incorporating the cleavages and political fluctuations of Iraq's society and the changes in the regional environment since the advent of Nasirism. This naiveté on behalf of the civilian politicians staffing the monarch's state apparatus would eventually lead to their final overthrow in 1958.

The union of Egypt and Syria on February 1, 1958 heralded the formation of the United Arab Republic (UAR), and Iraq criticized the merger. On March 3, 1958 Nuri Al-Said became Prime Minister for the thirteenth time (Haddad 1971: 78). The military had enough with the system that they were sworn to protect. Iraq's flirtation with liberalism under the monarchy was rejected as it was associated with a system imposed by

Britain with an Arab façade (Simon 1986: 169). The Free Officers' reaction was to abolish this system entirely, prosecute the supporters of the monarchy and the old elite for collaborating with imperialists and establish a Republic. The plan for a coup was set in motion.

The 1958 Iraqi coup and revolution

After the formation of the United Arab Republic in February 1958, Iraq had formed a Hashimite Union with Jordan to counter the perceived threat from Nasir. In order to protect Jordan from the chaos ensuing in Lebanon between Nasirist and anti-Nasirist factions in the summer of 1958, the Iraqi Hashimite monarchy dispatched a brigade of the Army to protect the other Hashimite monarchy based in Amman. The Iraqi leadership chose the 20th Brigade of the Third Division for this task. The Brigade was stationed at Jalawla, 160 kilometers north-east of Baghdad near the Iranian border. In order to reach Jordan the unit had to pass through the capital, which it planned to do on the night of July 13 (Khadduri 1969a: 38). Prime Minister Al-Said, who had given these commands to the Twentieth Brigade to move to the Jordanian border, placed too much confidence in the military and had not predicted the danger of these troop movements so close to the city.

Generally ammunition had not been issued to Iraqi army units, except for limited supplies during military maneuvers. Brigadier Naji Talib, one of the first Free Officers who was made the Director of the military training branch of the Staff College secretly supplied the Brigade with live ammunition. Qasim and a committee of officers who had been planning a coup decided to launch it on July 14 as they could trap the King, the Regent and Al-Said before they left for a Baghdad Pact meeting in Istanbul (Khadduri 1963: 45). Capturing the leadership was necessary as both Al-Said and the Regent had managed to escape in 1941 and proved to be a leadership-in-exile to the army officers who had seized power then.

On July 13, the commander of the Third Division, Major General Ghazi Daghistani left for Baghdad, unaware that one of the three battalions of the Twentieth Infantry Brigade of the Third was planning a coup under Arif's leadership (Be'eri 1970: 176). Daghistani had left temporary control over the entire Division to Abd Al-Karim Qasim, commander of the Nineteenth Brigade, and also one of the coup planners. Qasim's forces were based in Baaquba, north of Baghdad, and Arif's forces would reach that town on the night of July 13. Once the Twentieth Brigade reached Baaquba, Arif detained the battalion commanders and assumed command of the entire brigade. It was planned that Qasim would maintain his Nineteenth Brigade at the Al-Mansur camp in the vicinity of the capital, to prevent any force from attacking Arif from behind as he led the first assault into Baghdad (Khadduri 1969a: 38). By five in the morning of July 14, Arif's brigade reached a bridge over the Tigris and the units moved to seize the radio station, as the coup planners' first priority was to seize a means of mass communication to announce the putsch. Then the coup planners sought to take hold of the main government buildings. The battalions successfully secured the radio station, and surrounded Al-Said's house and the Royal Palace (Batatu 1979: 797).

In a standoff outside the Palace, the twenty-three year old King Faisal II, Crown Prince Abd Al-Ilah and the royal family was killed. A mob had gathered outside and proceeded to mutilate the Prince's body and hang it at the gate of the Ministry of Defense, in apparent retaliation for the Regent's role in hanging Al-Sabbagh in the same place. Despite the troop blockade around his house, Al-Said was able to escape. He was eventually spotted in Baghdad in disguise, wearing a woman's black cloak, but unfortunately for him part of his men's pajamas were showing underneath (Haddad 1971: 98). Differing accounts state that he either committed suicide after being discovered or was executed during the coup.

Arif declared on the radio that the monarchy had been overthrown and called on the masses to show its support for the new Republic. The coup had been planned by military officers who had contacts with civilian party leaders, but these leaders were uncertain about the exact date of the coup. While political parties were active in the events surrounding the July 1958 coup, it was the military officers who made the crucial decision of when and how to strike at the monarchy. The involvement of the opposition political parties gave the coup the semblance of popular support and hence it took on the name of the 1958 Revolution. The opposition parties envisioned establishing a parliamentary democracy with a civilian at its head. They had expected the officers to play a role similar to the Four Colonels, where they would sit behind the scenes, but a civilian premier and other civilians would form the cabinet (Khadduri 1969a: 27–8). It was only once they were in power that the military ruler regime began to form.

5 Military coups and the ruler regimes 1958–1968

Defining the military ruler regime

Nordlinger wrote, "Once the officers have become politicized as moderators it is a relatively small step to exercise governmental power themselves" (1977: 23). Indeed the Iraqi officers made this jump to the next step in 1958. The officers from 1936 to 1941 emerged as a moderator regime by acting as a politicized pressure group, at times threatening the government, preventing the accession of another government and replacing one civilian government with another. The officers of 1958 carried out a coup and became the government. Opposed to moderator regimes, the military as ruler regime dominates the state and political, economic and social life. They enact fundamental changes in regime structure according to their own preferences. These changes are usually carried out to establish an authoritarian system that is closed to competition from civilian political parties (ibid.: 7). While moderator regimes tend to preserve the status quo, ruler regimes enact radical changes in the political and socio-economic system, often seeking to improve the lives of the poor and disenfranchised. Changes include redistribution schemes, nationalization of industry, land reform and providing low income housing. The ruler regime argues that such reforms will extend over indefinite periods of time and thus legitimizes and perpetuates military rule. Unlike guardian regimes, which return power to civilian authority after a few years, ruler armies do not or rarely act on such promises. Ruler regimes do allow civilians into the government particularly if they possess their technocratic skills or financial expertise that are beyond the capabilities of the military officers in power. Incorporating civilian ministers in the government also provides the ruler regime a façade of civilian rule to the public. Despite the presence of civilians, the ruler regime is defined by the paramount power of the officers. In these regimes it is the civilians that are subordinate to military governors (ibid.: 26–8).

The Free Officers in power

The civilians who took part in the coup expected to rule and form a Council of Revolution, but the Free Officers took the most important executive posts for themselves, despite their claims that they sought to replace the monarchy with a government of the people. During this transition, the Free Officers had envisioned that they would assume the role of a guardian regime where they set a new political process in motion, designing the structure of a new government, carrying out reforms and then withdrawing to the barracks. As Khadduri wrote of the officers, "Once in the saddle, they found themselves just as capable of governing their country as anyone else and were tempted to remain in power" (1969a: 66). This transitional period eventually became indefinite allowing Qasim to consolidate a military ruler regime.

The officers began to take on the characteristics of a ruler regime when they drafted a provisional constitution in just barely over a week after the coup (Khadduri 1969a: 64).

Qasim assumed the title of Prime Minister and Acting Minister of Defense, and Arif became Deputy Prime Minister and Minister of the Interior. Qasim also assumed the position of Commander-in-Chief of the armed forces, while Arif became Deputy Commander-in-Chief. Arguably the two most important executive portfolios had been taken by the architects of the coup. The other spoils of the coup, the executive posts, were distributed to the Free Officers. Two of the three members of the Sovereignty Council, designed as an executive office, were themselves officers, General Al-Rubayi of the Staff College and of the Arab Rubayi tribe, and Colonel Khalid Naqshabandi, a Kurdish officer from a prominent Sufi family.

The machinery of state was soon crippled as every director general in the civil service of the monarchy was dismissed. The Free Officers faced several administrative challenges once in power, inexperienced in running a state, but unwilling to allow qualified civilians to run the country in a proposed Revolutionary Council. The civilians felt that officers usurped power and some declined cabinet posts under his authority. For example, Kamil Chadirchi of the NDP declared he could never become a member of a military government (ibid.). However, some civilians did assume cabinet posts, such as Muhammad Hadid of the NDP, who became Minister of Finance, Fuad Rikabi, head of the Baath Party, became Minister of Development, Ibrahim Kubba, a Marxist, Minister of Economics and Siddiq Shanshal of the Istiqlal Party became Minister of National Guidance (Be'eri 1970: 177–8). While Qasim sought to award cabinet posts to the parties that took part in the revolution, the most important positions were still in the hands of the Army. What united the Army and these parties was their opposition to the monarchy, but once the Free Officers were in power, they had no systematic program, nor ideology to unite these factions. Even the officers themselves were part of a military government that had its own divisions between Iraqi nationalists, pan-Arabists, Baathists and Communists. The Free Officers had to deal with the emergence of rival political parties and factions that erupted on the scene after the collapse of the monarchy, and strife between Arab nationalists and Communists was a dominant feature of Qasim's ruler regime.

One of the first actions taken by the new administration of Free Officers was to consolidate their control over the military by purging all possible supporters of the monarchy. Most of the generals in the military were dismissed and were replaced by Free Officers. Colonel Abd Al-Aziz Uqayli commanded the First Division, Brigadier Nadhim Tabaqchali the Second, Colonel Khalil Said the Third and Brigadier Muhyi Al-Din Hamid the Fourth, and Captain Jalal Al-Awqati commanded the Air Force. The officers who were dismissed under the monarchy were de-purged and reappointed (Khadduri: 1969a: 71).

Qasim declared martial law, strengthening the military grip over Iraq. Brigadier Ahmad Salih Al-Abdi was declared Military Governor-General and reported directly to the Ministry of Defense, which was also headed by Qasim (ibid.: 72). In August 1958, Qasim's ruler regime tightened its hold over the country through establishing two institutions, the Popular Resistance Forces and the Special Military Court. The Forces were organized to train civilians in maintaining domestic order, similar in scope to the *Futuwwa* of 1939, and soon it emerged as a tool of Qasim to eliminate political opponents. The Special Military Court, which later became known as the People's Court, was headed by Colonel Fadhil Abbas Al-Mahdawi, Qasim's cousin (Davis 2005a: 127). While it originally was designed as a legal–military institution to convict royal loyalists that could threaten the Republic, it soon turned on the military itself, convicting officers who opposed Qasim.

Relations with the UK were strained after the coup, although Qasim advocated a neutralist policy where Iraq would not side with either camp during the Cold War. The military government of Qasim reoriented Iraq's foreign policy, resulting in Iraq's withdrawal from the Baghdad Pact. The USSR replaced the UK as Iraq's primary supplier of arms (Abbas 1989: 219). The ground forces would thereafter be equipped with a combination of Soviet T-54 and British Centurion tanks, and the Air Force included a mix of Soviet MiG-17s and British Hunter aircraft (Be'eri 1970: 186). A total of 500 Soviet military advisors came to Iraq, and Iraqis were sent to Moscow for military training (Haddad 1971: 120). By January 1959, the Iraqi military had created a new Fifth Division (*The Times*, January 7, 1959: 9). During the expansion to create this new division Iraq was reportedly still approaching the UK for arms, demonstrating Iraq's neutralism (*The Times*, May 12, 1959: 11). However, in June these approaches to the UK seemed to have ended given Al-Mahdawi's comments in the People's Court, where he described Iraq's freedom from imperialism because it no

Table 5.1 Officers who participated in coups during the military ruler regimes 1958–1968

Name of officer	Year of birth	Place of birth	Sectarian affiliation	Ethnic affiliation	Political affiliation	Tribe/clan	Number of coups in which they participated
Najib Al-Rubayi	1904	Baghdad	Sunni	Arab	Independent	Rabiya	1958
Muhyi Al-Din Hamid	1914	Baghdad	Sunni	Arab	NDP		1958
Naji Talib	1917	Nasiriyya	Shia	Arab	Arab nat'list		1958, Feb. 1963, Nov. 1963
Abd Al-Karim Qasim	1914	Baghdad	Sunni/Shii	Arab/Kurd	Iraq firster		1958
Abd Al-Salam Arif	1921	Baghdad	Sunni	Arab	Arab nat'list	Jumayla	1958, Feb. 1963, Nov. 1963
Abd Al-Rahman Arif	1916	Baghdad	Sunni	Arab	Arab nat'list	Jumayla	1958, Feb. 1963, Nov. 1963
Nadhim Tabaqchali	1913	Baghdad	Sunni	Arab	Arab nat'list		1958
Aziz Al-Uqayli	1920	Mosul	Sunni	Arab	Arab nat'list		1958, Feb. 1963
Rifat Al-Hajj Sirri	1917	Baghdad	Sunni	Arab	Arab nat'list		1958, 1959
Tahir Yahya	1913	Takrit	Sunni	Arab	Baathist	Al-Bu Nasir Shiyasha	1958, Feb. 1963, Nov. 1963
Wasfi Tahir	1918	Baghdad	Sunni	Arab	Communist		1958
Jalal Al-Awqati	1914	Baghdad	Sunni	Arab/Turkmen	Communist		1958
Abd Al-Wahhab Al-Shawwaf			Sunni	Arab	Nasirist		1958, 1959
Ismail Arif	1921	Al-Khaliz	Sunni	Arab/Turk			1958
Ahmad Hasan Al-Bakr	1912	Takrit	Sunni	Arab	Baathist	Al-Bu Nasir Bayjat	1958, Feb. 1963, Nov. 1963, Jul. 17

Name	Year	Place	Sect	Ethnicity	Affiliation	Tribe	Dates
Salih Mahdi Ammash	1925	Baghdad	Sunni	Arab	Baathist		1968, Jul. 30 1968
Abd Al-Sattar Abd Al-Latif	1926	Baghdad	Sunni	Arab	Baathist		1958, Feb. 1963, Jul. 17 1968
Hardan Al-Takriti	1925	Takrit	Sunni	Arab	Baathist	Al-Bu Nasir	1958, Feb. 1963, Nov. 1963
Rashid Muslih	1917	Takrit	Sunni	Arab	Baathist		1958, Feb. 1963, Nov. 1963, Jul. 17 1968
Arif Abd Al-Razzaq	1922	Rammadi	Sunni	Arab	Nasirist		1958, 59, Feb. 1963, Nov. 1963, 1965, 1966
Abd Al-Latif Al-Darraji	1913	Rammadi	Sunni	Arab	Nasirist		1958, Feb. 1963
Subhi Abd Al-Hamid	1924	Baghdad	Sunni	Arab	Nasirist		1958, Feb. 1963, Nov. 1963, 1965, 1966
Abd Al-Karim Farhan	1922	Sawayra	Shia	Arab	Nasirist		1958, Feb. 1963, Nov. 1963, 1965
Abd Al-Razzaq Al-Nayif		Rammadi	Sunni	Arab	Independent	Jumayla	Jul. 17 1968
Ibrahim Al-Daud		Rammadi	Sunni	Arab	Independent		Jul. 17 1968
Sadun Ghaydan	1929	Baghdad	Sunni	Arab	Independent		Jul. 17 1968, Jul. 30 1968
Abd Al-Ghani Al-Rawi	1917	Rawa	Sunni	Arab	Independent		1958, Feb. 1963, Nov. 1963, 1970

Sources: Al-Qazzaz (1985: 350–1) and Batatu (1979: 778–82, 810–13). Tribal and political affiliations provided by the authors.

longer needed British arms, going as far as to describe the British Centurion tanks and Hawker aircraft as "scrap bought at fantastic cost" (*The Times*, June 26, 1959: 12).

The ruler regime began to rule by instituting several reforms, such as providing housing for the poor or paving streets. Most prominent among these reforms began on September 30, 1958, when an agrarian reform law was passed limiting the amount of property the landowners could posses, with the excess distributed to landless farmers (Haddad 1971: 104). However, the revolutionary changes promised by the new government materialized quite slowly, especially the agrarian reform, which suffered from bureaucratic mismanagement (Lenczowski 1965: 284). Qasim's ruler regime was preoccupied with its survival and fighting enemies, both internal and external. Most of Iraq's oil revenues was spent on the military in order to placate the officers, rather than being allocated to development projects.

One of the weaknesses of the Qasim-led ruler regime became evident when he failed to develop a base among the Iraqi parties. Qasim and the Free Officers around him seemed unable to transition successfully into the roles of statesmen. In order to buttress the strength of his own ruler regime, Qasim balanced the parties against each other without depending on one particular group. Unlike Nasir's Egypt, he failed even to develop a party of his own, or successfully create a single party system. Addressing the issue of political parties on May 1, 1959, Qasim declared that the Army and the people had merged into a single entity after the Revolution and hence, his party was the party of the people (Haddad 1971: 102). In another speech to the officers, he stressed his lack of ideological commitment to any one party, and stressed his bonds with the military: "Brother officers. I being one of you, state publicly before you that I carry no principle of any specific nature, but I proceed in the light of freedom" (quoted in Lenczowski 1966: 54). In a government sponsored book celebrating the achievements of the Revolution, it was written:

> The triumphant 14th July Revolution which the Iraqi army exploded under the leadership of Maj. Gen. Abdul Karim Qassim, had realised miraculous achievements which we are all proud of. All army members, officers and ranks, are one hand to protect the homeland from the sabotage of saboteurs, plotters, and the conspiracies of imperialists. This army had the power to realize this noble aim.
>
> (High Committee 1961: 16)

From the aforementioned communication Qasim conveyed an idealistic polity, where he sought to cement ties between his office as both General and leader, with the military, and the military with the people and the nation. The structural flaw in his military government was that Qasim's support rested on a divided core of officers who presided over a divided army and an Iraqi populace rife with the political divisions swirling around the region at the time, such as Communism, Baathism and Nasirism. Officers who sought to satiate their own political ambitions would legitimize their future attempts to unseat Qasim by adopting these various ideological platforms. Rather than a "consolidated military ruler regime," Iraq at this juncture was ruled by a "contested military ruler regime," plagued by persistent military coups to follow.

The Free Officers themselves were not a monolithic group and did not have a clear vision of what type of government would succeed the monarchy. Qasim and Arif, the two architects behind the July coup, emerged as the main contenders for power. One of the reasons behind the Qasim–Arif tensions resulted due to their differing policies, where Qasim adopted the Iraq firster approach of Hikmat Sulayman, which stressed Iraqi unity and Kurdish-Arab cooperation. His priority was inward-looking nationalism (*wataniyya*), as opposed to an outward-looking pan-Arabism (*qawmiyya*) adopted by his coup partner, Colonel Abd Al-Salam Arif.

Qasim had failed to build up a sustainable patronage network in the officer corps based on ideological, tribal, clan or regional belonging. He had promoted officers that served with him in the 1948 war to key positions, such as Ahmad Salih Al-Abdi, the Chief of Staff and military Governor General, and Staff Brigadier Ahmad Muhammad Yahya, the Minister of Interior. Qasim's relatives such as Brigadier Abd Al-Jabbar Jawad became commander of the newly created Fifth Division, and Colonel Fadhil Abbas Al-Mahdawi operated the People's Court. He also tended to support the "Iraq firster" camp, such as the Shia Colonel Muhsin Al-Rufaii, who later became Director of Military Intelligence and the Shia Staff Brigadier Hamid Al-Sayyid Husayn who later became Commander of the First Division. However, none of these networks proved to unite or cut across a large group within the military based on religion, sect, ethnicity, regional affinity or ideology. These alliances Qasim formed only alienated the pan-Arab group in the military, which was much larger than the Iraqi firster group (Batatu 1979: 845–6).

Arif was influenced by the Baath, although was not a member of the Party. At first it appeared to the Arab world that the 1958 coup would follow the example of Egypt and Syria, constituting part of a trend of nationalist revolutions led by military officers, eliminating corrupt oligarchies subservient to foreign powers. The sequence of these anti-imperialist coups led by military officers culminated in the United Arab Republic (UAR). However, Qasim chose not to follow this path of unity with the UAR. Arif and his supporters in the military viewed Qasim's attempts to meet the needs of not just Arab Sunnis, but Shia and Kurds as confessional politics that contradicted their vision of an Arab Iraq, striving for a modern republic and unity with Egypt and Syria (Lukitz 1995: 141). As Qasim seemed to abandon Arab unity, Arif forged an alliance with the pan-Arabists to further their own personal ambitions of emerging as the true power in the military ruler regime.

However, not all of Iraq's pan-Arabist officers supported unity with the UAR. Some of these Iraqi officers had heard complaints from their Syrian colleagues about Egyptian engulfment and domination of Syria and did not pressure Qasim to pursue this path. Some of the pan-Arabist officers close to Qasim, such as Major General Ahmad Salih Al-Abdi was anti-Nasirist and defended Qasim's decision not to join the UAR (Shwadran 1960: 20). Qasim, who had struggled to overthrow the monarchy, was unwilling to subordinate himself to Nasir. According to one Iraqi official, Qasim's view on unity with Nasir was articulated as: "We have just rid ourselves of the Hijazis who ruled us for the last thirty-seven years. Now why for God's sake should we turn around and deliver ourselves to foreign domination [again]?" (ibid.: 141). The "Hijazis" was a reference to the Hashimite royal family originating from this area in what is today Saudi Arabia.

As the gulf grew between Qasim and Arif and his pan-Arabist allies, the latter began campaigning for unity with Egypt around the country with Fuad Al-Rikabi of the Baath Party (Khadduri 1969a: 88). Qasim tried to weaken Arif's networks on September 12 by dismissing him from his post as Deputy Commander-in-Chief of the armed forces. Qasim then transferred many of the officers loyal to Arif in his Twentieth Infantry Brigade away from Baghdad. Two weeks later Qasim relieved Arif of his executive positions of Deputy Prime Minister and Minister of the Interior, and simultaneously deployed Arif's brigade back to its original position in Jalawla, where it was stationed prior to the July coup. Qasim further promoted Communist colonels loyal to him to the highest commands in Arif's Brigade (Batatu 1979: 835). Qasim then appointed Arif as ambassador to West Germany in an attempt to exile his opponent. Arif refused and a crisis erupted between the two. The Iraqi leader convened a meeting of the powers behind the ruler regime, the Free Officers and the commanders of Iraq's five army divisions, to persuade Arif to accept the post. Arif eventually left for Europe but returned on November 4, 1958 whereupon he was arrested. On November 27, 1958, his trial began and was accused of harboring sympathies to both the Baath Party and Nasirism. Arif was sentenced to death. Qasim then arrested several other Baathist officers, including Salih Mahdi Ammash and declared membership in the Party illegal (Be'eri 1970: 181–2).

The conflicts within Iraq's ruler regime were representative of a greater rivalry between Qasim's Iraq and Nasir's UAR. A war of the airwaves began between the two leaders, where Qasim delivered public speeches broadcast on the radio calling Nasir the "Protégé of American Imperialism," "McNasir," "the Pharaoh" and "Hulagu," a reference to Genghis Khan's grandson who sacked Baghdad in 1258. In the proceeding of the People's Court, broadcast live to the region via radio, Colonel Al-Mahdawi described Nasir as having "a trunk-like nose with which he will continue to sniff at our oil until he dies." In March 1959, Nasir struck back, playing on Qasim's name which means "divider," to mock him as the "Divider of Iraq," and ridiculing Qasim's title, "the Sole Leader," by deeming him "the Sole Divider of Iraq" (Shwadran 1960: 54, 68). These tensions between the two leaders would manifest themselves in the Iraqi military with events that would unfold in March 1959, ushering in the era of Iraq's contested military ruler regimes.

The March 1959 coup attempt

Qasim's ruler regime was threatened by an ongoing confrontation between Communists and the Baathists. Qasim tended to tilt towards the Communists during these confrontations, and his closest supporters, Colonel Wasfi Tahir and Colonel Fadhil Abbas Al-Mahdawi were both Communist sympathizers. Qasim was also aware that the Communists had influence among the lower ranking soldiers and non-commissioned officers, which could rival the strength of the pan-Arabists in the military (Batatu 1979: 847). This period saw a rise in Communist papers such as *Ittihad Al-Shaab* (*The Union of the People*) and *Al-Thawra* (*The Revolution*). Pan-Arabist papers were also prevalent, such as *Al-Hurriyya* (*Freedom*) and *Al-Fajr Al-Jadid* (*The New Dawn*), which were popular among pan-Arabist officers (Lukitz 1995: 142).

Qasim's suspicions of the pan-Arabists increased after an alleged coup attempt in December 1958. Rashid Ali Al-Gaylani had returned from exile in Egypt to Iraq after the 1958 coup and was accused by the Directorate of Military Intelligence of plotting to overthrow Qasim. In the People's Court Al-Mahdawi declared that Al-Gaylani had forged links with pan-Arabist officers Tahir Yahya and Abd Al-Latif Al-Darraji. (These allegations ultimately proved correct as these two officers eventually conspired to overthrow Qasim in 1963.)

Qasim soon became aware that the primary threat to his military regime came from factions within the military itself demonstrated by events that would unfold in Mosul a few months later. Ironically, the planned pro-Nasirist coup involved the chief of Military Intelligence Rifat Al-Hajj Sirri, himself a pan-Arabist who had taken part in foiling the pan-Arabist coup of Rashid Ali (Khadduri 1969a: 102–3). On March 8, 1959 the attempted coup was led by Colonel Abd Al-Wahhab Shawwaf, commander of the Fifth Brigade of the Second Division and the commander of the Mosul garrison. Shawwaf was one of the fourteen members of the Free Officers Central Organization and had sought to become the leader of the movement while it was in opposition as well as in power. Shawwaf was a pan-Arabist officer, and General Nadhim Tabaqchali, the commander of the Second Division was also sympathetic to the Arab nationalist cause and was also anti-Communist. Qasim had suspected Tabaqchali and two months prior to the coup had tried to eliminate his power base in Mosul by transferring his command to the Fourth Division in the south, but

Tabaqchali refused the orders and stayed in command of the Second (Be'eri 1970: 183).

The networks involved in the March 1959 coup involved a disparate coalescing of opportunism, nationalism, class and tribalism. It was believed that Nasir had begun to make inroads with the officers based in Mosul, who were disgruntled over Qasim's ties with the Communists and his unwillingness to devolve more power to them. The coup planners could also count on the support of the Shammar tribe of Shaykh Ahmad Ajil Al-Yawar, a landowner who opposed Qasim's support among the leftists. The Arab Dulaym and Muntafiq tribes were also expected to rally their men in a revolt against Qasim. While this coup would eventually be known as the "Shawwaf revolt," as he was the first officer who announced the uprising, it actually involved a network of disgruntled officers. Shawwaf, while he professed Arab nationalism, also resented that Qasim had passed him over for a prominent role in the military. Captain Mahmud Aziz of Shawwaf's Fifth Brigade was also a pan-Arabist and sympathized with the Baath Party. Colonel Sirri, the Director of Military Intelligence was also an avowed pan-Arabist, and upon hearing the communiqué announcing the coup, Sirri was supposed to move against Qasim in the capital (Batatu 1979: 871–3).

The spark for the coup occurred in Mosul after a clash between the pan-Arabists and Arab tribesmen on one hand, and Qasim supporters, including leftists and Kurdish factions. Inter-communal violence erupted in the multi-ethnic city. Kurdish and Arab tribes settled scores with one another, peasants revolted against the landowners and the lower ranks of the Fifth Brigade comprising mostly Kurds revolted against their Arab officers (ibid.: 866).

All preceding coups had demonstrated the necessity of securing communication facilities to announce the putsch, and Shawwaf was able to deliver a national communiqué broadcast from a transmitter provided by Nasir's UAR. In his statement, Shawwaf accused Qasim of handing Iraq over to the Communists and deviating from its pan-Arab destiny. However unlike the coup that began in Mosul in August 1937, elements of the military in the central region of the country proved loyal to Qasim. The Iraqi Air Force bombarded Shawwaf's headquarters and government troops surrounded Mosul. Shawwaf was ultimately killed in the fighting between his forces and government loyalists and Sirri never acted in Baghdad. Qasim initiated a renewed purge of alleged pan-Arabists in the armed forces and promoted the Communists to powerful positions in the military. Communist sympathizers either dominated or commanded units based in Kirkuk, Mosul, and in the Abu Ghurayb and Al-Washshash camp. Communists also had a following among the troops in units based in the south in Basra, Al-Nasiriyya, and Diwaniyya (ibid.: 891).

However, by 1959 Qasim soon perceived that the waning influence of the pan-Arabists in the military was replaced by the rising strength of the

Communists. In June 1959, he declared that "I do not wish parties or tendencies, whatever their color, to penetrate into the ranks of the armed forces under any circumstances." He began to retire officers with suspected Communist sympathies in June, including Staff Brigadier Daud Al-Janabi, who had replaced Tabaqchali as Commander of the Second Division (ibid.: 907). These purges would continue as long as Qasim felt that the Communists challenged his authority. Armed disturbances broke out in Kirkuk in July 1959, with Communists taking part in bitter fighting between Kurds and Turkmen. Rather than ending the riots, the troops in the Second Division also took part in the violence (Be'eri 1970: 187). The Communists and soldiers, many of whom happened to be Kurdish, targeted the Turkmen community in Kirkuk (Batatu 1979: 913). Because of the Communist atrocities during these events, their bitter rivals, the Baathists, began to enjoy growing support among various Iraqis. Qasim, angered by the role of the Communists and Kurds in the Army in the massacres of Turkmen, declared, "Are your Turkmen brethren the enemies of the people?" (Shwadran 1960: 45). Qasim sought to use the Kirkuk violence as a further pretext to move against the Communists, and their alleged sympathizers in the Army were purged. The Popular Resistance Force, which had emerged as a people's militia after the revolution, had been infiltrated by the Communists who turned it into an armed wing of the party. The Force had taken part in the Communist inspired violence and Qasim disbanded it in another tactic to weaken the Party (Lenczowski 1966: 53). The Force's dismantlement was significant as it would be the beginning of a trend where party militias would challenge the role of the Iraqi Army.

On the other hand, Arab nationalist officers expelled from the Army after the Mosul revolt were allowed to return in August 1959 in order to placate this group that had otherwise opposed the Qasim government. One of the officers readmitted into the military was Major Salih Mahdi Ammash, who had served as a conduit for the Baath Party to infiltrate the armed forces. Other key pro-Baathist military officers included Ahmad Hasan Al-Bakr, Abd Al-Sattar Abd Al-Latif, Hardan Al-Takriti and Mundhir Wandawi (Farouk-Sluglett and Sluglett 1987: 69–73).

Instead of relying on the pan-Arabists, Qasim at the same time also turned against some of the Arab nationalist Free Officers who had taken part in the Shawwaf coup. General Nadhim Tabaqchali, Commander of the Second Division was blamed for allowing the March 1959 Mosul revolt to occur under his watch. One of the first Free Officers, Rifat Al-Hajj Sirri, Director of Military Intelligence had conspired with Shawwaf. On September 16, 1959 Sirri was executed followed by the execution of Tabaqchali on September 20 (Shwadran 1960: 59). Sirri was replaced as Director of Military Intelligence by the Shia Colonel Muhsin Al-Rufaii.

Despite the readmission of some Baathists into the military, the failure of the Shawwaf coup convinced the civilians in the Party that they would have to eliminate Qasim themselves. They had determined that Qasim's regime was alienated and still too close to their rivals, the Communists. Fuad Al-Rikabi began the preparations for an assassination attempt in April 1959 and ten Party members were selected to carry out this plan. Al-Rikabi was in contact with the Baathist officers in the military, such as Salih Mahdi Ammash, to ensure his military units would prevent a Communist seizure of power if the plan succeeded. On October 7, 1959, the Baathists struck at Qasim while he was driving from his office. Two of the assassins' guns jammed, and when one of the attackers, Abd Al-Wahab Ghariri rushed at Qasim's car, was mistakenly shot dead by another Baathist assassin firing from the other side of the street (Khadduri 1969a: 128–30). After the failed attempt, the attackers dispersed including a young Saddam Hussein who took part in this attack. Members of the Iraqi Baath fled to either Syria or Egypt, where they would continue plotting against the Iraqi government from exile.

The Mosul revolt and the ensuing assassination attempt on the Sole Leader led to a heightened megalomania and paranoia. His Minister of Foreign Affairs wrote of him: "And so the unopiniated, unassuming Qasim whom I knew in 1958 gradually got the taste of being the only man in the country. In other words, we built a dictator.... Our people are in truth builders of dictators" (Batatu 1979: 836). Qasim's portraits were omnipresent in Iraq. Qasim was soon referred to in Iraq as "the Genius Leader," "the Immortal" and "the Savior," and after the failed Baathist assassination attempt, a public holiday was declared in his honor known as "The Day of Safety and Rejoicing" (Haddad 1971: 119). As the military ruler regime began to take on the attributes of a cult of personality, dissention increased within the ranks of the officers. Nevertheless, despite Qasim's megalomania, as an officer in power he did not tamper with the Iraqi Army's promotion guidelines, requiring a senior officer to wait four years before a promotion to a higher rank. Qasim, who was promoted to the rank of lieutenant general in 1959 would be promoted to brigadier general in 1963, just a month before his execution by another faction of revolting officers (Al-Khafaji 2000: 285).

The Kurdish revolt and Kuwait crisis of 1961

Qasim, embroiling Iraq in a conflict with Nasir's UAR, had also raised tensions with its neighbor Kuwait. After Kuwait became independent from the British in June 1961, Qasim renewed Iraq's claim to its neighbor as King Ghazi had done in the late 1930s. The Iraqi military was mobilized to the Kuwaiti border, but British forces deployed to Kuwait to prevent a possible invasion. Qasim's actions alienated him in the Arab world, humiliated the Iraqi military and weakened his position domestically (Davis 2005: 139).

Mulla Mustafa Barazani, the leader of the Kurdish Democratic Party (KDP) had returned to Iraq from the Soviet Union after 1958. Qasim originally embraced Barazani and his Party as an ally of the Revolution, but soon the Iraqi leader began to use his divide and rule tactics among the Kurds as well. Mulla Mustafa opposed Qasim's overtures to the Zebari tribe in 1959, one of the rivals to the Barazanis (Be'eri 1970: 190). When intra-Kurdish fighting began between factions allied with the Barazani tribes versus the Herki and the Surchi tribes in the summer of 1961, the military intervened on the side of the latter by attacking a pro-Barazani village. The armed forces found itself embroiled in a fight with the Kurds once again, unable to score a decisive victory due to the difficulty of combating guerrillas in the mountainous terrain of the north (Farouk-Sluglett and Sluglett 1987: 81).

Close to two-thirds of the military were deployed to the north, which further led to Qasim's growing unpopularity in the Army. Officers on the northern front accused Qasim of failing to devote enough troops to quell the revolt, but the Sole Leader's fear was that too many troops outside of his control would eventually lead to revolt against him (Haddad 1971: 118, 121). Military officers also advocated a military offensive against the KDP, however Qasim opted for a defensive strategy, pinning his hopes on the Kurdish infighting and an embargo on food and arms that would cause the revolt to collapse. However, it was the Kurdish militias who proved that they could prevent food from reaching the Iraqi military garrisons, causing more discontent among the Army stationed in the north (Pollack 2002: 158–9). The concentration of the Army forces outside of Baghdad, particularly in the north would eventually facilitate the overthrow of the Qasim government by nationalist and Baathist factions of the military in February 1963.

Divisions within the military: 1958–1963

The fighting in the north created tensions between Arabs and Kurds in the ranks of the military. The 1961 Barazani revolt resulted in a number of desertions among both Kurdish officers and conscripts sympathetic to his cause. However, there were Kurdish soldiers who remained loyal to the Iraqi state and fought against the KDP, recruited from tribes opposed to the Barazanis. Those Kurds in the military whose loyalty was in question were monitored closely by the state.

While the number of high-ranking Kurdish officers declined during this period, the few numbers of Shia officers remained constant. Sectarian prejudices were prevalent among the Sunni Arab officers towards the minority of Shia officers, who were often deployed on extended campaigns in the restive north, and rarely rotated to other bases in the Shia south or in the vicinity of Baghdad. There was also a limited number of Shia graduating from the military academy. During this period the number of military academy graduates was estimated at 70 percent Sunni Arabs, mostly coming from the town of Mosul. A total of 20 percent were Shia Arabs and 10 percent were Kurds, Turkmen, Christian and Yazidi (Hashim 2003a: 32).

Qasim tried to enhance his own patronage network among the officers, appeasing the military establishment by allocating 40 percent of the national budget to it. He had increased the number of promotions and the pay of the officers, and provided them with housing compounds with their own schools, cinemas, swimming pools and health facilities in Officers' City (*Madinat al-Dhubbat*) (Al-Khafaji 2000: 265). Yet his network of supporters was far outnumbered by his enemies. There were 8,000 officers in the military before Qasim's tenure. He had purged more than 2,000 of these officers creating a formidable network of opponents (Heller 1977: 84). In 1958, Qasim was the center of a military ruler regime that appeared to have the support of the masses. By 1963, Qasim's priority was to ensure its own survival, to the neglect of the reforms promised after the Revolution (Be'eri 1970: 189). Without a base of popular support, military loyalty had propped up Qasim's regime, but that loyalty according to Haddad "was more to military principles of discipline than to Kassem's own person" (Haddad 1971: 119). His fatal flaw in solely relying on the armed forces was that he failed to create an overarching network that incorporated all the officers. His divide and rule tactics applied to political parties also affected the officer corps, many of whom were political partisans themselves. He continued to alienate the officers through his incessant shuffling of commanders at all levels, and appointing three of Iraq's five division commanders who did not graduate from the Staff College, a violation of the Officers Service Law (Batatu 1979: 846–7).

In November 1961, Qasim released Colonel Arif, his co-conspirator in the 1958 overthrow of the monarchy, a move that would ultimately seal the Iraqi leader's fate two years later (Haddad 1971: 109). By 1959 he had already released Baathist officers such as Ahmad Hasan Al-Bakr, Abd Al-Sattar Abd Al-Latif, Hardan Al-Takriti and Mundhir Wandawi. One of the escapees of the 1959 assassination attempt on Qasim's life, Ali Salih Al-Saadi, had returned to Iraq from Syria in April 1960 to mobilize key supporters of the Baath Party, including those in the military. By 1961, they began secretly disseminating their underground newspaper *Al-Ishtiraki (The Socialist)*, which was gaining a growing readership among the military (Khadduri 1969a: 189). In 1962, Al-Saadi convened a secret meeting of the Baathist Command in the Iraq Region, otherwise known as the Iraqi Regional Command (Batatu 1979: 967). The core of the Iraqi Baath Party began their plans for seizing power. The number of active members in the Baath at this juncture was relatively small, estimated at 700 members (Helms 1984: 75). The Party began to establish a clandestine network of Alarm Committees in Baghdad and other Iraqi towns. These Committees would wait for the day when the Baath Party Command would give them the order to take to the streets with arms and support a Baathist uprising.

As a civilian party, the Baath realized that it would be impossible to overthrow Qasim's military ruler regime with civil resistance alone. In order to bring down the regime, the Baath would have to instigate a civilian uprising that would be so widely spread that the military could not suppress it. Even with its network of Alarm Committees, the Baath did not command a significant following among Iraq's population to spark a nationwide revolt. After the Baathist assassination against Qasim had failed, he was heavily guarded at all times by an entourage of loyal soldiers and secret police. In order to bring down a military ruler regime, the Baathists settled on the one tactic that could undermine it from within: instigating its sympathizers to foment a coup against Qasim. In 1962 the Baath formed its six-man Military Bureau that included a civilian, Al-Saadi as its secretary and other retired Baathist officers who had just been released from prison. The Bureau's strength was amplified by their network in the military. Some of the officers in the Bureau were Brigadier Ahmad Hasan Al-Bakr and Lieutenant Colonel Abd Al-Sattar Abd Al-Latif. Staff Lieutenant Colonel Salih Mahdi Ammash, a member of the Party since 1952 was still in active service in the Air Force, serving under its Communist commander, Jalal Al-Awqati (Batatu 1979: 968–70). Unlike the Communist Party, which sought a wide base among the lower ranks, the Baathists sought alliances with officers who commanded units that could strike swiftly into the capital. These officers did not necessarily have to be Baathists, such as Abd Al-Salam Arif, but sympathetic to their views and most importantly opposed to Qasim.

In December 1962 they began to plan the coup. The Bureau decided that if their coup was to succeed, they would have to first secure the radio station in Abu Ghurayb, fourteen kilometers west of Baghdad and another radio station in Baghdad itself. They would also have to take the Defense Ministry complex, which served as Qasim's headquarters. The Ministry itself was guarded by three infantry battalions from Qasim's Nineteenth Brigade, 2,500 men loyal to the Sole Leader and an array of anti-tank and anti-aircraft guns. The coup would also have to strike at the Rashid Camp, which had a counter-coup force including tanks and fighter aircraft piloted by a detachment of Communist air force pilots. The Baathists could rely on a network of supporters in the Fourth Tank Regiment stationed at the Abu Ghurayb base, a position that allowed the coup plotters quick entry into the capital. They also had supporters among the mechanized Eighth Infantry Brigade and the Sixth Squadron of the Air Force, both stationed at the Habbaniyya base. Qasim had allowed a concentration of Arab nationalist pilots to be stationed in Habbaniyya as part of his policy of balancing them against the Communist pilots at the Rashid base. Since most of Iraq's coups had taken place at dawn, it was decided to begin at nine in the morning to take advantage of the element of surprise, as well as on the Islamic day of rest, Friday, when officers and soldiers would be at home (ibid.: 970).

The February 1963 military ruler regime

Qasim's intelligence network provided him with information about a possible coup within the military and on February 3, 1963 he ordered the arrest of Salih Mahdi Ammash of the Baath Military Bureau. The civilians in the Baath planned to hold an emergency meeting the next day, but it was foiled by Qasim's intelligence network. Ali Salih Al-Saadi, one of the prominent civilian agitators of the Party was also arrested. Ahmad Hasan Al-Bakr, the head of the Party's Military Bureau, working with a network of officers that included Abd Al-Salam Arif and pro-Nasirists, decided to organize the coup on Friday February 8, before Qasim moved against the remaining Baathists (Khadduri 1969a: 190).

At 8:00 A.M., Arif and Al-Bakr led a tank column made up of the Fourth Tank Brigade from Abu Ghurayb into the capital. Thirty minutes later, rebel soldiers assassinated the Communist commander of the Air Force, Jalal Al-Awqati, killing him near his home in front of his children. A Nasirist colonel at the Habbaniyya base, Arif Abd Al-Razzaq took control over the aircraft of the Sixth Squadron, and his fighter jets took off to support the coup. By 9:00 A.M., the coup preceded on schedule as the planes, one of them flown by the Baathist Captain Mundhir Wandawi, attacked the Rashid air base, destroying its runway and depriving the Communist pilots from taking off. Afterwards the aircraft flew to the Ministry of Defense and began their attack. The rebels moved to secure the radio stations in Baghdad and announced the coup (Be'eri 1970: 193).

The coup plotters released their first communiqué, a personal attack against Qasim and his deviation from Arab unity. Just as in 1958, Arif made the first radio announcement, but prematurely declared over the radio that Qasim had been captured. The masses would otherwise have no way of knowing that Arif was lying. Upon news of the coup, Baathist irregulars of the Alarm Committees, now calling themselves the National Guard, moved into the streets and supported the Army units involved with the coup (Be'eri 1970: 194–5). Crowds, including Communists and the urban lower classes, gathered in neighborhoods of Baghdad and around the Ministry of Defense to defend Qasim. While the coup plotters had secured the radio station, they had forgotten about the other important medium – TV. Qasim in fact had not been captured, and was shown on TV being applauded by his supporters. By 10:30 he had reached the Ministry of Defense where he began organizing a counter-coup. It may appear odd that the Communists had come to Qasim's aid, as they had been targeted during his rule. However, they realized that if the pan-Arabist/Baathist coup were to succeed, the Communists would face harsh reprisals from their arch rivals. The Communists could mobilize people on the street, but the crowds could not prevent the rebel tanks from approaching the Ministry of Defense complex by 11:30. The pro-Communist Brigadier Taha Al-Shaykh Ahmad suggested that Qasim rally his loyalists at the Ministry and launch an offensive counter-attack. Qasim however decided to defend the compound and resist the attackers from within its confines (Batatu 1979: 976).

Qasim had requested that the mostly Communist troops from the Rashid base, which had just been attacked, come to his aid, but only a few units were able to make it outside when they were attacked by elements from the rebel Fourth Tank Brigade and Baathist militias. The Rashid base fell to the enemy military units, and officers at the other military base, the Washshash camp north-west of Baghdad, joined the side of the coup plotters (Batatu 1979: 979–80).

The standoff in front of the Ministry of Defense continued until the following day, February 9, when a group of rebel soldiers made a final assault on the facility. It was reported that Qasim resisted until he ran out of bullets for his pistol. He was taken to the radio station where the coup planners were. Arif was face-to-face with the man he once considered his father. It was Qasim who had supported Arif's membership to the Free Officers and convinced other officers skeptical of Abd Al-Salam's qualifications to let him join. Arif even declared to the other Free Officers when they were planning their coup in 1958, "*maku za'im illa Karim*" or "There is no leader other than Karim" (ibid.: 798). Qasim had spared Arif's life by revoking his death sentence, but that favor was not returned, and the Sole Leader was executed on that day (Be'eri 1970: 195).

On the same day, fighting between Communists and the Baathist National Guard continued to rage. Vitriolic radio communiqués labeled the Communists as "agents" and "the partners in crime of the enemy of God Qasim" and called for military units and the National Guard to "annihilate anyone that disturbs the peace" (Batatu 1979: 982). A post-1963 periodical would glorify the actions taken by their supporters on that day in the following terms:

> Until came the dawn of the blessed 14th Ramadhan (February 8th, 1963), when the vanguards of the Army and the people rose to raze the tyrant's fort and eliminate him once and for all, so as a new society may rise, after being cleaned from the venoms of Qassim and the communists.
>
> (*Iraq*, May 1, 1963: 7)

Since the Communists were the only organized party left, they had to be eliminated to consolidate Baath rule, and the National Guard militias went on a rampage in the days following the coup, establishing a reputation for their excessive use of violence. Communist military officers were also executed in the following days after the coup.

After the successful coup, Abd Al-Salam Arif was promoted to the highest military rank of Field Marshal and assumed the title of President. The pro-Baathist Ahmad Hasan Al-Bakr became a Brigadier General and

Prime Minister. Tahir Yahya was promoted from colonel to major general and became Chief of Staff, and Salih Mahdi Ammash was promoted from lieutenant colonel to lieutenant general and became the Minister of Defense (Batatu 1979: 1,003). While Qasim did not tamper with military promotion guidelines, the officers in the 1963 coup had no compunction about skipping ranks. Most of them were colonels and became generals overnight.

The new military ruler regime was a coalition of military officers, Nasirists and Baathists. The Baath was the first ideological party to rule Iraq, but its support within the state essentially emanated from the military. Arif in the early days of his presidency invoked the Baathist slogans of "unity, freedom and socialism" (Haddad 1971: 128). However Arif only used the Baath to seize power and was not a member, but rather sympathized with their ideology as did other non-aligned officers.

The Baath sought to expand their power by creating an even more pervasive network in the Army, winning over more adherents in the officer corps to their ideology, as well as strengthening their own paramilitary organization, the National Guard. The Baathists soon established their own network in the military to counter Arif's. Ammash held the portfolio of Minister of Defense and a Baathist major, Muhyi Al-Din Mahmud, was the chief of the Military Intelligence Directorate. Another Baathist, Hardan Al-Tikriti commanded the Air Force, and Abd Al-Karim Nusrat, who led the charge against Qasim in the Ministry of Defense, commanded the Fourth Armored Division (Batatu 1979: 1011).

Other officers in the Army began to resent the Baathist patronage networks that developed almost immediately after the coup. Baathist officers would often receive military promotions based solely on their political merit. In addition to patronage networks based on Party membership, regional networks were also established in the military. Al-Bakr, coming from Takrit, promoted a number of his townspeople to prominent positions in the military, as well as the government. The Chief of Staff, Tahir Yahya and Commander of the Air Force Hardan Al-Takriti also came from Takrit, but were from the Shiyasha clan opposed to Al-Bakr's Bayjat clan (Be'eri 1970: 200). According to one account, one official dropped his last name, "Al-Takriti," which indicated his origins, as not to affiliate himself with the numerous other Takritis infiltrating the security and governing apparatus. Another patronage network from Mosul was also dominant and resented the dominance of the Takritis (Marr 1970: 287).

Arif also sought to consolidate his military ruler regime by creating a network based on support of his family. His brother, Colonel Abd Al-Rahman Arif was promoted to the rank of brigadier and would command Iraq's recently formed Fifth Division. Colonel Said Sulaybi who came from the Arif's Al-Jumayla tribe was made commander the military police (Sakai 2003: 140). While the Baathist Abd Al-Karim Nusrat commanded the Fourth Armored Division, Arif placed men loyal to him as the commanders of the three of the remaining Army divisions (Be'eri 1970: 198).

After the coup, the Baathist National Guard, a militia whose numbers increased from 5,000 to 34,000 from the months between February and August 1963, continued to persecute all suspected Communists, Qasim sympathizers and anyone who posed a threat to the new government (Parasiliti 2001: 86). The emergence of a paramilitary force, alongside the regular Army would serve as a precedent to a trend that would continue under the rule of Saddam Hussein. The commander of the militia was the twenty-eight year old Baathist pilot Wandawi. The National Guard appeared to be similar to the youth *Futuwwa* of the 1930s in its role as a militant student militia: "Most volunteers are part-time. Previously mainly students were given weapons and green armbands, but less educated youths and workers are being recruited" (*The Times*, May 24, 1963: 10). Their excessive use of violence led to the public appropriating a euphemistic title to describe them – *Bashi Buzuk*, a reference to the undisciplined irregular troops of the Ottoman Empire stationed in Iraq (Haddad 1971: 135). As Be'eri (1970: 198) noted, "The National Guard was a military organization without military discipline whose mission was to terrorize the population." The description seemed apt to say that the National Guard was similar to the Fidayin Saddam that was created in the late 1990s. The National Guard alienated the military, even the Baathist career officers, who resented the arbitrary actions of the Guard, such as setting up checkpoints and even checking vehicles that belonged to the officers (Batatu 1979: 1012).

The Army was divided between Baathists and Nasirists who still sought union with Egypt. Even though the pan-Arab Baath had been allies with the pan-Arab Nasirists, the former was reluctant to advocate unity with Nasir once they had achieved power. Eventually the Nasirists emerged as a threat to the Baathists and in May several pro-Nasir officers were purged. On May 25, the Baathists announced a thwarted plot by Nasirist officers in the Twenty-fifth Armored Corps based near Baghdad. Eleven officers were executed and eighteen officers were arrested, among them Colonel Arif Abd Al-Razzaq, the commander who provided the air support for the anti-Qasim coup and who would later re-emerge to challenge the Arif ruler regime (Haddad 1971: 131–2).

The Kurds under Mulla Mustafa Barazani had asked the Arif government for autonomy, and when this request was not met the Kurds began a new offensive on June 10, 1963. The pro-Baathist officers were kept in Baghdad where they could protect the regime, while officers whose loyalty was suspect were dispatched to the front lines. This tactic was reported to have led some of the anti-Baath officers in the north to defect to the Kurdish side (ibid.: 134). Once again the military deployed in the north grew disillusioned, especially after hearing empty promises from the Baathist Minister of Defense, Salih Mahdi Ammash of a "crushing victory." However a quick victory did not materialize before the winter had begun in the mountainous north, making it difficult for the Army to pursue Kurdish rebels.

The November 1963 coup

In September 1963, an internal crisis within the Baath emerged between a radical left-wing faction led by the civilian agitator Ali Salih Al-Saadi and the moderate wing of the Party, which included the Prime Minister, General Hasan Al-Bakr. Al-Saadi's faction urged the Baath to adopt a platform of radical nationalization, to establish a party organization based on democratic centralism and to create a political structure less dependent on the military. The Bakr faction opposed nationalization and stressed the importance of the Army in Iraqi politics (Be'eri 1970: 199). Additionally, most of the moderate Baathists were military officers who felt that the more radical civilian Baathists were edging them out of power by not inviting them to the Baath Party Regional Command meeting (Khadduri 1969a: 204). Moderate Baathists at this point were also concerned about the continued excesses of the National Guard and that they may reflect negatively on the reputation of the Party. They feared that the Baath National Guard was beginning to usurp the role of the Army, and non-Baathist officers resented the militia as a manifestation of a Baathist lack of respect for the authority of the armed forces.

Arif would eventually call in the Army to check the excesses of the National Guard, which he despairingly referred to as the "un-national" National Guard (Lenczowski 1966: 287). Al-Saadi loyalists in the National Guard refused Arif's ultimatum to disband. The government exiled Al-Saadi to Spain, but even outside of the country, he was still able to mobilize the commander of the National Guard Mundhir Wandawi to launch a coup. On November 13 the National Guard seized the post office and telephone exchange in the capital, and Wandawi commandeered a fighter aircraft from the Habbaniyya base and strafed Arif's presidential palace (Be'eri 1970: 200).

The moderate wing of the Baathists in the military decided to forego Party loyalty and rallied behind Arif. On November 18, 1963 Arif's brother, Abd Al-Rahman, Commander of the Fifth Division, led his troops from the Baaquba base into Baghdad. He was supported by Colonel Said Sulaybi the commander of the military police. Two of the moderate Baathists, Chief of Staff Tahir Yahya and the Commander of the Air Force Hardan Al-Takriti, took part in leading the forces to suppress the radical Baathist rebellion. The combined firepower of tanks, aircraft and artillery pounded the National Guards' barracks in the Adhamiyya district in Baghdad in a battle that lasted two hours (Haddad 1971: 136). Arif's military ruler regime was based on his control over the military, and thus the coup attempt of November demonstrated to those officers the fate of those who favored their party ties over loyalty to the military. Wandawi's decision to side with the Baathists led to his elimination.

The moderate Baathist officers loyal to Arif were "rewarded" with promotions. Al-Bakr, who had been Prime Minister, became Vice-President, Tahir Yahya, the Chief of Staff became Prime Minister, Hardan Al-Takriti, the Commander of the Air Force became Defense Minister and another Takriti Baathist officer, Rashid Muslih, became Minister of the Interior. However, their promotions were part of Arif's plans to rid Baathist influence in the military ruler regime once and for all. These four Baathists demonstrated the nature of patronage networks in the military and why Arif perceived them as a threat. All four of the men had been members of the Party serving in its Military Bureau, and all of them were Takritis (Batatu 1979: 1028). Al-Bakr's post of Vice-President proved to be merely symbolic and Hardan Al-Takriti's promotion to Minister of Defense weakened his control over the Air Force. By January 1964, Arif abolished the office of Vice-President and transferred Al-Bakr to an ambassadorial post, essentially a political "kiss of death," ironically imitating Qasim's attempt to exile Arif as ambassador to West Germany. In March 1964 Hardan Al-Takriti lost his post of Defense Minister (Be'eri 1970: 201). He was later appointed as ambassador to Sweden, infuriating him to the point where he said in a meeting of exiled Baathists, "By the beard of the Prophet, I swear I will overthrow the traitor Aref" (Haddad 1971: 143). Only Tahir Yahya would survive in Arif's ruler regime, yet he was considered to be a nominal Baathist and thus posed no threat.

Arif also buttressed his military regime by introducing dual militarism in Iraq. First he strengthened the Twentieth Infantry Brigade, which he had commanded when he marched into Baghdad in July 1958. After the National Guard challenged the ruler regime in November, Arif created an elite military force, the Republican Guard, recruited mostly from the ranks of his trusted brigade (Batatu 1979: 1027–8). The praetorians under Arif essentially had created a special praetorian class within the Army. The strongest praetorian in Iraq, Arif had developed a force to protect his position, a system later developed to perfection by Saddam Hussein (Farouk-Sluglett and Sluglett 1987: 94). Arif filled the ranks of the Republican Guards with men from his Arab Sunni Al-Jumayla tribe. The Commander of the Guards, Colonel Said Sulaybi was also a relative of the Iraqi leader who demonstrated his prowess suppressing the National Guard coup in his capacity as commander of the military police. Arif also cemented his ties with the military establishment by appointing his brother Abd Al-Rahman to Chief of the General Staff, consolidating his ruler regime by creating a patronage network based on family and tribal ties within the military, in addition to building an elite corps whose loyalty was tied not to any political program, but their primordial ties to the leader. Despite these efforts there were still networks of Baathists and Nasirists in the Army that would later challenge the networks Arif had established to prop up his military ruler regime.

Further military coups attempts 1964–1966

Having lost his power after demonstrating his loyalty to Arif over the radical Baathists, Ahmad Hasan Al-Bakr avenged the betrayal by orchestrating a coup to overthrow the Iraqi leader in September 1964, when the President was scheduled to fly to an Arab League conference in Egypt. The pilots of the six aircraft assigned to protect Arif's plane belonged to a Baathist cell and they had conspired to shoot down the President's plane as it took off, and then attack the other fighter aircraft stationed at the airport and at the Rashid camp. While this attack was to occur, pro-Baathist Lieutenant Colonel Ahmad Jaburi would lead a tank column into Baghdad. However, one of the six pilots was in fact an Arif informer. The five other pilots were executed and Arif led a crackdown on the remaining Baathists in the military and Al-Bakr was imprisoned once again (Be'eri 1970: 202).

The other threat in the military emanated from the *wahdawiyyun* or "unionists," those officers who still favored Iraq's union with Nasir's Egypt. Two of the officers who were in the ruler regime, Brigadier Subhi Abd Al-Hamid, Minister of the Interior, and Brigadier Abd Al-Karim Farhan, Minister of Culture and Guidance, were pro-Nasirist. In February 1965 these men had suggested that Arif grant autonomy to the Kurds. Arif rejected their plan and on April 4, ordered the Iraqi Army to take part in a renewed campaign against the KDP. This decision proved unpopular as the military was again embroiled in a quagmire, leaving most of the Iraqi Army pinned down while fighting Kurdish rebels (Lenczowski 1966: 287).

In May 1964 Arif's government drafted a provisional constitution that cancelled the provisional constitution of July 27, 1958. The second military ruler regime had tried to undo the work of the first military ruler regime of Qasim (Haddad 1971: 141). This constitution, which was issued from a military government, forbade the military from engaging in politics, ostensibly directed to the factions of the Army that were not part of the state apparatus.

Ruler regimes often try to carry out grand programs of national reforms. Arif did make some efforts in this regard, announcing a five-year plan in January 1965 to improve socio-economic conditions through greater use of oil revenues (Khadduri 1969b: 81). However, Nasirist officers in the government demanded more radical nationalization and further socialist reforms. In July a new crisis erupted when Arif had failed to nationalize Iraq's oil, and most of the Nasirist officers resigned from the government in July. As a result of disarray in the cabinet, Arif pressured Tahir Yahya to resign from his post as Prime Minister in September. In an attempt to placate the unionist camp, the Iraqi leader appointed the Nasirist officer Arif Abd Al-Razzaq as the new Prime Minister. Abd Al-Razzaq was a pilot, promoted to commander of the Habbaniyya base after the July 1958 coup. He turned against Qasim for his failure to endorse Nasirism and took part in the failed Shawwaf rebellion in Mosul in 1959. He was retired from the military, but took his revenge against Qasim by piloting one of the planes that attacked the Ministry of Defense during the February 1963 coup. Abd Al-Razzaq later became Commander of the Air Force, replacing Hardan Al-Takriti. The Iraqi leader believed that appointing Abd Al-Razzaq as Prime Minister would deprive him of his network within a strategic branch of the military and thus he would not constitute a threat.

Appointing Arif Abd Al-Razzaq as Prime Minister proved to be a tactical error on Abd Al-Salam Arif's part. Abd Al-Razzaq began conspiring with the pro-Nasirist officers who had resigned in July over the failure to nationalize Iraq's oil. Arif's brother, Abd Al-Rahman, in his capacity as Chief of Staff relieved several Nasirist officers of their posts and a confrontation began to brew between Abd Al-Razzaq and the Arif brothers. However these tensions did not prevent Abd Al-Salam Arif from leaving the capital to attend another Arab League meeting in Casablanca on September 14, 1965 (Haddad 1971: 149).

With the President away, the coup planners struck in what had become an almost routine procedure. The plan of the coup was not discovered by the Military Intelligence Directorate, since its head, Colonel Hadi Khammas was a Narisist and supported the planned putsch. Brigadier Muhammad Majid, Chief of Operations of the General Staff and Colonel Irfan Wajdi led a tank column from the Abu Ghurayb base outside of Baghdad and proceeded to seize the radio station to announce Arif's overthrow and union with Egypt. Abd Al-Razzaq ordered the arrest of Arif's relative, Colonel Said Sulaybi, commander of the garrison in Baghdad and the first commander of the Republican Guard. The current head of the Republican Guard, Lieutenant Colonel Bashir Talib was also summoned by the Nasirist Prime Minister. The former sensed that there was a conspiracy that morning and led a tank column to interdict the renegade tank formation marching into the capital. They surrendered and Abd Al-Razzaq fled to Cairo. Arif returned to Baghdad as a victorious survivor, but the Army's prestige, the principal support of his military ruler regime, had been undermined (Be'eri 1970: 206).

Both Baathists and Nasirists had sought to bring the collapse of the military ruler regime through the vehicle of the Army. The Arif military ruler regime had depended on the support of a coalition of pro-Arif, Baathist and Nasirist officers. The Baathists and Nasirists had been eliminated due to their own attempts to use the military to overthrow Arif, while the other officers, mostly from the Al-Jumayla tribe managed to consolidate their power. The Republican Guard was in the hands of this tribe, and after the former head of Military Intelligence, Hadi Khammas had taken part in the pro-Nasirist coup, he was replaced with Lieutenant Colonel Abd Al-Razzaq Al-Nayif, also from the Al-Jumayla tribe (Sakai 2003: 140). (Abd Al-Razzaq Al-Nayif should not be confused with the Nasirist Arif Abd Al-Razzaq who had just fled to Cairo at this point.)

In September 1965, after Arif Abd Al-Razzaq, the last Nasirist officer/Prime Minister tried to overthrow him, Arif allowed a civilian, Abd Al-Rahman Al-Bazzaz to assume the post. Al-Bazzaz represented the first civilian to become Prime Minister since the chain of ruler regimes were established in republican Iraq as of 1958. While Arif still held the more powerful presidency, this appointment appeared as a move from the military ruler regime to devolve some power to the civilians. However, the other important government posts were still held by officers. The Minister of Interior was Brigadier Abd Al-Latif Al-Darraji (accused of plotting with Al-Gaylani against Qasim in December 1958) and the Minister of Defense was Major General Abd Al-Aziz Uqayli (Be'eri 1970: 207). Both of these officers had taken part in the July 1958 and the February 1963 coups.

The presidency of Abd Al-Rahman Arif

Arif and Al-Darraji were killed in a helicopter crash on April 13, 1966 during a sandstorm in the south of Iraq. By this time, the armed forces in Arif's ruler regime were subordinated under the National Defense Council dominated by twelve military officers, rather than under control of the cabinet (Hurewitz 1982: 149). The National Defense Council had a choice of appointing Abd Al-Salam's Arif's brother, the Chief of Staff, Major General Abd Al-Rahman or another officer Major General Abd Al-Aziz Uqayli, the Minister of Defense. Uqayli had a strong following among the officer corps but his position on the Kurdish issue alienated elements in the National Defense Council. Uqayli had called for a continued military campaign against Mulla Mustafa until his forces would collapse. By this juncture, others within the military had grown weary of the campaign in the north and sought for a settlement with the KDP (Khadduri 1969a: 265–6). Abd Al-Rahman seemed a more favorable candidate in accepting such a plan, in addition to the fact that he was the brother of the former President. Most of the National Defense Council had been appointed by Abd Al-Rahman's deceased brother, and Abd Al-Rahman also enjoyed the support of Brigadier Sulaybi, from the same tribe, who commanded military forces in Baghdad (Batatu 1979: 1062). Given the power of the familial and clan ties in the ruler regime, Abd Al-Rahman was appointed as President.

The pro-Nasirist Air Force officer and former Prime Minister Arif Abd Al-Razzaq continued his exile in Egypt until June 1966 when he sneaked back into Iraq in order to take part in another coup. He contacted another Nasirist Brigadier Yunis Attar-Basha commander of the Fourth Division in Mosul who had not raised the suspicions of the ruler regime. Another coup was scheduled for June 30. It began in Mosul where Attar-Basha took over the base, and Abd Al-Razzaq flew a Hunter fighter aircraft and advanced towards Baghdad. Pilots in support of the coup took off in their fighters from the Habbaniyya air base, and tanks deployed from the Abu Ghurayb base. The coup plotters seized one of the capital's radio stations and announced the coup in the afternoon. Just as in Abd Al-Razzaq's failed coup of September 1965, the Republican Guards rallied behind Abd Al-Rahman Arif during this second Nasirist coup, a demonstration of the Guards serving an effective counter-coup role. Upon landing back at the base in Mosul, Abd Al-Razzaq was arrested, as well as thirteen other officers taking part in the coup (Be'eri 1970: 208).

Abd Al-Rahman was unable to cultivate the ties of patronage that his brother had. His primary pillar of support was still the Republican Guard, where he shared the common tribal Al-Jumayla link, but he took their loyalty for granted (Tripp 2000: 185–6). Furthermore, the commander of the Guard, Brigadier Sulaybi saw in Abd Al-Rahman's weakness an opportunity for him to strengthen his own control over the armed forces. The new Iraqi leader did not invest the time and effort that his brother did in ingratiating himself with officers of the Guard, allowing them later to come under the influence of the Baathists. He also failed to overcome the divisions within the officer corps who managed to unite only in their opposition to Al-Bazzaz, the strongest civilian in Arif's government.

Since March 1965 close to 50,000 troops out of an Army of 70,000 were deployed in the north (Haddad 1971: 151). The Kurds had delivered a massive defeat to the Iraqi armed forces in May 1966 inflicting 2,000 casualties (Pollack 2002: 163). On June 29, in an attempt to end the crippling war in the north, the Prime Minister Al-Bazzaz announced a program attempting to grant the Kurds autonomy. However, the military decided to oppose this plan at this time. The Army had opposed long campaigns in the north in the past and at one time advocated a settlement with the KDP. Their opposition to a plan to end the fighting at this juncture was their fear that the officers and the military would appear to have lost to the Kurds. The officers had a professional identity to protect tied to the dominant political role of the military in politics. Such a defeat not only harmed their legitimacy as the protector of Iraq's national integrity but deprived them of a justification to rule. Negotiating with the KDP at this juncture would have also harmed the officer's personal honor and the prestige of the Army (Tripp 2000: 187).

What proved more disturbing to the officers was Al-Bazzaz's attempt to redirect the revenues from Iraq's oil from the defense budget to regenerating the economy. A continuing war in the north served as a pretext for the military to object to cuts in the military budget. One of the mistakes that Al-Bazzaz as a civilian had made was that he failed to develop a patronage network within the military, so that one faction could support him in his time of need. In fact, his survival was largely due to Abd al-Salam Arif's support, and with his death, Al-Bazzaz lost his strongest political patron. On August 6, Al-Bazzaz resigned under pressure from the officers in the ruler regime (Khadduri 1969a: 282).

After the resignation of Al-Bazzaz, the military eliminated a politician who threatened its influence over the government. However, the military officers themselves were still divided into rival camps, the strongest being the Nasirist *wahdawiyyun* or unionists, the Baathist *qawmiyyun*, who supported Arab unity but not under the leadership of Nasir, and the Iraq firsters or *wataniyyun*. The only candidate for the post of Prime Minster that all the officers could agree to was Brigadier Naji Talib, a Free Officer from 1958, and a Shia, who was also considered a moderate in terms of Arab unity. Talib formed the new government on August 6, 1966 (ibid.: 284–5). In May 1967, Arif dismissed Talib after a crisis with Syria over sharing oil revenues from the pipeline to the Mediterranean was concluded to Damascus' favor.

During the Six Day War of June 1967 Iraq did not have the opportunity to participate in an active combat role, although it belatedly attempted to send forces to the front. Military leaders criticized the inaction of the Arif regime and popular protests against the government emerged following the war. Iraq had emerged into an officers' state, yet even a government dominated by the military failed to take an active part in the war. The resentment towards the officers in power extended beyond Iraq's non-involvement in the war, as their reputation had been tarnished by involvement in politics and failure to bring stability to the political system. Ironically, the officers in power had weakened the institution of the armed forces itself. The officers had emerged as akin to the former, exclusive elites, devoted to enhancing their rent seeking opportunities, concerned for their own well being and growing ever so distant from the public. Merchants complained of officers whose only concern was selling import licenses and embezzling the state's funds. Military power, and thus control of the state rested with a clique that predominantly came from the north and north-west of Baghdad, from towns such as Ana, Falluja, Takrit, Rawa and Hit, another source of public discontent with their administration.

Soon protests led by trade unions and students began to demand of the ruler regime a constitutional democratic republic and free elections. Ahmad Hasan Al-Bakr of the Baath, who had been released from prison during an amnesty, sent a letter to the President asking for a coalition cabinet and the election of an assembly in two years. Arif ignored his request failing to appreciate the networks Al-Bakr and the Baathists had re-established in the military. The Baath was keen to return to power and realized that military means provided the only possible solution. While the Baathists envisioned themselves as a revolutionary party due to its calls for radical socio-economic change, they realized that they could not instigate a radical upheaval by the masses. It was military force that determined which Iraqi faction could attain and maintain power, and thus it was the allegiance and ambitions of the officers who determined if a government was to survive. However, the decade from 1958 to 1968 demonstrated to the Baath, as well as the Iraqi public that the constant military intervention in the political process led to a weak military force that could neither participate effectively in the 1967 War nor in suppressing a Kurdish insur-rection. Furthermore the military had failed to modernize the country as it promised and in fact only exacerbated domestic instability. The Party seemed to have heeded the words of its founder, Michel Aflaq: "There is no real revolutionary party in the world whose leaders are military men continuing to command army units" (Dawisha 1986: 25). While the Baath deemed the military as an agent inhibiting change, there was no other alternative for seizing power and implementing their reforms. The plans for a second Baathist military coup were set in motion.

Part III
The totalitarian military

6 The Baathification of the military 1968–1980

Defining the totalitarian-penetration military

> Power grows out of the barrel of the gun. Our principle is that the party commands the gun and the gun shall never be allowed to command the party.
>
> (quoted in Nordlinger 1977: 13)

Mao Ze Dung's aforementioned quote encapsulated the ethos of the totalitarian-penetration system, where the military, "the gun," is subordinated to the party. This model emerged in Nazi Germany, the Soviet Union, Communist China, North Korea, North Vietnam, Cuba and Baathist Iraq. Before applying this model to Iraq, the question arises as to whether Saddam Hussein's Iraq could be categorized as a totalitarian regime. Opposed to an authoritarian regime, a textbook definition of totalitarian regime is as follows:

> Whereas authoritarian regimes allow individuals and groups some independence of action, the central feature of totalitarian system is that the state attempts to control the whole of society, minds as well as bodies, and to this end mobilizes the population, youth as well as adults.
>
> (Curtis 2006: 22)

In addition to these characteristics, a totalitarian regime "makes deliberate use of terror as a controlling faction through the secret police, concentration of labor camps, and the completely amoral use of force" (ibid.). Iraq under Saddam Hussein took on all the aforementioned characteristics of a totalitarian state. Others who work on Iraq such as Kanan Makiya (1998), Ahmad Hashim (2003a: 35) and Faleh Jabar (2004: 132) have classified Iraq in totalitarian terms. However, some political scientists would disagree with this classification:

> By way of comparison, a country such as Iraq, although highly oppressive, cannot be described as totalitarian because it lacks a clear

ideology. Saddam Hussein's primary goal as Iraq's leader is simply to maintain and expand his political power as an end in itself.

(O'Neil 2004: 123)

However, all leaders in a totalitarian system "seek to maintain and expand political power." In addition to all of the characteristics of a totalitarian system, Hussein sought an ideological transformation of society. While some would say that Hussein deviated from some of the tenets of the Baath, we argue that Hussein sought to Baathify the military and society as he interpreted the foundations of the Party to suit the Iraqi context. In fact, after 2003 Iraqi politicians referred to a "Saddamist Baathism" or *Al-Baathiyya Al-Saddamiyya*. The Shia and Kurds were not oppressed in Iraq solely for their ethno-sectarian differences. They were persecuted since generally members of these communities rejected Saddam Hussein's vision of a Baathist Iraq. A regime adapting the political tenets of an ideology to suit a local context does not preclude a state from being totalitarian. Maoism emerged in Chinese context yet was still considered totalitarian.

The totalitarian-penetration model usually emerges where there is a highly centralized single party or a personal dictatorship, or a combination of both. Civilians from an authoritarian party ensure that the military remains loyal and obedient by penetrating the military with a political ideology. If the military is to be penetrated by a single package of political ideas, there cannot be other parties that can articulate competing ideologies (Nordlinger 1977: 15). The goal is to remove any tension between a civilian party and the military by ensuring political conformity through the creation of an ideological military. However, as Hashim pointed out, "Totalitarian regimes never achieve complete control over the armed forces; they simply cannot attain ideological uniformity among the officer corps" (Hashim 2003a: 35). Thus tensions between the military and the party are a defining feature of this relationship. Usually this model is a stark contrast to the liberal model, where:

> The government respects the military's honor, expertise, autonomy, and political neutrality. It does not slur the officer corps, interfere in professional military affairs, interject political considerations into the armed forces (e.g., by promoting officers because of their political loyalties), or use the army for domestic political advantage.
>
> (Nordlinger 1977: 13)

In the totalitarian-penetration system, the regime does not follow these guidelines and in Iraq, Saddam Hussein violated all of the defining features of the liberal model. The rise of Saddam Hussein marked the end of praetorianism in Iraq, and the restoration of civilian control with the totalitarian-penetration model. The military and militarism were dominant in Iraqi society, especially during its three wars, but it was Saddam Hussein and the civilian Baathists who exercised supreme authority.

One of the first tactics in creating a totalitarian military is infiltrating political commissars into the armed forces at all levels to disseminate an ideology and hold political discussions within the military units. Their responsibility is to the civilian leadership of the party, rather than to military officers or to a ministry of defense. The party commissars ensure that all decisions taken by the military meet the party's approval. Besides providing ideology, they are the "eyes and ears" of the party, ensuring that political ideas are put to practice. Nordlinger wrote "Surveillance is so extensive that suspicions might be quickly aroused if some officers got together for social occasion without inviting their (presumably not too popular) political commissar" (ibid.: 16). The armed forces are also monitored by secret police or military intelligence agencies separate from the party commissar network. Informers from these organizations also report directly to the party establishment or the military intelligence agencies that are under the control of the civilians in the government. These networks prevent the officers from launching a coup or conspiring with other civilians against the ruling civilian elite.

Other tactics include providing ideological education to both professional officers and the ranks of the enlisted through military academies or at mass indoctrination gatherings. Promotions are usually granted to officers who demonstrate political loyalty, often at the expense of their demonstration of military capability or experience (ibid.: 15). Loyalty within the military is also maintained through the use of surveillance and punishments ranging from purges, imprisonment or executions.

Janowitz described such regimes as "a revolutionary political elite of relatively low social status and based on an authoritarian mass political party," which molds a new type of officer and soldier (1977: 188–9). This revolutionary elite comes to power, "bedecked with paramilitary symbols," and promises their public to strengthen, revitalize and expand the military (ibid.: 80). The military is expanded as long as the armed forces support the strategic goals of the party in power. The party subsumes the military under its control by granting it extensive resources, such as advanced arms and higher salaries. At the same time, the party creates its own parallel military units to challenge the strength of the regular armed forces. The goal of this relationship is to ensure that the officers lack organizational independence, even if it means hurting their overall professionalism for the sake of keeping the armed forces out of domestic politics (ibid.).

The previous chapters demonstrated the essence of a coup in Iraq, which is defined by Quinlivan as the "seizure of the state by a small group within the state apparatus." Therefore coup-proofing is "the set of actions a regime takes to prevent a military coup" (Quinlivan 1999: 133). The creation of the totalitarian military in Iraq represented the successful efforts of the post-1968 Baath in "coup-proofing." Coup-proofing entails the creation of structures that prevents small groups, such as factions within the officer corps or clandestine parties, from overthrowing the system. The strategies a regime undertakes to prevent a coup include the recruitment of family, ethnicities or religious groups tied to the regime. They are placed in "coup-critical positions," such as those in the armed forces, to protect a state in which they share common origins. Second, the regime must create a counter-coup force through parallel armed forces to challenge the monopoly on physical coercion enjoyed by the regular military. Third, the regime creates multiple internal security agencies with overlapping jurisdictions to monitor not just the loyalty of the armed forces, but the other security agencies. These agencies must have an independent path of communication to the leadership that bypasses the military hierarchy. Finally, the rulers must foster expertness in the regular military and finally must have the means of financing such efforts (ibid.).

One of the areas where the military suffers in a totalitarian system is in professionalism. The totalitarian relationship that developed between the regime and the military after 1968 in Iraq witnessed a rise in arbitrary military appointments and promotions, as well as Baath Party interference in military affairs based on political considerations. Kamrava wrote that "professionalization enhances the autonomy of the military and, if politically unchecked, can increase its tendency to intervene in the affairs of the state" (Kamrava 2000: 69). Thus, the Baath sought to prevent fostering internal cohesion among the armed forces or bestowing upon it a greater sense of corporate identity. In the past, internal cohesion and corporate identity was deemed as the precursors to the military's forays into politics, which the Baath was keen to prevent. The Baath had to find a balance in providing new armaments to the military and expanding its size, while at the same time preventing it from emerging as a force that would threaten the power of the Party.

The July 1968 coup

Despite the ouster of the Baath from power in November 1963, the Party was still able to maintain networks within the military. The underground Party had established a three point plan to seize power, based on first infiltrating the armed forces, using the military to bring the Party to power, and finally ensuring the Baath would control the Army once they had seized power.

Brigadier Said Sulaybi, the military ruler regime's strong man, had exercised his power of patronage by appointing three officers to powerful positions in the armed forces. Lieutenant Colonel Abd Al-Razzaq Al-Nayif, from the Al-Jumayla, directed the Military Intelligence Directorate, Lieutenant Colonel Ibrahim Al-Daud had assumed the command of the Republican Guard, and Lieutenant Colonel Saadun Ghaydan, commanded the tank regiment of the Guard, the Tenth Armored Brigade. Hasan Al-Bakr was in contact with all three of these officers. However, these three conspirators did not necessarily subscribe to Baathist goals and had their own motivations for conducting the coup and betraying the President Abd Al-Rahman Arif. Once in exile, the former Iraqi President claimed that Al-Nayif was bribed by the Baathists to take part in the coup and Al-Daud was resentful of the Nasirist officers who were making their way back into the military. Ironically, Al-Nayif and Al-Daud were reportedly very close to Abd Al-Rahman Arif and one occasion before the coup proclaimed, "We are your brothers! You can count on us! We will risk our lives for your sake!" (Batatu 1979: 1073–4). Regardless of Arif's accusations, both officers had their own ambitions and realized that they would be the rulers of Iraq once the President was overthrown.

On July 17, 1968 the coup unfolded. Brigadier General Sulaybi who had been a key supporter of the Arif brothers was in the UK on the day of the 1968 coup and thus unable to offer any resistance (Farouk-Sluglett and Sluglett 1987: 112). Saadun Ghaydan, with the coordination of the Baathist officers Al-Bakr, Hardan Al-Takriti and Salih Mahdi Ammash, mobilized his Republican Guard tank regiment in the morning. Al-Nayif, head of Military Intelligence used his forces to take over the Ministry of Defense and Al-Daud, who commanded the Republican Guards, seized the key radio station to announce what was essentially a bloodless coup. However, unlike 1958, Arif, who had not committed any serious transgressions against the coup plotters, was not executed, but rather was allowed to go into exile.

On the day after the coup, Al-Bakr was declared President and Commander-in-Chief of the Armed Forces and head of the Revolutionary Command Council (RCC) of the Baath Party. The other three prominent coup plotters also assumed new roles. Al-Nayif became Prime Minster and Al-Daud headed the Ministry of Defense, and Ghaydan assumed the command of the entire Republican Guard (Farouk-Sluglett and Sluglett 1987: 113).

The secondary coup

The Baathists were more ideologically motivated and believed that the Army should be made subservient to the Party, as they were aware that the military been the primary force behind every regime change in Iraq since 1936. However, the Baath had followed the previous patterns by seizing power through military force. In fact, the Baathist civilians did not really provide any concrete role in helping their allies in the military taking power. The civilian Baathists were also cognizant that the officers could expel the civilians from the new government, as was demonstrated in 1963 when the symbiotic relationship between the Baath and armed forces did not endure. It was the tensions between the civilian and military wings of the Party that led to the Baathist purge in November of that year. The civilian Baathists' immediate priority would be to eliminate their allied military conspirators in the new regime, non-Baathist and Baathist officers alike.

Almost immediately after the coup, Al-Bakr, an officer, but also a loyal Baathist who sided with the civilian wing, sought to control the military by appointing officers from the Party to the Republican Guard and other units in the armed forces. Just two weeks after the coup, tensions emerged between Baathists represented by Al-Bakr and Al-Daud, as well as Al-Nayif who had declared his opposition to the socialism of the Party (Khadduri 1978: 26). The Baathists began to plan for their ouster. The Baathists sought to ensure that they had other key supporters in the military, including winning the support of Ghaydan from Al-Nayif and Al-Daud. The Baathists had also won over Hammad Shihab Al-Takriti, the commander of the Baghdad garrison.

Just two weeks after the takeover, the Baathists were ready to implement a follow-up coup to eliminate the two strongest non-Party officers who demanded greater roles for themselves in the new government. On July 30, an armored brigade loyal to the Baathists seized the strategic buildings in the capital on the day when the Minister of Defense, Al-Daud left Iraq to inspect formations of Iraqi troops in Jordan, leaving his key ally, Al-Nayif at the mercy of the Baathists. On the same day Al-Nayif was arrested and exiled to Spain, and Al-Daud was told not to return from Jordan (Farouk-Sluglett and Sluglett 1987: 113). The RCC then declared Al-Bakr both President and Prime Minister and appointed a twenty-six person cabinet. The Baath had managed to come back to power, ushering in a new phase in civil–military relations.

Creating the totalitarian army: 1968–1975

The Baathists combined executive and legislative power in the RCC, a five man body made up of Baathist military officers. RCCs emerged in other countries where Arab officers sought to create a political body to dominate the executive. The RCC was designed as the ultimate decision-making body in Iraq essentially ruling by decree. The RCC was created by praetorian soldier-politicians to counter as a body other politicized officers who sought to seize power for themselves. The RCC served as a military instrument to control and eliminate opposition within the government, the military and society at large (Perlmutter 1977: 136). The RCC in Iraq was a product of its military ruler regimes, first emerging under a different title in Qasim's government, and then evolving under the Arif officers. Even though the strongest non-Baathist officers had been purged from the new government, the civilian faction of the Party, represented by Saddam Hussein, was wary of the threat still posed by the military and would replace all the officers in the RCC with civilians.

President Hasan Al-Bakr, forged a tactical alliance with his younger cousin Saddam Hussein. Hussein who had been in charge of internal security in the Party during its exile, continued his role of eliminating political rivals within the Party and from without. Even though Al-Bakr was a military officer himself, Hussein had never served in the military. However they shared the same goal of ensuring that the military returned to the barracks, guaranteeing civilian domination of the Iraqi political process and the subordination of the armed forces to a civilian administration. By Baathifying the Army into an Ideological Army, or *Al-Jaysh Al-Aqaidi*, they sought to prevent the possibility of another military takeover and to unify the fractious officer corps. Fostering a Baathified military was to eliminate a sense of collective corporate identity among the armed forces independent of the Party's control. Creating the Ideological Army sought to demilitarize politics, and to politicize the Army, albeit with a homogeneous Baathist doctrine. Anyone in the military engaging in political activity or that was a member of a party other than the Baath would face the death penalty (Farouk-Sluglett *et al.* 1984: 24).

Following the expulsion of powerful non-Baathist officers in July 1968, the Party began to rotate, expel or retire officers deemed threatening to the new government. Officers whose loyalties were in question, particularly those with alleged Nasirist, Syrian or Communist sympathies, were purged from the military and replaced with Baathists regardless of their military experience. Taha Yasin Ramadan, a Baath party loyalist oversaw a purge of 2,000 officers during this period (Baram 1991: 16). By December 1968, the Baathification of the armed forces led to the dismissal of the Chief of Staff Faysal Al-Ansari and eight commanders at the division level, who were replaced by officers trusted by the Baathists. Major General Saadun Husayn and Brigadier Said Hammu of the Fifth Division stationed in the north were executed in June 1969 after they were accused of plotting against the government. In October 1969 Baathist rivals in the commanding forces in the east of the country also died in mysterious circumstances. Major General Muhammad Nuri Khalil died in a car accident while Major General Ali Rajab died of a heart attack, both believed to have been orchestrated by the state. While the deaths of senior officers took their toll on the operational readiness of the armed forces, at this juncture the priority lay in consolidating Baathist control over the state (Hashim 2003b: 19).

Salih Mahdi Ammash, one of the Baathist coup plotters, who had assumed the post of Minister of the Interior, still had a strong following in the Army and Hardan Al-Takriti, the Minister of Defense, had a similar following in the Air Force. Even though both officers had been involved in the 1968 coup, Al-Bakr and Saddam Hussein feared that the two were seeking power for themselves and thus could not trust the armed forces entirely (Farouk-Sluglett and Sluglett 1987: 129).

Saddam Hussein consolidated his control in this year through two maneuvers. In November 1969, Hussein became Vice-President, and the

RCC was expanded to fifteen members, for the first time including civilians like Saddam. While Al-Bakr focused on establishing control of the military, Hussein developed his power by taking control over the Iraqi security apparatus and ensuring that Baathists loyal to him held prominent positions in Iraq's Military Intelligence Directorate and the General Security Directorate. Hussein also controlled the Baath Party's National Security Bureau that formed as an umbrella to coordinate the activities of these security services (Batatu 1979: 1085).

By the end of 1970, 3,000 Baathists were granted military ranks, giving the Party a network of political commissars interspersed within all units of the armed forces. Baath Party ranks, which included "active members," "member-trainees" and "partisans first grade," were given intensive courses at the Military college so that they could serve in the armed forces. A Baathist who had studied for two years at the college would receive the rank of lieutenant. These tactics led to the formation of an informal parallel chain of command that led to the Party opposed to the formal military hierarchy (Farouk-Sluglett and Sluglett 1987: 120).

Other changes were made to further the leadership's control over the armed forces. The Baath Military Bureau was connected with renegade officers in the military, when the Party was an underground opposition movement. After the 1968 coup, it became a formal organization, made up entirely of civilians, to ensure Baathist control over the military (Middle East Research and Information Project 1973: 17). It was similar to the Main Political Administration of the Soviet armed forces. The Bureau scrutinized the armed forces in addition to developing strategies of ideological indoctrination. Political guidance commissars were delegated this responsibility, as well as serving as an internal source of surveillance for the Party. These Party loyalists in the military would watch over ammunition storage facilities as well as monitor all air bases to prevent coup attempts (ibid.: 16). The Bureau watched over officers and suggested their promotion based on their political loyalty, and withheld advancement from other officers who failed to demonstrate the requisite fealty to the Baath. Furthermore, career officers could not implement important orders from their superiors without getting approval from this Bureau (Heller 1994: 44). For those officers that did not follow the Baathist line, it was told to them in the Iraqi dialect, "*Illi ma yimshi 'ala sichchitna yuruh yugud wiya marta*" or in other words, "Who does not take our path, stays at home with his wife" (Batatu 1979: 1095). Unfortunately for most officers, not following the Baath line led to imprisonment or execution rather than the option of sitting home with their wives.

Takritization of the military

The military was still the strongest barrier protecting the Sunni Arabs as a minority from Shia and Kurdish opposition. Sunni Arab hegemony in the military had been a constant feature in Iraq's history, even though the coups often brought Sunni Arabs from differing classes, tribes and regions into power. Hussein continued the same practice as his predecessors by ensuring that the officer corps would serve as an extension of the political elite, professing their allegiance to the Baath, while in many cases sharing the same class, ethnic and sectarian origins of the new Iraqi leaders.

The Baath Party in Iraq was founded by a Shia, Fuad Al-Rikabi and at first attempted to recruit the impoverished Shia who were looking for organizations beyond those of the clergy to advance their interests. By the time of its involvement in the 1963 coup, the Baath had been transformed into a party dominated by Arab Sunnis, particularly dependent on their army officers, mostly originating from Takrit. As Ahmad Hasan Al-Bakr assumed a more prominent role in the Baath in 1964, he tended to recruit men he could trust, and those he could trust shared his personal origins, either coming from Al-Bakr's tribe or town. Saddam Hussein also began to play a prominent role in the Party by 1964. He did not share Al-Bakr's military background, nor came from the same generation as he was twenty-three years younger. What they had in common was that Hussein was Al-Bakr's cousin and they both belonged to the Al-Bayjat clan of the Al-Bu Nasir tribe, dominant in Takrit. Most of the officers that had survived the purges or coups of the last decades came from families, clans and tribal networks from the provincial Sunni Arab north-west of Iraq, which included towns such as Takrit, Rawa and Falluja. It was this area where a large number of Iraq's officers were recruited from after Iraq's independence. Due to the number of Takritis who entered the military academy during and after the monarchy, by 1968 many of them had become high-ranking officers (Baram 2003: 94). The promotion of these members of the same tribe coming from Takrit represented what Finer defined as the "sectional" or "regional interest" and provides one of the underlining motivations of a coup (Finer 1962: 39–40). Coups are usually announced by a group of officers who are acting in the name of the masses, and who are unlikely to admit publically that such actions serve to further the interests of a particular in-group coming from a particular town, tribe or region.

After the Baathists consolidated political power through a secondary coup on July 30, power in Iraq was concentrated in a five member RCC. The Council was made up of five generals, including the President, Ahmad Hasan Al-Bakr, Salih Mahdi Ammash, Hardan Al-Takriti, Saadun Ghaydan and Hammad Shihab Al-Takriti. All of the RCC members were officers, educated in the military academies. Their origins also revealed a trend in the armed forces that would be perpetuated by the Baath. Ammash and Ghaydan were from Baghdad, but the other three officers were from Takrit (Baram 1989: 450). The disproportionate number of officers from a small provincial town north of the capital demonstrated the dominance of Takritis in the armed forces at the time of the 1968 coup.

In addition to consolidating political control of the armed forces, the top leadership also sought to control the armed forces by placing loyal tribal and clan members in key positions at every level. Takritis were given priority in promotions, resulting in officers with higher ranks due to their origins rather than their military credentials. The Al-Bu Nasir tribe had some 20,000 people at that time and served as loyal network who sought to benefit from the favors that could be accrued from their fellow tribesmen's rise to power (Tripp 2000: 199). In return they could be trusted to defend their leaders against any threats that could undo their privileged status. By 1973, Takritis such as Major General Hammad Shihab Al-Takriti held the portfolio of Minister of Defense, Brigadier Husayn Hayawi was commander of the Air Force, Brigadier Umar Muhammad Al-Hazza was commander of the Baghdad garrison, Colonel Bassam Atiyya the Habbaniyya air base and Major Hamid Al-Takriti commanded the Republican Guard Tank regiment (Batatu 1979: 1092). As Batatu wrote at that time, "Their role continues to be so critical that it would not be going too far to say that the Takritis rule through the Ba'th party, rather than the Ba'th party through the Takritis" (ibid.: 1088).

Nevertheless, coming from Takrit did not guarantee protection at the highest echelons of power. While Al-Bakr and Hussein were from Takrit, so were their personal rivals in the military such as Hardan Al-Takriti (Galvani 1972: 17). While coming from Takrit facilitated one's promotion in the military, one also had to demonstrate fealty to Baathist ideals, and more importantly the power coalescing behind Al-Bakr and Hussein to survive. This failure on Hardan Al-Takriti's part ultimately led to his downfall.

Divisions within the military: 1968–1971

Civilian Baathists would eventually assert their control of the armed forces as a result of divisions within the officer corps. Major General Salih Mahdi Ammash, a Baathist officer-politician who held the portfolio of Minister of the Interior still maintained a network of followers in the Army. Major General Hardan Al-Takriti, another Baathist officer-politician held the portfolio of Minister of Defense and had established a network in the Air Force. The civilian Baathists were convinced that the two were creating their own power bases in the military, and thus could not trust the armed forces entirely, especially during a renewed Kurdish revolt (Farouk-Sluglett and Sluglett 1987: 129).

Al-Bakr, promoted to the rank of Field Marshall in 1969 was able to balance the rivalries that soon erupted between Ammash and Hardan Al-Takriti. As long as the officer corps was united, the military wing of the Baath and the military itself remained the strongest force in the country. However, the factionalism among the military officers and their ensuing struggle for power proved to be an advantage for the civilian wing of the Party. After 1968 a delicate balance was reached between the civil and military wings of the Party that prevented one from dominating the other, represented by the working partnership between an officer, Al-Bakr, and a civilian, Hussein. Dissension within the military provided the opportunity for the Baathist civilians to gain control over the armed forces. The civilian Baathists eventually won this struggle over the military faction of the Party, but the civilians' concerns about the threat of the military would remain constant.

During the struggle between Hardan and Ammash, the civilian wing supported the latter, as Hardan was seen only as a nominal Baathist and as the more threatening of the two. Ammash hoped to assume the post of Prime Minister; however Al-Bakr held both the presidency and the premiership. In 1969, the portfolio of Prime Minster was fused into the office of the presidency, and to appease the two officers, Al-Bakr made them both into Vice-Presidents in April 1970. In doing this, Al-Bakr had promoted them and at the same time disconnected them from their power bases in the military. Hardan was no longer Minister of Defense, severing his link with the Army and Air Force and Ammash was no longer Minister of Interior, severing his link with the police and internal security forces. Al-Bakr appointed two loyalists to replace them: Chief of Staff Lieutenant General Hammad Shihab Al-Takriti became Minister of Defense and the commander of the Baghdad garrison Saadun Ghaydan assumed control of the Ministry of Interior (Khadduri 1978: 58–9). While Hardan came from Takrit and tried to maintain his own patronage network by placing loyal fellow townsmen in high positions, Al-Bakr was also from the same town and could offer better protection and patronage to Takritis due to his superior position in government. Al-Bakr's network was also more pervasive as he tried to cultivate a following among the clans from Mosul, Samarra and Ramadi, the latter of which had served Arif in the past.

In September 1970, King Hussein of Jordan regarded the Palestine Liberation Organization (PLO) based in his country as a risk to his authority, and his forces began to attack the Palestinian guerrillas, beginning a series of events thereafter referred to as "Black September." Iraq had stationed its Salah Al-Din contingent in Jordan, which included 12,500 Iraqi troops and 100 tanks (*The Times*, September 5, 1970: 12). Hardan Al-Takriti however argued that Iraq was not ready to go to war with Jordan due to Baghdad's conflict in the north with the Kurds. While other military officers shared Hardan's assessment, Iraq's failure to aid the PLO during the conflict proved to be unpopular with the Iraqi masses. The civilian wing of the Baath expressed their support for the PLO and by creating a scapegoat in Hardan, they could eliminate a rival. His "inaction" provided Al-Bakr and Hussein with the justification they needed to remove Hardan Al-Tikriti from his position and expel his followers in the military. Hardan was exiled to Algeria and his followers in the military were purged thereafter. They were replaced by loyal Baathist officers who supported the civilian wing of the Party. Hardan eventually left Algeria and then moved

to Kuwait, where he was assassinated in March 1971. With Hardan eliminated, the other rival to Al-Bakr and Hussein who still had a following in
the armed forces was Salih Mahdi Ammash. He held his post of Vice-
President but the civilians in the Party felt he was still a threat and was
removed from the political scene in Baghdad in 1971 and given a diplomatic post abroad (Khadduri 1978: 59–61).

By 1971, Al-Bakr was the only remaining high ranking military officer
in a position of executive power. Despite his bonds with the military, Al-
Bakr did not rule through the military nor establish a military ruler regime.
Rather than use the armed forces to control the country, he used his position as chairman of the RCC, allowing him to cooperate in a collective
decision-making body with the civilian wing of the Baath, and thus maintaining Party unity. He also depended on his clan and family networks
through his alliance with Saddam Hussein. In 1971 Hussein became vice-
chairman of the Revolutionary Command Council, the second most
powerful position in Iraq at this time. While all the staff of the RCC after
the coup came from the armed forces, by this year only five out of the
fifteen RCC members were military officers (Jabar 2003a: 117). On
November 17, 1971 al-Bakr declared, "The responsibility for leading the
Army and directing it politically falls on the RCC alone ... no Party other
than the Ba'th Party will be able to carry out any forms of political or
organisational activity within the armed forces" (Farouk-Sluglett and Sluglett 1987: 157). The British journalist David Hirst also noted that
Hussein made a similar declaration in the same month stating "with party
methods there is no chance for anyone who disagrees with us to jump on a
couple of tanks and overthrow the government" (Hirst, *Guardian* 1971:
15). Hussein's quote denied the fact that the Baathists themselves came to
power with a couple of tanks, but nevertheless served as an indication that
Baathifying the military was still a concern for the regime.

Coup attempts: 1970–1973

The fear of foreign inspired coup attempts, particularly from its regional
rival Iran, was prevalent in Iraq in the early 1970s. Whether Iranian
attempts to foment instability in Iraq were perceived or actual, the accusations were linked to the tensions between Socialist Soviet-leaning Baathist
Iraq and the pro-Western Shah of Iran. A long lasting disagreement re-
emerged over the Shatt al-Arab waterway where shipping rights were disputed by both sides. The first victims in a crackdown on alleged military
conspirators were First Lieutenant Jawad Abd Al-Majid and Chief
Sergeant Ahmad Al-Alwan, who were found guilty of providing intelligence on the Iraqi military to Iran and the CIA (*The Times*, April 18,
1969: 5).

One of the documented coup attempts during the early years of the
Baath government was that of Major General Abd Al-Ghani Al-Rawi and

Colonel Salih Mahdi Al-Samarrai. Al-Rawi was a retired officer who was loyal to the Arif regime and Al-Samarrai had served in the military since the monarchy. On January 20, 1970 Al-Samarrai led a contingent from the Rashid Camp to the Republican Palace, unaware that the regime had uncovered their plans and ambushed the coup plotters once they were in motion. After hearing the news of the failed coup General Al-Rawi fled to Iran. A Special Court led by Taha Yasin Al-Jazrawi of the RCC and Nadhim Kazzar, Director of the General Security Directorate (*Mudiriyyat Al-Amn Al-'Amma*) ordered the execution by firing squad of twenty-seven military men involved in the coup (Khadduri 1978: 54–5). The coup attempt was followed by purges and executions of officers accused of belonging to Islamist organizations, and Sunni generals such as Muhsin Al-Janabi and Shia generals such as Muhammad Faraj were among the victims of these purges (Tripp 2000: 202–3).

The Baath argued that Iran had orchestrated the coup and it became ever more so fearsome of foreign attempts to subvert their government. The paranoia became all pervasive where officers' interaction with foreign contacts was severely circumscribed to the point where they were discouraged from studying in the USSR for fear they would become Communist agitators upon their return. The Baath also perceived an omnipresent threat from an American–Iranian plot to subvert the military. Such fears were made clear after the US backed the Chilean military to overthrow the leftist Allende government in September 1973, causing Saddam Hussein to remark that the "anti-Allende experiment" would not succeed in Iraq (Hashim 2003b: 18).

Ironically, Nadhim Kazzar, who had a role in prosecuting the 1970 coup planners, orchestrated a coup attempt himself. Kazzar had served as Director of the General Security Service since 1969, an appointee of Saddam Hussein. By 1973, Kazzar feared that Al-Bakr and Hussein would no longer allow him to develop an independent power base in the security services. Kazzar, himself a Shia, apparently said during his attempted coup that he would "wipe Takrit off the map," acknowledging his umbrage at the Takriti domination in the military and higher echelons of the state (Kelidar 1975: 9). His coup unfolded on June 30, 1973 and ultimately failed, and while it did not originate from within the military it did have ramifications for the armed forces. First, Kazzar realized that the remaining officer politicians, Lieutenant General Hammad Shihab Al-Takriti, Minister of Defense, who controlled the military and Lieutenant General Saadun Ghaydan, Minister of Interior, who had controlled the police, would have to be eliminated for the coup to succeed. He invited them to one of his headquarters on the day of the coup and detained them. Afterwards he had planned to assassinate Al-Bakr in the airport after arriving from a trip to Poland. As the plane was delayed, Kazzar's men at the airport dispersed fearing the coup had been discovered, but failed to inform Kazzar. Upon hearing of the delay, Kazzar took the Ministers of

Defense and Interior hostage and made an escape attempt to the Iranian border. After landing and discovering the coup, Al-Bakr ordered his loyal units to intercept Kazzar. During a standoff, Hammad Shihab Al-Takriti was shot dead and Saadun Ghaydun was wounded (Middle East Research and Information Project 1973: 17). Kazzar failed to gather the support of the military, based on his assumption that assassinating the President would lead to the armed forces rallying behind him. Along with Kazzar, Muhammad Fadhil of the Baath Military Bureau was also found guilty of taking part in the coup and both were executed (ibid.).

The Kazzar coup provided the pretext for Hussein to expand his intelligence network not only to check the General Security Service, but to counterbalance the Military Intelligence as well. A new Department of General Intelligence (*Mudiriyyat Al-Mukhabarat Al-'Amma*), usually referred to as the "Mukhabarat," was established as a response to the 1973 coup. In the same year, the Directorate of Political Guidance (*Mudiriyyat Al-Tawjih Al-Siyasi*) was established to monitor the military (Bengio 1998: 149). These institutions further strengthened Hussein's position vis-à-vis the regular military and ensured his eventual control over the armed forces establishment.

In order to prevent further coup attempts, Al-Bakr also took direct charge of the Ministry of Defense (its Minister was killed in the standoff during the Kazzar coup) and an amendment was made to the provisional constitution where the President would also serve as Commander-in-Chief of the armed forces (Farouk-Sluglett and Sluglett 1987: 162–3). The Baath also continued what had become an Iraqi tradition of preventing military units' access to ammunition and fuel. Such measures prevented large scale movements of military units outside of their garrisons and marching into Baghdad, the key target in most of Iraq's coup attempts. The only units that had access to ammunition were the elite praetorian guards inside the capital such as the Republican Guards, armed to serve as a counter-coup force. The Baath's priority was also to take over the key military facilities in the capital. By 1973 the Baath had felt secure that its loyalists were in control of the Ministry of Defense, the Habbaniyya air field outside of Baghdad, the military garrison in the capital and the Republican Guards brigade. By doing so, the Party had control over the key security institutions in Baghdad, as well as the strategic approaches into the capital (Hashim 2003b: 21). This process demonstrated that the Baathification of the military establishment was a continuous process that was still in motion five years after the Party's coup.

The 1973 Arab–Israeli war

It does not seem that the Baath had prior knowledge when Egypt and Syria launched a surprise attack against Israel in October 1973, as Iraq's participation lacked any planning or coordination. The Iraqis did dispatch a significant force – two armored divisions and three infantry brigades, in all 60,000 soldiers and 700 tanks to the Syrian front (Pollack 2002: 167). However, the Iraqis did not have the proper logistical equipment to transport many of its tanks to the Golan Heights where the fighting was taking place. Without enough tank transporters, some of the tanks attempted to travel the entire distance from Iraq to the front and broke down along the away. Iraqi forces supported the Syrians in deterring a potential Israeli push on Damascus after the Israeli forces secured the Golan. On October 13, an Iraqi armored brigade suffered heavy losses after an Israeli attack, and the Syrians and Iraqis attempted a counter-attack but these measures were unsuccessful due to their lack of coordination. In November, the Iraqi forces withdrew after the fighting had ended, losing 480 troops, 111 tanks and armored personnel carriers and twenty-six fighter aircraft in the war (Wagner 1979: 68). While technically a military defeat, the deployment in and of itself was enough for the Baath to boast of their Arabist credentials and commitment of using Iraq's armed forces in an armed engagement with Israel. The engagement was a symbolic victory, as the loss of the Golan could be blamed on the Syrian forces (Chubin and Tripp 1988: 22).

The Kurdish revolt: 1974–1975

By December 1968 Barazani's forces resumed their attacks, breaking the peace that existed since early 1966. In March of 1969, the Kurdish Democratic Party (KDP) forces were able to launch an attack against the oil facilities in Kirkuk, disrupting the flow of Iraqi oil for days. Three Iraqi divisions, 48,000 troops were deployed against the Kurds (*The Times*, March 19, 1974: 7). The fighting at this stage would last until 1970, and followed the same patterns of the two previous Kurdish uprisings from 1961 to 1964 and 1965 to 1966. The Kurds besieged isolated military garrisons in the northern mountainous terrain, and then moved into the northern plains were they were in position to attack Kirkuk and its oil facilities. The military would counter-attack by securing urban centers, pushing Kurdish militias back into the mountains with aerial and artillery bombardments. Iraqi armored forces secured the low areas of the valleys, but infantry forces could not effectively combat the Kurdish guerrillas in the mountainous terrain, particularly during the winter (Wagner 1979: 66). In each case, the government in power would then seek some kind of arrangement with the Kurds, only to have the fighting resumed a few years later.

Negotiations between the KDP and the Iraqi government broke down after failing to reach an agreement on power sharing and autonomy, particularly over Baghdad's refusal to grant Kurdish control over Kirkuk and its oil facilities. In April 1974 Barazani renewed the Kurdish revolt and mobilized 50,000 to 60,000 *peshmerga* fighters with an additional

50,000 irregulars, while the Iraqi military at that point had 90,000 men. The armed forces also had 1,200 tanks and armored vehicles and 200 aircraft at its disposal (Farouk-Sluglett and Sluglett 1987: 168–9). Eight Iraqi army divisions were deployed to the north, a major proportion of the state's military, and reservists had to be mobilized. Unlike the previous campaigns, the military had better equipment and used aircraft to attack Kurdish artillery positions, which also resulted in civilian casualties as well. The armed forces was able to press the campaign through the winter and overtook several KDP positions in the mountains over Irbil in December 1974 (Wagner 1979: 66). The Iraqi leadership tried to maintain the loyalty of the Kurds in the military, even allowing one Kurdish officer to become commander of a division (Ghareeb 1982: 168). The fighting resulted in a stalemate once again, with heavy financial costs incurred by the government. At the same time, the Iraqis were short of ammunition, which was kept secret to prevent the loss of morale in the armed forces (Abdulghani 1984: 156–7).

Saddam Hussein, in his capacity as Vice-President, sought a solution to this crisis by negotiating over the Shatt Al-Arab waterway. Iran and Iraq came to an understanding over the waterway after signing the Algiers Agreement in March 1975. Much to Iraq's dismay, both states agreed to shared sovereignty over the waterway and that the border between the two countries would be split between the middle of the Shatt. In return, Iranian support for the KDP was discontinued and the Kurdish revolt quickly collapsed. After signing the agreement, the Iraqi military conducted a final successful offensive against the Kurds (O'Ballance 1996: 98). The Iraqi military mobilized its infantry, armored and air forces and began scoring decisive victories against the KDP, pushing them back to the borders between Turkey and Iran. Despite this victory, Hussein's signing of the Algiers Declaration was deeply resented by the military, which believed it was close to scoring a victory without giving into Iran's demands (Helms 1984: 118). Following the defeat of the Kurds in 1975, Jalal Talabani broke ranks with the KDP, forming the rival Patriotic Union of Kurdistan (PUK). Mulla Mustafa Barazani of the KDP passed away in 1979 leaving the leadership of the organization to his sons. After the defeat of the Kurds in 1975, Iraq, which had devoted its manpower to infantry units to fight in the mountains, could now transform its military into an armored military force.

The expansion of the armed forces: 1975–1980

The expansion of Iraq's armed forces was made possible by Iraq's poor performance in the 1973 war, a renewed Kurdish revolt and perceived threats emanating from Israel and Iran, the latter also engaged in building up its military forces. The emergence of Iran as a regional power in the Gulf clashed with Iraq's attempt to enhance its position not just in the

Gulf, but the entire Arab world. The expansion was also facilitated by the increase in Iraqi revenues after the oil crisis following the 1973 war, which allowed for surplus funds to be devoted to a significant increase in the hardware needed to project Iraq's military power. Such expansion could have only occurred when the Baath was confident in its complete control over the military establishment (Chubin and Tripp 1988: 18). In the Baathist view an expansion of the emerging ideological army would allow the Party to strengthen its grip over the country by incorporating all of the nation's communities into an ideological army. Thus emerged two contradictory trends where the Baathists subordinated the regular Army under its control while militarizing Iraqi society through a massive expansion of its armed forces.

During the Eighth Baath Party Congress held in January 1974, Iraq's performance during the 1973 war was discussed and suggestions were made as to how to improve the military's fighting capabilities. At the Congress the goals of the Party were to ensure that the Army remained subordinate to the Baath by continuing to purge its "suspicious, conspiratorial and adventurous elements." The process of indoctrinating the armed forces would continue, an indication that the Party felt in control over the Army, but that Baathification would have to continue. In tandem with these efforts, the Party would restructure, modernize and expand the armed forces (Jabar 2003a: 116). In the Congress, the Party also criticized the former Arif regime, labeling it a "military aristocracy" and alluding to the officers that the Baath would never let Iraq to be ruled by such a clique in the future (Jabar 2003b: 81).

The increase in oil prices after the 1973 oil embargo provided the government with the revenues to expand the military. The influx of currency allowed Iraq to increase the defense budget, which would in turn finance universal conscription. Between 1973 and 1980 the Iraqi military expanded on a level unlike that of any other Arab military during those years. The size of the Iraqi military doubled to 210,000 men, with the addition of nine divisions. After signing a Friendship Treaty with the USSR in 1972, the Iraqi military took possession of 1,600 tanks, including at that time, the advanced T-72 tank, in addition to armored infantry fighting vehicles, anti-tank, surface-to-surface and surface-to-air missiles, and self-propelled artillery and anti-aircraft guns (Wagner 1979: 71–2).

While the USSR remained the primary supplier of military equipment, by September 1976, the military began to receive arms shipments from France, the first time since 1958 arms were provided from a Western power. These deals allowed for Iraq to take possession of between sixty and eighty Mirage F-1 interceptor fighters and 200 AMX-30 tanks, as well as armored fighting vehicles from Brazil and naval vessels from Italy (Farouk-Sluglett and Sluglett 1987: 181). Given that the government was becoming dominated by civilians, the provisions of advanced equipment to the military was a tactic to placate the armed forces. Prior to this build-up, the military had primarily served as a counter-insurgency force deployed in the north of Iraq, with minor engagements in three Arab–Israeli wars. The expansion was designed for the armed forces to maintain its traditional role of preserving internal security and projecting Baathist power against Kurdish guerrillas. Second, the expansion allowed the Baath to construct an image of the most powerful military in the Arab world, allowing Saddam Hussein to fulfill his ambitions of emerging as the dominant regional player.

Even though the Iraqi Communists had joined the Baath in an alliance known as the National Progressive Front, such a body was designed for public consumption, as parties besides the Baath were strictly forbidden from proselytizing within the armed forces. In May 1978, twenty-one Communists were executed for conducting subversive activities within the military, and the Baath stated that, "deterrent measures should be taken against violators, namely to execute anybody who commits such idiotic action" (*The Times*, June 1, 1978: 6). The qualitative and quantitative expansion of the military indicated that the Baath government felt secure enough that the Army did not pose an immediate threat if it were strengthened, but the executions of the Communists demonstrated that the Party maintained its vigilant monitoring of the armed forces. The government allowed the expansion of the military within a security network that would allow Al-Bakr and Hussein to exert ultimate control and discover subversives within the military ranks.

Parallel militaries in the totalitarian-penetration system

The centralized authoritarian party in the totalitarian-penetration system creates other military forces to counter the autonomy of the regular army. Such anti-armies serve as an ideological extension of the party in power and challenge the monopoly of coercion enjoyed by the regular military. After 1968 the Republican Guard, inherited from the Arif military ruler regime, still functioned as the Baath's praetorian guard. The higher echelons of the Guard were still recruited from the Arab Sunni tribal areas north of Baghdad, forming a confessional link with the leadership. The Guard, rather than tasked with a traditional role of defending the state from foreign adversaries, was deployed to protect the Baath Party from internal threats, particularly military coups.

Iraq, as a rentier state, was able to draw up a vast surplus of funds, independent of generating revenues from public taxation. As Quinlivan noted the accessibility to funds created a steady flow of subsidies that bound the military to the leadership (1999: 153). The windfall from the oil embargo provided extra funds to the Baath to allow it to purchase weapons both for popular militias and the regular military, while increasing the salaries and benefits to higher ranking officers.

During the expansion in the 1970s, the Party created an ideological paramilitary unit, the *Al-Jaysh Al-Shaabi*, or the Popular Army (also known as the People's Army or the People's Militia). The Popular Army was structured as a parallel army whose loyalty rested with the Baath and was subordinated to the Party opposed to the Ministry of Defense. In states that have a totalitarian-penetration military structure, these mass mobilization militias are a means to arm the citizens, including them in a collective effort to defend the party. Such militias also cultivate in its soldiers the tenets of the party, serving as a means of ideological education. As Kamrava wrote, "The militia is thus one of the crucial links through which the emotionally-laden nexus between the state and society is maintained" (Kamrava 2000: 84). While the regular military also provides such a link between state and society on a professional basis, these militias serve as a reserve, allowing all citizens to contribute to the defense of the party for short periods during the year, usually ranging from two weeks to two months. While such militias are often incapable of fighting on the battlefield, they offer a means of cementing the political loyalty of the masses with the state. In Iraq's case, the forced conscription of the masses into the Popular Army during the Iran–Iraq War was a testimony in itself of the Party's coercive ability to force the people to defend it, buttressing the perceived legitimacy of the Baath.

These popular militias serve as "anti-armies," communicating to the regular army that a counter-coup force is in place to protect the party. During the expansion phase, the Iraqi state could invest in strengthening the technical skills of regular military officers and provide them with advanced hardware to deal with threats emanating from foreign militaries. With the creation of Baathist anti-armies, the regular military realized that a coup would be a risky endeavor. If rebellious military officers were successfully to carry out a coup, they would have to coordinate their actions with these parallel militaries inside of the capital, increasing the chances that their plan would be uncovered. If officers of the regular military tried to move against the leadership without the help of these anti-armies, then they would have to fight their way into the capital, increasing the risks of such a move.

The Popular Army's predecessor was the National Guard, a party militia that sought to supplement and check the power of the Army in 1963. The Popular Army was formed on February 8, 1970 to provide military training to Party members (Segal 1988: 955). While the leadership felt it had secured control over the armed forces, it was still convinced in 1975 that it faced opposition in the regular armed forces and that the Popular Army could counter such threats as the regular army underwent its expansion (Cordesman and Wagner 1990: 69). Hussein could weaken the political power of the regular Army by strengthening a militia that he alone created and that would be loyal to him personally. One account of the Popular Army also noted that it allowed Hussein, a civilian Baathist, to live as a soldier vicariously: "It did, however, permit party functionaries who were not from the military wing of the party (including Saddam Hussein) to dress up in elaborate general's uniforms replete with aiguillettes and swords" (Quinlivan 1999: 145).

In 1975 Hussein delegated his protégé RCC member Taha Yasin Ramadan Al-Jazrawi to double the size of the Popular Army by enforcing compulsory military training for all Party members between the ages of eighteen and forty-five. As commander of the Popular Army, Al-Jazrawi reported to the Party, and by doing so, the Popular Army was not a branch of the armed forces, nor did it fall under the command of the Ministry of Defense. Hussein and his clique of civilian Baathists could mobilize the Popular Army armed forces outside of the military chain of command, and it could also monitor the general political atmosphere, reporting any subversive activity directly to the Party HQ (O'Ballance 1988: 55). The Baathists created the Popular Army out of political motives, by giving it an internal security and civil defense role in every Iraqi city, town and village. In 1978 Al-Jazrawi boasted that "Popular Army formations have steadily expanded to cover the whole of Iraq, reaching the smallest village and the remotest point" (*Iraq Today*, January 16–31, 1978: 4).

Even its education apparatus was separate from the military college. The Popular Army School provided courses on politics, as well as the use of small arms and air defense training to every male member. Their units had trained twice weekly for three hours, as well as participated in an annual two-week summer camp on combat techniques. Similar youth programs were also established to provide exposure to military training for those aged nine and above. The leadership's provision of mass paramilitary training co-opted civilians into a Baathist endeavor of protecting the nation from threats, both real and imaginary. By 1975 the Popular Army's numbers had reached 50,000 and by 1979 it had 75,000 men, yet the leadership solicited Cuban assistance to triple its size further (O'Ballance 1988: 55).

Saddam Hussein's political consolidation over the military

The Slugletts had characterized the Iraqi regime as neither purely military, nor purely civilian by the late 1970s. Military regimes were dominated by a few generals who seized power and ruled, such as the ruler regimes from 1958 to 1968. Some military regimes went through the motions of establishing a single party to give the semblance of civilian rule, although this was not attempted in Iraq. However, the regime in post-1968 Iraq was not purely civilian. The regular armed forces were one of the main pillars on which it rested, quelling the Kurdish insurrection in the north and serving as a means to deter a potential Shia revolt in the south. The civilian and military spheres were closely intertwined, and Hussein obsessed over ensuring that the civilian leadership remained dominant. As long as he was ruling with Al-Bakr at his side, the latter could balance relations between officers in the military and the civilians in the government. However the continued Baathification process of the armed forces strengthened Saddam Hussein's position vis-à-vis the military and made Al-Bakr's role redundant.

In 1976, perhaps to boost his own military credentials, Saddam Hussein, who had not served in the armed forces, assumed the rank of Lieutenant General. His "promotion" was justified after receiving an honorary degree from Iraq's military college (Cordesman and Wagner 1990: 59). In January 1977 Adnan Khayrallah Talfa was promoted to the Regional Leadership of the Bath Party (Baram 1989: 453). The promotion was significant for Talfa, a military man who had received an "accelerated promotion" to Staff Colonel even though he was not a senior military officer like Al-Bakr. Al-Bakr, who also held the Minister of Defense portfolio after the attempted 1973 coup, gave the position to Talfa in October 1977, who was then promoted to the rank of general (Baram 2003: 95). Talfa was the son-in-law of Al-Bakr, having married his daughter. At the same time Talfa was Hussein's brother-in-law as Saddam had married his sister. Talfa and Hussein were also maternal cousins and childhood friends. This relationship exemplified the use of Hussein's relatives to control the armed forces. It also demonstrated that Hussein was cultivating connections at the expense of his elder cousin Al-Bakr. However, rather than removing Al-Bakr at that point, Hussein further sought to consolidate his control over the armed forces and Talfa, as Minister of Defense helped Saddam establish further networks in the military. Talfa's rapid promotions to political positions represented Hussein's rising strength rather than that of the military in the top leadership.

On July 17, 1979 General Al-Bakr resigned from his post as President of Iraq due to "health reasons," abdicating in favor of his Vice-President, Saddam Hussein, the first civilian to rule Iraq in two decades. With Al-Bakr's "resignation," Hussein assumed the title of President of the Republic, Chairman of the Revolutionary Command Council and Commander-in-Chief of the armed forces. Hussein was also promoted to Field Marshal in the process, the highest military rank in Iraq (Chubin and Tripp 1988: 115). Hussein finally presided over a military that was deemed politically reliable and with enough parallel military forces to deter any faction of officers from challenging his position. Due to years of purges, the high command of the military was concentrated in Hussein's hands, in addition to those of his closest Baath allies, most of whom were civilians with little military experience. The generals and officers who had survived the purges owed their positions to loyalty to Hussein rather than to any military competence. In order to celebrate his accession to power, in August 1979 Hussein increased the salaries of the military, further solidifying his subsidization of the officer corps. By the time Hussein assumed the helm of chairman of the RCC, he had ensured that no career military officers were allowed into what was Iraq's most powerful institution.

The Baathists under Saddam Hussein had managed to do what no party had done in Iraq's history: it brought the military under civilian control.

The expansion of the military served as a means to buttress Saddam Hussein's leadership, projecting the image of an Arab regional leader and demonstrating the development and technological strength of the armed forces to the Iraqi public. According to Chubin and Tripp (1988: 243), the massive modernization and expansion of the military also presented Hussein with a dilemma: creating such a force was of little use to the Iraqi leader unless he could employ it in a decisive demonstration of his power. The threat to Iraq emanating from Khomeini's Islamic Revolution ultimately provided Hussein with the opportunity to use this expanded military in such a demonstration of power.

7   The totalitarian military and the Iran–Iraq War 1980–1984

Targhib and *tarhib* in Baathist Iraq

The ethos of Iraq under Saddam Hussein can be summarized by two Arabic concepts, *targhib*, or "enticement" and *tarhib*, "intimidation" (Batatu 1982: 7). *Targhib* and *tarhib* could ultimately be translated as a "carrot and stick" policy conducted vis-à-vis the military. These two pillars capture the means and methods in which Hussein assured the survival of his rule from 1979 to 2003, and how he maintained control over the military. The leadership in Baghdad employed a sustained propaganda campaign to maintain the loyalty of all sectarian and ethnic communities in the military through *targhib*, emphasizing the unity of Iraqis and stressing the threat from an Iranian victory and an "Islamic Republic of Iraq." *Targhib* included addressing the needs of the military, at times granting promotions, pay raises, lavish housing facilities and restraining the heavy-handed tactics of the Baathist minders in the armed forces. Iraqi combatants resisting government overtures suffered the brunt of the policy of *tarhib*. The state set out to eliminate opposition within the military to Hussein's policies through sustained, institutionalized repression. The state's mammoth, all pervasive security apparatus implemented this more aggressive aspect of his policy. Such tactics included the intensification of the use of informants and security services to monitor the military, and the use of rotations, arrests and executions to eliminate seditious and subversive soldiers and officers. In other words, the state created a pervasive sense of internal fear by penetrating the Iraqi military at every level.

During the Iran–Iraq war, the state developed a strategy maintaining loyalty, morale and discipline in the military. Hussein's priority was to maintain a base within the armed forces to prevent dissension that could threaten his rule. The leadership created parallel military structures to contribute to the war front and to serve as a counter force in case any armed faction within the military attempted a coup. Second, the armed forces were supplied with the most advanced weapons it could acquire, financed partly with aid from the Gulf states. Hussein's strategy of war populism was designed to inspire all segments of Iraqi society to continue fighting.

Such tactics particularly targeted the Kurdish and Shia communities who were giving their sons as conscripts in a costly war. Security within the military was guaranteed by Hussein's Takriti and Sunni Arab networks, which had the most to lose with an Iranian victory. Another strategy that does not necessarily deal with the military itself, but rather national morale and the families of the soldiers, was the government's attempt to isolate the Iraqi public from the war. This tactic was achieved through a "guns and butter" policy where the Iraqi leadership financed the war without imposing any hardships on the Iraqi population at least in its initial years (Gongora 1997: 325). While cities such as Basra received the brunt of the fighting, the leadership tried to shield major urban centers such as Baghdad from the conflict. Additionally, the state embarked on massive public projects, improving education and housing opportunities for the masses, but particularly for the families of the troops and officers on the front lines.

Saddam Hussein's most important constituent group during the war was the elite group of insiders whose loyalty he cultivated. This in-group was made up primarily of civilian Baathists, including members of his own clan that he promoted to key security positions once he was in power. The other constituents formed clusters around this inside group, including the higher echelons of his security services, tribal leaders who declared and proved their loyalty to the President, a new class of economic entrepreneurs who benefited from Hussein's patronage and the officers who represented the interests of the military. Hussein never allowed himself to be threatened by any of these collective interests, particularly those of the military at a time when Iraq was facing setbacks on the battlefront. Rather than becoming dependent on any one cluster during the war, he played one off against the other, applying *targhib* and *tarhib* where he saw fit. This policy particularly affected the military as Hussein would select officers for special favor or disgrace, thus communicating to any commander his dependence on the President alone. The Iraqi leader practiced *targhib* by promoting key members of his inner core to strategic and prestigious positions within the military. At the same time he played off his loyal core of insiders against the military, convincing the former of their common plight of losing their status and privilege if the career officers of the armed forces were to launch a coup in response to their failing fortunes on the battlefield.

The advance on Iran: 1980–1981

The expansion of the mid-1970s provided Iraq with the means to conduct an offensive operation against Iran, the largest operation ever undertaken by the military. After the Iranian Revolution, Ayatollah Khomeini declared he sought an Islamic Republic in Iraq, if not the rest of the Middle East, and publicly called for the overthrow of the Iraqi President. The Iraqi

Baath government, a secular regime that nominally promoted socialism and Arab nationalism, felt besieged by Khomeini's ideology, which divided Iraq's heterogeneous communities of Shia, Sunnis and Kurds. Given that political survival of the Baath government was one of Saddam Hussein's primary political objectives, his goals in invading Iran were to contain a revolutionary threat emanating from Iran, as well as seizing full control of the Shatt Al-Arab waterway and demonstrating Iraq's role as the regional hegemon.

Prior to the war, the Iranian leadership sent messages to the Iraqi military to overthrow the ruling party: "The war the Iraqi Baath wants to ignite is a war against Islam ... the people and the Army of Iraq must turn their backs on the Baath regime and overthrow it" (quoted in Hiro 1992: 28). As a response, in April 1980 Hussein declared that the Iraqi Army was bound to perform its "national duty" by fighting Iran (quoted in Sari-olghalam 1997: 107). By May 1980 General Shansal, the Chief of Staff, began preparing for an invasion of Iran based on an exercise conducted at Iraq's War College in 1941, when British military instructors trained the Iraqi cadets to capture the Iranian urban centers of Abadan, Khorramshahr and Dezful within ten days. While the initial plan had been provided by the British, the Iraqi Army at this time had been restructured under the guidance of advisors from the USSR and Iraqi tactics reflected Soviet influence (O'Ballance 1988: 48–9). The Soviet doctrine, concepts and training had been modified by the Iraqis, and envisioned using heavy bombardments and slow, methodical advances over enemy territory. The Iraqi modifications however featured a heavy reliance on tank warfare without the adequate number of infantry to accompany the armored units. The invasion plan called for an initial thrust into Iran's south-western Khuzestan province. These divisions would secure the major cities and roads in the province and seize the mountain passes in the Zagros range to prevent Iranian forces from retaking any of Iraq's gains. To the north Iraqi divisions would take the other passes through the Zagros to prevent an Iranian counter-strike in the direction of the Iraqi capital. According to some Iraqi generals this military action was envisioned to last no more than two weeks (Pollack 2002: 184).

This attack would have to be quick and decisive due to the imbalances in population. Iran's population at that time was forty million opposed to Iraq's fourteen million (Sterner 1984: 130). The fact that Iran's population offered a three-to-one advantage in manpower, meant that a protracted war would give the Iranians the upper hand. At this point Iraq had 2,750 tanks, 2,500 armored fighting vehicles and 920 artillery pieces. Iran on the other hand had 1,700 tanks, 1,700 armored fighting vehicles and 1,000 artillery pieces, but most of its equipment was inoperable due to lack of spare parts from the US and Europe. While Iran had 447 aircraft only half of those were operational while Iraq had close to 300 planes that could be deployed (Karsh 1988: 89–90). As for the regular military, Helms gave a breakdown of the Iraqi military structure in the first years of the war. An Iraqi battalion (*katiba*) had 600 to 700 men. A brigade (*liwa*) had 2,700 to 3,500 men and a division (*firqa*) had 11,000 to 12,000 men. Three divisions formed a corps (*faylaq*) of approximately 36,000 men (1984: 172). On the eve of the Iran–Iraq War, the Iraqi Army consisted of twelve divisions. Considering that an Iraqi division has close to 12,000 men, approximately 200,000 men were put on alert on the eve of the war. Combined with the forces from the Popular Army, the Iraqi armed forces had 330,000 men ready for combat (Cordesman and Wagner 1990: 69).

On September 21, 1980 Iraqi forces were able to cross the Shatt Al-Arab with little opposition from Iran, since its military had deployed only light defenses along the waterway and stationed only a few battalions in the southern province of Khuzestan. Six out of the twelve Iraqi divisions were used in this attack and were able to occupy 1,000 square kilometers via two thrusts into the Khuzestan province (ibid.: 92–5). The Iraqi forces headed for Abadan, the center of Iran's oil industry and Ahvaz, the capital of the province and where a major air base was located. The Iraqi military fought and prevailed during a major battle near the southern town of Dezful also in Khuzestan, however the Iranian air force, managed to provide some resistance to the Iraqi advance. Just weeks after the initial invasion, the Iraqis fought a major battle for Abadan in November 1980. On November 3 Iraqi forces prepared to penetrate the city but faced stiff resistance from the Iranian Revolutionary Guards. By November 10, the Iraqi military scored a victory after capturing the border town of Khorramshahr, after Iraqi troops engaged in intense street fighting. The heavy casualties incurred at this battle perhaps compelled the Iraqis to consider laying siege to Abadan, rather than directly taking the city in order to avoid deadly urban combat. Hussein mistakenly believed that the close to three million Arab inhabitants of Khuzestan would rise up to support an invasion from an Arab country. However, many fled to Teheran and other Iranian Arabs fought alongside the Iranian military in Abadan and Ahvaz.

This initial offensive proved to be the largest operation conducted by the Iraqi armed forces. Some 70,000 troops and 2,000 tanks had taken part, with three additional divisions of 35,000 soldiers and 40,000 militia men providing reinforcements by November (Wagner 1979: 68). While the Iraqi military was able to assemble a massive fighting force, reaching sixty-five kilometers into Iran, it failed to follow up tactical successes as its command structure ultimately led to Baghdad, were decisions had to be taken by the political establishment, namely Saddam Hussein himself. Commanders on field were prevented from taking the initiative due to political dictates. The Iraqis suffered from a failure to integrate their new modern weaponry into combined-arms operations, with a lack of coordination between armored and infantry forces or air forces and ground forces. Years after the war a former Iraqi general complained about the planning behind this initial offensive:

Our troops were just lined up on the border and told to drive into Iran. They had an objective, but no idea how to get there or what they were doing, or how their mission fit the plan, or who would be supporting them.

(Pollack 2002: 184)

Of course, no officer dared criticize the President's handling of the war in a direct manner as that would have cost him his career or even his life. However, one of the first critiques of Hussein's repeated intervention in the war planning occurred in the winter of 1980, when the Iraqi leader ordered the troops to dig in and strengthen their positions. The commanders argued that these political orders deprived the Army of any momentum, forcing it to sit out a long wasteful interval of inactivity, where the troops' morale deteriorated (Pellitiere 1992: 65).

The primary assault in the first months of the war bore all the trademarks of an invasion designed within a totalitarian-penetration system. Political factors would debilitate Iraq's fighting capability throughout the first years of the war. The political leadership expected that Iraq's lightning attack on Iran would lead to victory within a matter of weeks, and made an immediate offer to negotiate while Iraq still held the advantage, as the Iraqi military had secured the Shatt and held swaths of Iranian territory. Teheran rejected any settlement with Iraq based on exchanging captured land for a peace settlement. Hussein's offer to Iran to exchange land it held for a promise of non-aggression proved demoralizing. The officers saw the men under their command die to capture those pieces of foreign territory and were perplexed to hear their leader's willingness to grant them back to the Iranians for what merely constituted an assurance from the clerics to abstain in interfering in Iraq's affairs (ibid.).

The political leadership had envisioned a show of force of Iraq's military might to intimidate Iran into submission. The land attack across the Iranian border and pre-emptive air strike were the key elements of this demonstrative onslaught:

This seems to be quite likely in a war which was largely regarded in Baghdad not as a fight to the death with Iran, but simply as a means of compelling the Iranian leadership to give official recognition to Iraqi might.

(Chubin and Tripp 1988: 54)

Hussein failing to order his forces to proceed any further into Iran indicated that he was pursuing a policy similar to Anwar Sadat in the 1973 war, where the Egyptian seizure of parts of the occupied Sinai Peninsula was a tactic to force the Israelis to negotiate with him to the advantage of Egypt. The Iraqi leadership would naturally have an aversion to fighting a protracted war with the Iranians, as the Army was predominately Shia fighting against another Shia army; another political consideration. Significant casualties on the front would have incited sedition among Iraq's Shia population within the armed forces and society at large. Iraq's first foray into Khuzestan had cost it considerable casualties, which was unacceptable to Hussein. The political leadership was cognizant of Iraq's limited population base in comparison to Iran and sought to minimize casualties in order to maintain public morale. Hussein stressed in his speeches that as the supreme military commander he would not waste the lives of soldiers on the front lines. In the beginning of the conflict one source wrote how the Iraqi media portrayed the conflict with an "absence of any representation of war as a bloody pursuit" (Pellitiere and Douglas 1990: 30). Iraqi troops and officers were shown in the media dressed in finely pressed uniforms and were rarely shown in trenches, and the public was certainly insulated from the footage of casualties from the front. The news from the front was delivered on television in a matter-of-fact manner with live combat footage rarely shown (ibid.).

A lightning military victory over Iran was worth the price as it would demonstrate to the Iraqi Shia that it was not in their interest to emulate the revolution of a defeated, humiliated regime. The notions of Iraqi "rights" emerged when Saddam Hussein in a speech to the National Assembly in November 1980 declared that he would hope that "the war to last a week, provided we gain all our rights" (British Broadcasting Company (BBC)/Summary of World Broadcasts (SWB)/Middle East (ME), November 6, 1980: A/5–10). Just a month into the war, Hussein said, "We have taken a protracted war into consideration ... We will continue to fight until the enemy says: 'Yes, we have agreed to your rights'" (ibid.). The Iraqi leader had signaled to the public that the Iraqi military's demonstrative war was to be a prolonged military engagement.

The nature of the totalitarian military and the highly personalized leadership of Saddam Hussein resulted in an Iraqi leadership that received non-critical input from its military commanders. The prevalent assumption was that the initial incursion into Iran would be a "walkover" was based on faulty military intelligence and an inflated expectation of Iraq's military capabilities. Hussein, although a civilian, portrayed himself as a grand military strategist and envisioned a war with overwhelming Iraqi military might and new technology acquired from the USSR and France leading to a decisive victory over Iran with a minimal shedding of blood on the Iraqi side. The Iraqi President failed to anticipate that the invasion would inflame Persian nationalist feelings, ultimately benefiting Khomeini who could rally the nation, preventing Hussein from obtaining an immediate victory, never mind an exit strategy from the conflict. On the contrary, the invasion did not spark an overthrow of the Khomeini government, but ironically strengthened it, as the invasion fit into the Ayatollah's world view that the Islamic Republic was threatened by secular regimes. The war gave Khomeini a platform to export the Islamic revolution through an armed struggle, with the promise that if he could defeat Iraq, it could spread throughout the Gulf, if not the entire Middle East.

By January 1981, the Iranian military was able to organize a counter-attack, albeit an uncoordinated one, but the Iraqi Army was able to repulse Revolutionary Guard advances in the northern and central fronts. During the fighting near Susangerd in January 1981, the Iraqi forces used tactics learned from the 1973 Arab–Israeli war, by conducting ambushes and flanking maneuver tactics and employing ambushes against the Iranian forces (Wagner 1979: 69). However, political constraints on the officers affected their fighting capability on the ground. Iraqi troops entered Susangerd twice and then abandoned it, as well as giving up critical positions near Dezful and Bostan because they lacked clear orders from an unresponsive command in Baghdad. After the fighting near Bostan in Khuzestan, Saddam Hussein declared, "that our forces did not enter Bostan for special reasons," an example of a systematic campaign of military spin that would be utilized throughout the war (Cordesman and Wagner 1990: 421). The Iraqi leader dismissed some senior officers and demoted others for their failings in these engagements.

In September 1981, Iraqi soldiers abandoned their siege of Abadan after an Iranian counter-attack. The Iraqi forces also suffered losses around the Qasr-e Shirin area in the central front in December 1981, and with the winter rains rendering most of the muddy terrain impassable to tank and vehicular movement, the conflict came to a brief halt.

War populism during the Iraqi advance

The Iraqi leadership developed a symbolic and rhetorical strategy of imbuing the military with a fighting spirit, as well as the society as a whole. Workman defined this tactic as "war populism," which was designed as "a strategy that partially overcame the fissured character of Iraqi society and enhanced the regime's images as 'defender of the Arab nation'" (1994: 2). There were reports emerging of sedition within the military concerning the legitimacy of war against Iran. Even the leadership realized that the conflict not only had to be won on the battlefield but through an ideological campaign that could spark enthusiasm in Iraqi society and the military tasked with combating Iran.

Militaristic values were penetrated into Iraqi society on a par with the era of Husri's and Shawkat's glorification of Iraq's pan-Arab army. Part of the war populism directed towards Iraq's fighting ranks included the label for the Iran–Iraq War and the symbols surrounding it. The official Iraqi term for the Iran–Iraq War became *Qadisiyyat Saddam*, a reference to the first battle between the Persians and Arabs in which the Arab Muslims emerged victorious. The battle, which took place in AD 637, led by the Arab General Saad ibn Waqqas lasted for three days, resulting in the end of Persian Sassanian rule in Iraq. The collapse of the Zoroastrian Iranian forces at Qadisiyya allowed the Arabs to spread Islam eastward, thus giving this battle a religious significance, an analogy that Hussein hoped the Iraqis would make (Al-Marashi 2003c: 2–3).

The other symbolic element of the war was the depiction of Saddam Hussein as a capable military leader, leading the nation on the road to victory. He invested in his image as a general, always dressed in an army uniform and a beret, visiting the war front and giving combat orders, surrounded by subservient officers (O'Ballance 1988: 98). All civilian members of the Baath RCC also appeared only in uniforms during the war, with special ranks to demonstrate their supremacy over the officers (Baram 1989: 466–7).

In the Iraqi media, the theme of Hussein directing the war was part of a strategic communication campaign directed towards the Iraqi public. The state owned daily, *The Revolution* (*Al-Thawra*) boasted of Saddam Hussein's strategic vision and his development of "new concepts in military principles." One such article further stated, "We have to be proud that His Excellency is enriching military ideology and drawing new experience from the lessons of war" (Abbas 1989: 223). The portrayal of the military commanders in the Iraqi media followed an almost formulaic pattern. Generals were rarely mentioned in the news, to prevent anyone emerging as a war hero, challenging Hussein's image of the military champion of Iraq (ibid.). During the initial victory in Iran, Iraqi officers were never identified by name to the public, serving as another example of political center sidelining the Iraqi military.

The use of Air Force and Navy

Prior to the war, the Iraqi Air Force lacked experience in air-to-air combat or air-to-ground combat, and its role had been restricted to attacking undefended targets such as Kurdish villages in the north of Iraq. The Iraqi Air Force high command had little notion of how to use air power to reach a wartime objective in the initial phases of the war. Characteristic of a totalitarian military, all Air Force sorties had to be approved by the higher echelons of political commanders, and permission often took hours or even days to be granted (Cordesman and Wagner 1990: 83). This relationship could not keep up with the fast paced events unfolding on the battlefield, where air support was often needed within minutes, rather than hours. This relationship between the central authority in Baghdad and the Air Force suffered from political over-centralization and rigid Baathist planning. Combat aircraft were dispatched on preplanned missions that came from political authorities after long periods of deliberation. The Air Force could not respond to the immediate tactical situation and was unable to exploit targets of opportunity that became available during the course of combat. For example, in the initial pre-emptive Iraqi air strikes in the first days of the war, aircraft failed to attack unsheltered Iranian planes and helicopters on the ground because the pilots were not ordered to do so. Rather they had to focus on the mission given to them of bombing the runways and creating craters so Iranian aircraft could not take off (ibid.: 458).

The craters were quickly repaired and with its US supplied planes intact, the Iranian Air Force launched a counteroffensive. The Iraqi pilots subsequently dueled with Iranian pilots in air-to-air combat, the latter winning most dogfights in the early war phase. The Iraqi pilots, with less practical training than their Iranian counterparts, proved to be less aggressive after the Soviet Union imposed an arms embargo on Iraq for failing to inform Moscow of the invasion, and the Iraqi Air Force could not afford to lose aircraft. Instead of engaging the Iranian Air Force, most Iraqi planes were dispersed to airfields among its allies in Saudi Arabia, Kuwait, Jordan and North Yemen – a decision also made due to political considerations. Hussein needed to ensure that the Air Force would serve as a reserve for the ultimate defense of the Iraqi nation in case an Iranian counter-attack would undermine his regime.

The Iraqi Air Force had few reconnaissance aircraft, which were rarely used or dispersed to other countries (Pollack 2002: 190). Due to political pressures, pilots often exaggerated the success of their missions and the higher echelons of the Air Force further compounded these exaggerations for the purpose of pleasing their political minders. As Air Force commanders often accepted delusional reports of success, they would underestimate the number of aircraft needed to achieve objectives in future combat missions. The misinformation designed to appease the political authorities would continue to plague the Air Force, depriving it from learning from past mistakes (Cordesman and Wagner 1990: 84).

The role of the Iraqi Navy was even more limited. Lacking a large harbor to develop a massive fleet, the Iraqi Navy was stationed at a small naval facility at Umm Qasr at the base of the Gulf. The Navy's ranks included 3,300 personnel, with close to thirty Soviet missile boats and Italian naval vessels (O'Ballance 1988: 25). However the role of the Iraqi Navy in the first phase of the war was negligible as it proved no match for the superior Iranian Navy.

The retreat of the Iraqi military and the Iranian advance: 1982–1984

Iran began preparations for a counteroffensive against Iraqi forces, after its earlier battles failed to produce any decisive results. The Iraqi military had been deployed along the Iranian border to prepare for such an offensive. The Second Army Corps protected the capital from an Iranian attack, guarding the Baghdad–Teheran highway. It was based near the town of Khanaqin and had seized the Iranian town of Qasr-e Shirin, and was responsible for defending it (ibid.: 58).

The Fourth Army Corps in the south had made the initial advances into Iranian territory in the Khuzestan province. At this time it consisted of eight divisions, with seven of them, totaling 75,000 men, deployed on Iranian territory. Three divisions occupied the town of Khorramshahr, while another three divisions secured the Khorramshahr–Ahwaz road. Since they were responsible for defending large swaths of foreign territory, units of the Popular Army were stationed in between the regular Army formations. The remaining Fourth Army Corps divisions held rear positions to defend Basra, stationed along the Basra–Baghdad road (ibid.: 79).

In March 1982, Teheran declared a new offensive called "Undeniable Victory." The forces of the Iraqi Fourth Corps came under attack near Susangerd in Khuzestan, suffering heavy losses. In a totalitarian system that took him close to a decade in building, Saddam Hussein retained control over every strategic and even tactical military decision during the first years of the conflict. During the fighting, which began around March 21, the Iraqi President dictated battlefield tactics from his position in Baghdad, through a cumbersome and inflexible decision-making process. Hussein ordered the headquarters of the Fourth Army Corps to defend its territory and avoid withdrawal from forward positions at all costs. This order prevented commanders from ceding captured land to redeploy in more defensible terrain (Pollack 2002: 201). Hussein's command overrode any decisions that could be made on the front lines, however he could not possibly comprehend how the battle was developing and the effects that Iranian "human-wave" attacks were having on the forces in the south. Hussein ordered in reinforcements but due to his distance from the battlefield, it was not until five days later that he realized the massive scale of the Iranian attack.

Wary of the political fallout from a total defeat on pubic morale, Hussein ordered on March 26 for the Iraqi forces to withdraw to prevent being encircled by the Iranian forces. He commanded the Iraqi forces to regroup and form a defensive line around Khorramshahr from the north. However his belated decision had little tangible effect on the fate of the Iraqi forces. Hussein's initial command to hold territory at all costs resulted in forces staying in static positions rather than conducting mobile exploitation of the battlefield, and the Iraqi forces were subsequently overwhelmed by the human-wave assaults. By March 29 Iranian forces had encircled two Iraqi armored divisions and one mechanized division, and captured several thousand prisoners. In eight days Iranian forces reached to a point where they were twenty-five kilometers from the Iraqi border (O'Ballance 1988: 80–1).

During these battles, Iran used human-wave attacks, recruited from the *Basij* that included youths and elderly Iranians. Initially the human-wave attacks were a tactical success on the battlefield, and psychologically demoralized the Iraqi troops. The Iraqi high command told the military the invasion of Iran would be a lightning victory against an Iranian army in disarray. Iran had not only organized a sustained counter-attack, but had employed several tactics that paralyzed the Iraqi forces. First, the Iranian forces usually attacked at night, since the Iraqi military had failed to develop night-fighting capabilities and to take adequate security precautions once the sun had set. At night, the Iraqi troops often panicked and their dependence on heavy armor was handicapped due to the lack of visibility facing off against masses of Iranian infantry. Disoriented Iraqi commanders often committed their reserves prematurely in these battles and this disarray allowed Iranians to break through their enemy's defenses (Pollack 2002: 201). Second, the spectacle of masses of Iranians seeking only martyrdom on the battlefield served as a shock tactic to the Iraqis. As one Iraqi commander put it, "It's horrifying; they swarm at you like roaches" (Pellitiere and Douglas 1990: 52). Another Iraqi officer described the attacks as following:

> They came at us like a crowd coming out of a mosque on a Friday. Soon we were firing into dead men, some draped over the barbed wire fences, and others in piles on the ground, having stepped on mines.
>
> (O'Ballance 1988: 81–2)

In these battles the Iraqis did not have enough ammunition to hold out against these assaults. The number of Iranian bodies charging towards the front simply overwhelmed the Iraqi soldiers.

During these setbacks Hussein continued to invest in a rhetorical campaign to imbue the armed forces with a fighting spirit through a series of speeches. As the Iraqi military found itself on the defensive in March of 1982 Hussein delivered a speech to the besieged Fourth Army Corps stating, "The General Command decided to rearrange defensive position to the rear after your strong blows absorbed the advance of the enemy" (Cordesman and Wagner 1990: 130–1). This speech was indicative of a campaign of state sponsored spin using Orwellian double-speak to maintain military morale. The leadership was adept at scripting any defeat into a victory. However, to the Iraqi officers and soldiers, no amount of political semantics could hide the fact that Hussein's obsessive supervision over military operations had a debilitating effect on their performance. Following the setbacks in 1982 commanders were executed for their shortcomings on the battlefield. Saddam Hussein himself even boasted of the execution of two generals and one field commander for "disgracefully" retreating from Iran (Axelgard 1988: 52).

The role of the military in Iraq's defensive strategy

As of 1982, when Iran took the war into Iraqi territory, Hussein, the Baath leadership and the officers could agree on a common goal: ensuring the survival of Iraq. Tripp stated, "The Iranian threat was very real and the Iraqi officer corps, as professionals occupying a certain position within the Iraqi state, regardless generally of their backgrounds, were determined to deny Iran a military victory" (2000: 237). The predominantly Arab Sunni officer corps emerged as one of the elites in the political system Saddam Hussein had nurtured and feared that its collapse due to a Shia Iranian victory would spell the end of their privileged status. The survival of what had been deemed a "community of interest," "a community of trust" and "a communality of guilt" formed an unspoken contract between the officers and the Iraqi leader.

In the summer of 1982, Iraqi forces began an organized retreat from Iranian territory. As Iraqi troops began to withdraw to their pre-war positions, the military began constructing a line of defense along the Iraqi border to repulse the inevitable Iranian offensive. The building of the defensive line had begun before any public announcement of the scale of Iraq's defeats as the recent events had repudiated Hussein's earlier claims of success. Despite the leadership's attempts to portray their defeats as victories, it had eventually to admit that it was on the defensive. The Iraqi military's new static defense strategy further enhanced Hussein's management of the war from Baghdad as very little movement would occur on the front. The defensive line stretched from the Shatt Al-Arab in the south to the Qasr-e Shirin theater in the center, with the mountainous north forming a natural defensive barrier. The World War I-like trenches featured lines of barbed wire in the front, as well as minefields. The main trench was linked with communication trenches leading back to underground shelters, which were used as resting quarters for the soldiers. The troops were provided with comforts such as air conditioning and TV, as well as telephones so that they could speak with their families (O'Ballance 1988: 101).

After the loss of Khorramshahr in May 1982, the Iraqi government reiterated its willingness to negotiate a settlement in June. Iran, emboldened by their success and taking Iraq's attempts to negotiate as a sign of weakness, demanded that Hussein step down from power. During this crisis in June, Hussein convened the Ninth Regional Congress of the Baath Party. The overarching theme of the Congress was the need for Party supremacy over the military at a time when the Baath's future under Hussein's helm was in question. According to the Congress' *Report* the goals of the Party regarding the military were:

> To consolidate the Party's leadership of the army, and disseminate in its ranks Ba'thist principles as well as nationalist and socialist culture; to strengthen the military and the principled criteria and discipline which enable the army to fulfill its duties satisfactorily; to protect it against deviation and error; to ensure its correct and effective contribution to revolutionary construction and the fulfillment of national tasks.
>
> (cited in Hashim 2003b: 17)

In order to stress the Party's credentials vis-à-vis the military, it reinterpreted its history from the 1968 coup, disregarding the role of the officers in the takeover. The session highlighted the role of civilians, like Saddam Hussein "the struggler" (*munadhil*) over the armed forces. In fact the Party accused some unnamed senior officers in the Party in 1968 of trying to undermine the "Revolution," an indirect reference to Hardan and Ammash. This allusion to unmentioned officers was a means of attacking the lack of ideological zeal and integrity of the entire officer corps (Baram 1989: 466). Glorifying the civilian wing of the Party came at a time when it was assumed that Al-Bakr, a Baathist officer may return to power to appease Iranian demands of Hussein stepping down. Al-Bakr died suddenly in October 1982 and while the causes of his death are unknown he conveniently passed away at a time when Hussein was under increasing pressure to abdicate power.

The Iranian "Operation Ramadan" began in July 1982 with an offensive in the direction of Basra, defended by the Third Army Corps, consisting of seven divisions, or 70,000 troops (O'Ballance 1988: 93–4). The Iraqis had repulsed these offensives and by the end of year, Iraq had fortified its defenses. The Iraqi leadership continued to "spin" defeat for the military by countering rumors that the armed forces suffered from low morale and weak leadership. The successful defense of Basra, Iraq's second largest city, was victory in itself. The ability of Iraq's defensive positions to blunt the Iranian offensives in late 1982, renewed hope in the Iraqi leadership that the enemy may tire of these tactics and seek an end to the war. The Party encouraged the Iraqi military that their tactics should not only focus on defending the nation, but inflicting enough casualties to end the conflict: "should the enemy be destroyed to the same degree as in previous attacks, the Iraqi leadership would consider the battle over from a military viewpoint" (BBC/SWB/ME, 1 September 1982: A/2). Iraqi leaders had used the Iranian failures as an indication that enemy morale would deteriorate and the war was coming to a near conclusion.

However, the Iranian advance continued on February 7, 1983, when Iraqi forces came under attack in the vicinity of Al-Amara, a town in the south-east of the country. The Iraqi military came under attack during another Iranian offensive in April 1983 near the road that leads to Baghdad, a maneuver attempting to cut off the capital from Basra. This 80 kilometer front was commanded by General Hisham Sabah Al-Fakhri, leading the Fourth Army Corps that had withdrawn from Iran, and which had been reorganized into six divisions. Al-Fakhri had managed to fight back the Iranian infantry attacks, and on April 9 led an armored counterattack bringing a lull to the fighting on the following day. Saddam Hussein was aware of the Western media's reporting of the war and believed that they were exaggerating Iraq's loses. He allowed foreign journalists to be flown into the battlefield, although only during cessations of hostilities. As part of a renewed demonstrative war to international media, Al-Fakhri gave a tour to journalists at the Fourth Corps Headquarters showing off captured Iranian tanks. Following the victory close to a 1,000 Iranian prisoners were paraded through the streets of the capital as evidence of victory to the Iraqi public (O'Ballance 1988: 115–16).

In the north the Iraqi military suffered defeats as a result of combined Iranian–KDP offensives. In the beginning of the war, the activities of the KDP were limited to hit-and-run tactics against the Iraqi government forces and combating its Kurdish rival, the PUK. The intra-Kurdish fighting allowed Iraqi military forces to concentrate on the central and southern fronts, while leaving the pro-government Kurdish forces, the National Defense Battalions to maintain order in the north. As Iran began to take the war into Iraqi territory in the south, Iran also opened up a front in the north, causing anxiety in Baghdad, as to whether the Iraqi Army could prevent further losses of territory to joint Iranian–Iraqi Kurdish attacks. The losses in the north increased as of 1983, and by June 23, Iranian forces were positioned on the strategic heights overlooking the Iraqi urban centers of Qalat Diza and Kirkuk. A few days later, the Iraqi government called on Kurds born between 1963 and 1964 in the north to report for military service (Baghdad Voice of the Masses, June 26, 1983 in BBC/SWB/ME, June 28, 1986: A/2–4). On July 22, 1983 the First Iraqi Army Corps, led by General Mahir Abd Al-Rashid had lost nineteen kilometers of Iraqi territory during the Iranian Val Fajr 2 campaign, pushing it back to the towns of Qalat Diza and Rawanduz and eventually they lost the military base of Hajj Umran. The Iranian campaign of Val Fajr 4 was launched on October 20, 1983 near east Sulaymaniyya and the Iraqi First Army Corps fell back, but continued to defend the town of Panjwin from Iranian advances (Trab-Zemzemi 1986: 116).

By the end of 1983, little territorial advances were made on the front lines in the north and south, and both sets of combatants absorbed and tried to inflict massive casualties on each other. Iranian forces still maintained their positions on the outskirts of Basra, but successive human-wave attacks failed to produce any territorial gains. The stalemate was due to structural deficiencies on both sides as political centers managed the war. Just as Baathist politics conflicted with decisions of the Iraqi military, on the Iranian side the clerics interfered with military operations.

The Iraqi military had doubled the size of its Army, from 242,250 (twelve divisions) before the war to 475,000 (twenty divisions) by 1983, as part of the first major expansion of the war (see Table 7.1 on Iraqi military growth 1980–1987). The second expansion would come three years later in 1986, after the Iraqi defeat in the Faw Peninsula.

In order to deflect criticisms from the military over Hussein's handling of the war, the Iraqi President lavished the military with material assets, both lethal and non-lethal. The state provided the armed forces with advanced weapons systems. This tactic was employed during the expansion of the military in 1975, but was made more difficult during the first

Table 7.1 The growth of the Iraqi armed forces 1980–1987

Force category	1980	1987
Total regular armed forces	242,250	850,000
Land forces		
Regular Army		
Active	200,000	805,000
Reserves	250,000	230,000
People's Army	250,000	500,000
Divisions		
Armored	4	5
Mechanized	4	3
Infantry	4	10
Special Forces	0	2
Republican Guard	1	1
Reserve, People's Army, Volunteer	–	8
Major equipment		
Main battle tanks	2,500	4,800
Armored fighting vehicles	2,000	3,800
Major artillery	1,000	5,200
Air Force		
Manpower	38,000	40,000
Combat aircraft	335	400–500
Combat helicopters	40	100–180
Total helicopters	250	360–400
Surface-to-Air missile batteries	28	75
Force category	1,980	1,987
Navy		
Manpower	4,250	5,000
Frigates	1	2
Corvettes	0	6
Missile patrol craft	12	10
Other patrol craft	25	12
Minesweepers	8	7
Landing craft and other ships	4	8

Source: Chubin and Tripp (1988: 294).

two years of the war. The USSR withheld supplying arms to Iraq to protest Iraq's escalation of tensions in the Gulf, as well as the fact it had failed to consult the Soviet Union prior to its invasion. The Soviets feared that the war would provide a pretext for the US to intervene in the Gulf and project its power in the region, at a time when the USSR was involved in a war in Afghanistan. However, by 1982 the USSR resumed large arms shipments to Iraq after the Iranian government cracked down on the Iranian communist party known as Tudeh and Iraq began suffering setbacks on the battlefield. In 1984 the USSR provided the Iraqi military with 200 T-62 tanks and 100 more advanced T-72 tanks, and the Air Force was given a further thirty MiG-23s and MiG-25s (Sajjadpur 1997: 35). France emerged as the second largest supplier of arms for the Iraqi military. Iraq provided France with what amounted to a shopping list of arms that the French were eager to provide in the beginning of the war, including thirty Mirage F-1 interceptors and 200 Exocet anti-ship missiles. During this period, a group of fifty Iraqi pilots trained in France to use the Mirage F-1E would form Iraq's best trained pilots (Eisenstadt 1993: 54).

Targhib *and* tarhib *applied to the officer corps*

The state lavished the officers with monetary incentives, giving them a stake in a system that they could defend in earnest. Hussein often provided pay raises to the officers and they were given priority for automobile and home purchases. Even on the front line, the officers' quarters were carpeted and fully furnished and included luxuries such as color TVs, which also served a political agenda as it allowed them to watch Hussein's speeches on the war (McKnight 1991: 95). Further luxuries included video cassette machines, air conditioning and phone lines. When time permitted they also had access to a week's leave a month, where they could arrive at a privately owned parking lot, identify their parked car and drive home. When returning from leave, they were informed of the current location of their unit and would return to the front (Pellitiere and Douglas 1990: 57). The state even practiced posthumous *targhib* by compensating the families of non-commissioned officers killed on the front with a Toyota vehicle and a plot of land, while the families of officers were given a Chevrolet and a larger piece of land (Jabar 2004: 130).

The patronage of tribes, ethnicities and sectarian groups within the officer corps served as another means of *targhib*. Nepotism was rife and generals related to Hussein were promoted overnight. They were reliant upon the Iraqi leader for their survival, and if Hussein fell in a coup, so would they all. Junior and middle-grade officers were discontent as relatives and clansmen of Hussein were promoted more rapidly and in many cases without enduring the fighting on the front.

Familial and regional origins were another factor that affected military professionalism, as *targhib* resulted in patronage of Sunni Muslim officers, particularly those from Takrit.

The highest ranks in the armed forces and in the Guard were staffed by members of Hussein's Takriti Al-Bu Nasir tribe. The exploitation of special loyalties formed a "community of trust" among those privileged officers from Takrit, as well as the surrounding Sunni Arab areas that staffed the state's central administration, the security organizations and the top echelons of the officer corps (Quinlivan 1999: 135).

The social networks from the provincial Sunni Arab areas were drawn from the towns of Ana, Dur, Sharqat, Huwayja, Bayji, Samarra and Ramadi, located in what became known as the "Sunni Arab Triangle" (Baram 1998: 26). Sunni Arab tribes and families that were part of these networks included the Dulaym, Jabur (mixed Shia/Sunni), Azzawi, Ubayd, Dur and Samarrai tribes and clans (Dawood 2003: 121). The state used the Iraqi media to cultivate the loyalty of the tribal elements within the military. Iraq's media broadcasted tribal poetry that glorified war and emphasized tribal concepts such as manly honor, military strength, bravery and revenge against the "enemy" (Yaphe 2000: 5).

While most of the lower ranks of the military were made up of Arab Shia and Kurds, there were distinguished officers from these communities as well. Prominent Shia commanders included Lieutenant General Abd Al-Sattar Ahmad Al-Muini who commanded the Second Army until January 1987 and Lieutenant General Saadi Tuma Abbas Al-Jaburi who had commanded the First Army, Third Army and Seventh Army at various times. Other Shia commanders included Major General Nimat Faris Hussein Al-Mihyawi who led the First Army and later served as the President of the Al-Bakr University for Higher Military Studies, Hamid Ahmad Al-Ward who served as the commander of the Anti-Aircraft Defense Forces and Zayd Jawwad Hasan Al-Rubayi, Mahmud Hammadi Al-Juburi and Abd Al-Jabbar Abd Al-Rahim Al-Asadi. One of the most prominent Kurdish generals was Husayn Rashid Wandawi Al-Takriti who commanded the Republican Guard that was responsible for protecting the President (Baram 1989: 471).

In totalitarian militaries, the ruling regime often uses rotations, retirements, purges or executions of officers as a means of control. The most benign element of *tarhib* is the failure to grant promotions. During the first years of the war, demonstrated fealty to the Baath or kin relations to the President, rather military competence, usually guaranteed promotion, a factor that proved demoralizing for numerous commanders whose careers stagnated. *Targhib* or promotions of officers beyond the rank of captain were based on the membership in the Party, as well as the ability to demonstrate support of the Iraqi President. The political leadership also failed to promote officers with combat acumen to the rank of general out of fear that their talents could be used in a coup. This trend led to personal factionalism among the officers who tried to garner attention of the Baath leadership.

The rotation was used to pre-empt an officer from developing his own network within a unit. Since coups are orchestrated by close-knit factions within the military, a rotation removes a high-ranking officer from this base of support so that he can no longer forge a personal relationship with the men under his command. Military competency was neglected in the face of creating a politically reliable military force, and the constant shuffling of officers on political grounds ultimately affected the professionalism of the officer corps.

A purge is a more extreme form of *tarhib*, serving as a punitive tactic for officers who may have failed on the battlefield, or losing the confidence and favor of the political leadership. Purges were also employed against officers suspected of disloyalty or who were of questionable reliability. After the reversal of Iraqi fortunes in Khuzestan in mid-1982, approximately 300 generals were purged. The execution was the most drastic tactic of *tarhib* used against officers who were suspected of attempting to overthrow the regime or who had failed spectacularly on the front. It was reported that formations known as the Punishment Corps (*Fayaliq al-'Iqab*) were also stationed in the rear lines to execute military commanders who performed poorly. During the debacle of mid-1982, it was believed that fifteen generals were executed (Al-Khafaji 1988: 36). The executions sent the message to disgruntled officers that the ultimate punishment would be enforced for failure on the battlefield or subversive activities.

The party's use of intelligence networks ensures the loyalty of the armed forces. Multiple security services are essential to a coup-proof system and are a defining characteristic of a totalitarian-penetration system. According to Quinlivan, coup-proofing is maintained by a security apparatus devoted exclusively to the physical protection of the leader. The hub of such an intelligence network must be stationed in the immediate vicinity of the leadership, as assassination attempts against a ruler are likely since the regime produces disenfranchised segments in the nation seeking revenge. The funds from a rentier state such as Iraq provided the resources to staff such an all pervasive security network (Quinlivan 1999: 135).

In Iraq, an intelligence network expanded during the conflict to monitor the military and to prevent dissension through the use of *tarhib* or instilling fear into the ranks, a critical asset at a time when the nation was engaged in a war. In 1983, Saddam Hussein fired his half-brother Barzan Al-Takriti as Director of the General Intelligence Directorate, which was seen as a "tremendous liberation for the officers." Lieutenant General Al-Fakhri, former commander of the Fourth Corps replaced him, and his status as a professional officer appealed to the officers (Pellitiere and Douglas 1990: 30). By 1984, Al-Fakhri, a Sunni Arab from Mosul was replaced by Lieutenant General Dr. Fadhil Al-Barrak Husayn, a Takriti from the Iraqi President's Bayjat clan. Al-Barrak was an example of an Army officer who benefited from Hussein's patronage due to his origins. He was rapidly promoted from the rank of major to general, not as a commander of troops in the field but rather as the military attaché in Moscow from 1972 to 1977, where he received a Ph.D. in political science (Baram 1989: 469). Al-Barrak benefited from Hussein's patronage policy as *targhib* guaranteed that his relations with the President would trump Al-Fakhri's military experience. Al-Barrak, however, was executed years later on charges of spying for the Soviets demonstrating that coming from Takrit did not guarantee one's survival.

The General Military Intelligence Directorate (*Mudiriyyat Al-Istikhabarat Al-'Askariyya Al-'Amma*) was created in 1932, in Iraq's first year of independence (Al-Marashi 2002: 7). Although initially under the Ministry of Defense, during the Iran–Iraq War its importance grew substantially and it was re-subordinated to report directly to the Presidential Palace. Its responsibilities included tactical and strategic reconnaissance of regimes hostile to Iraq and assessing threats of a military nature. In terms of local duties, it was responsible for monitoring the military through a network of informants and ensuring the loyalty of the officer corps.

The Special Security Apparatus (*Al-Amn al-Khas*) emerged during the Iran–Iraq War to serve as an overarching organization to monitor the security apparatus that continued to grow as a result of the war. The demonstration of familial patronage networks during this period can be evidenced by the rise of Hussein Kamil. Kamil was the Iraqi President's cousin and son-in-law and was instrumental in the creation of this agency. He selected loyal and devoted agents from the other security agencies to serve in this unit. In terms of the Iraqi military, its duties were to monitor the leadership of the armed forces, purchasing foreign arms and technology, and securing Iraq's most critical military industries, as well as supervising the activities of the Republican Guard. Just after its creation in 1984, the Special Security Organization thwarted a plot of disgruntled Army officers, who objected to Hussein's management of the Iran–Iraq War (ibid.: 2–3).

Hussein's intelligence network, charged with detecting political threats within the military, resulted in competing intelligence agencies vying to demonstrate their loyalty, rather on focusing on the tactical information gathering from the front. Intelligence agencies, particularly military intelligence, exerted more efforts on their *tarhib* duties, internal security and monitoring the loyalty of the armed forces, rather than gathering external technical intelligence on Iran. Information from these agencies tended to be ideological, lacking reconnaissance and target acquisition intelligence and objective observation, reporting and analysis of Iran's military. Due to this politicized intelligence network, military intelligence officers often distorted its information to report whatever Saddam wanted to hear. This intelligence was often collected from officers who boasted that they had defeated Iranian attacks when they had not done so, or exaggerated the number of Iranian forces that attacked them to justify their defeats. While the intelligence passed up the chain of command was misleading, the political leadership also restricted what intelligence they possessed. Controlling the dissemination of information served as a means of manipulating the military during the war. Tactical field commanders rarely received timely intelligence down from the chain of command and thus never had a full picture of the nature of the Iranian forces in their theater and were constantly hit by surprise attacks. Some Iraqi officers noted that they received more accurate intelligence from the media than from their own commanders (Cordesman and Wagner 1990: 80).

The Party also applied *tarhib* and *targhib* as a means to control the military. The stress on Party loyalty can be evinced from an Iraqi Army Training Command manual. The volume identified the central duties of the Iraqi officer, writing that loyalty to the Baath party was his foremost obligation. In a section entitled "General Duties of Officers" with the subheading, "Duties of the Unit Commander," it wrote:

> Unit commanders are responsible in front of God, the people, and the President of the Republic, the leader of the armed forces, to work according to the principles of the 17th to 30th Tammuz [July] Revolution of the Arab Socialist Baath Party, to raise the competency of their units in all fields of training, administration, technical and morale, with all loyalty and devotion to the level that empowers them to carry out the national duties with high proficiency.
>
> (Iraqi Army Training Command 1985: 15)

This training literature indicated the levels of Baathist indoctrination in the military. One of the characteristics of a totalitarian military was the pervasive infiltration of the ruling party in the armed forces. Baathist political officers, analogous to the Soviet commissars, were stationed anywhere from corps headquarters to detachments on the front line, ensuring that officers "worked according to the principles" of the Party (Dawisha 1986: 26). These Baathist minders, as an extension of the political center emanated *tarhib*, projecting fear and serving as a reminder that General Saddam could watch the officers at all times. The report of a slightest hint of disloyalty would ultimately lead to a commander's dismissal, imprisonment or execution.

Any indication of criticism among the officers and troops of the leadership's management of the war could be reported by these political officers through their own lines of communication directly to the Baath Party. They served as a conduit to the leadership in Baghdad by ensuring that all military actions taken on the war front had the political authorization of the Party. They scrutinized the commanders' activities and at times could override their decisions. This relationship proved not only humiliating for the officers, but cumbersome on the battlefield. The political minders enhanced the strained relationship between professional officers and the Baath, as the commissars represented the continued distrust of the Party towards the military.

The state's application of targhib *and* tarhib *towards the infantry*

While the above deals with the military at the elite level, the following analyzes the relationship between the state and the bulk of the armed forces: the conscripts and those who formed the lower ranks. The Iraqi leadership had to devise mass mobilization strategies towards the masses including propaganda and myth-making as well as surveillance. Inclusionary polices sought to increase public participation in the military and its rival paramilitary force the Popular Army. Youth aged between nine and fourteen would join the Vanguards, modeled after the *Futuwwa* of the 1920s and 1930s. This body was designed to provide military training and Baathist indoctrination.

The war effort placed huge demands on Iraq's population for manpower, requiring calls up of eligible males to serve in the armed forces, with the security services ensuring that they would not evade the draft. Military service for conscripts comprised anywhere from two to three years of active duty and close to 85 percent of the army consisted of draftees (ibid.). While some Arab Shia and Kurds held senior positions in the armed forces and performed well on the battlefield, the vast majority of the lower ranks, close to 85 percent, were filled by Kurds and Shia (Pelitiere and Douglas 1990: 11). The state sought to prevent the Shia from deserting en masse in a war against their co-religionists in Iran, and ethnic Kurds from abandoning their posts in a war that took on ethnic proportions of the population in defending the "Arabness" of Iraq. The state's application of *tarhib* to these communities could only achieve minimal success as a coerced fighting force would also be a demoralized fighting force. The state had to employ the tactics of *targhib* to ensure these ethnosectarian communities gave up their sons in a fight they believed in.

Populism directed towards the infantry and society

The war began as a demonstrative war designed to communicate the strength and military prowess of Saddam Hussein and the military at his disposal. The military had been a mere instrument with which the Iraqi leader sought to intimidate Iran and impress his public, bolstering his domestic legitimacy. By 1982 the war had evolved into a war of survival and emerged as a collective endeavor shaping a reinvigorated Iraqi identity. *Tarhib* did not only emanate from the regime of Saddam Hussein. The leadership also used *tarhib*, or instilling terror, by playing on fears of an imminent Iranian threat after the debacle in 1982, when Iraq was clearly on the defensive. While Iran insisted that it would end the war if Hussein stepped down, the Iraqi leader had to convince the soldiers that he was not merely fighting to protect Saddam's position as President, but the nation itself from an inevitable Islamic Revolution were he to abdicate power.

While Hussein invested in inspiring the officers through a mix of intimidation, coercion and cajoling, the Iraqi leader had to employ the same efforts with regards to the lower ranks of the military, including conscripts and those in the Popular Army. The troops were reminded of their loyalties to the Party through their training manuals, which identified the central duties of the Iraqi soldier:

> The central duties of a soldier is loyalty and devotion to the principles of the 17th to 30th Tammuz [July] revolution of the socialist Arab Socialist Baath Party, and it is prohibited to associate with any party

and secret or public group except the Arab Socialist Baath party, and that they have to distance themselves from persons suspected of hostility to the revolution or the Party to avoid suspicion.

(Iraqi Army Training Command 1985: 75)

After the reverses of 1982, Hussein conveyed a sense of public Baathist belonging, delivering a series of communications to appeal to the masses to defend the Party: "Every Iraqi who took up arms and fought in defense of the homeland was an organized Ba'thist whose record was similar to that of the brave Ba'thist who continued struggling at the time of the secret work" (quoted in Chubin and Tripp 1988: 95). The invocation of popular solidarity with the Party may have not achieved the desired results. During the war the Army served as a renewed means of socialization of Iraqis, harking back to the days of King Faysal and his coterie's vision of the role of the military in early Iraqi society. During the war young conscripts come into contact with Iraqis from various parts of the nation and engaged in a collective endeavor of defending the nation. This common bond forged among fighting men strengthened their sense of Iraqi nationalism, although it did little to strengthen Baathism. The values of Arab socialism and defense of the Party had little emotional value to the men on the front, as the Baath was blamed for poor battlefield management, interference in military affairs and the presence of ubiquitous Party commissars.

Afterwards, the troops were hailed by the leadership into defending the beleaguered nation by appealing to their sense of nationalism. In Hussein's appeal to the masses, he sought to dispel the fact that the country was ruled by a clannish clique and often stated that he punished "my relatives, including my nephews, brothers and my son, who sometimes behaved badly" by failing in their military service (Dawisha 1986: 29). In a 1982 speech addressed to the Second Army Corps, Hussein even admitted that the task of mobilizing the troops would be easier as Iraq was on the defensive and the nation faced a collective threat (BBC/SWB/ME, 7 September 1987: A/3–4).

The leadership was primarily concerned with recruiting Kurds to fill Army ranks and keeping KDP and PUK activities to a minimum. It increased material assistance to the Kurdish areas and maintained a conciliatory tone towards the Kurds to prevent their desertion from the military. In 1983, Saddam Hussein admitted that there were 48,000 mostly Kurdish deserters (MacDowall 1996: 348). Not only did these desertions drain the numbers of the Iraqi military, but they also could join the Kurdish guerrilla movements such as the Iranian-allied KDP. The state applied *tarhib* in the form of executions for desertion, but it had little effect. In April the government went even further by offering a concession of an amnesty and a promise that if the deserters returned they would not be sent to the front lines, but could serve in civil defense duties (Chubin and Tripp 1988: 107).

The Iraqi government also invested in a rhetorical campaign to appeal to the Kurds. In response to one military operation, a military communiqué read, "The heroes of Iraq, sons of Salah ad-Din Ayyubi, both Arabs and Kurds, fought bravely in the defence of our cherished homeland and inflicted on the enemy massive losses in both men and equipment" (Communiqué no. 1161, Baghdad Home Service, July 23, 1983).

On December 10, 1983, Jalal Talabani, leader of the PUK, had agreed to a ceasefire with Baghdad and Hussein tried to renegotiate a power-sharing arrangement (O'Ballance 1988: 138). In January 1984 negotiations with the PUK broke down after eleven PUK members were executed for desertion from the armed forces. Two months later, demonstrations broke out in Sulaymaniyya against conscription in the Popular Army, which led the PUK to attack an Iraqi garrison (Farouk-Sluglett *et al.* 1984: 26).

Even though the Iraqi Shia in the military were fighting other Shia from Iran, they did not rise up or defect in large amounts. The Shia failure to revolt en masse within the Iraqi public or within the ranks of the armed forces can be attributed to a multifaceted strategy conducted by the Iraqi state. In order to counter Iran's attempts to foster Shia unity between their co-religionists, the Iraqi state maintained a dual policy of *targhib* or appeasement and enticement towards the Shia, as well as *tarhib* or terrorizing those Shia who resisted the state's war efforts. Shia fighting alongside Sunnis on the battlefield forged a common sense of Iraqiness. Some Iraqi Shia may have loathed Hussein, but that did not preclude them from fighting out of a sense of Iraqi patriotism or to prevent Iraq from becoming an Iranian-styled Islamic republic, which would have been the most likely scenario had Khomeini emerged triumphant. Elements among Shia civilians feared that an Iranian invasion would result in a violent disruption of their lives that had also improved materially since the war began.

Targhib entailed the leadership's communicative campaign that stressed Iraqi unity, the Shia's Arab identity and the superiority of Arab culture. The Iraqi leader often invoked the two most emotive symbols of Shia Islam, the revered Imams Ali and Hussein reminding his Shia audience that they were ethnically Arabs, not Iranians (Dawisha 1986: 30). The state used such techniques to demonstrate both to the Shia in the Army and to society as a whole that Iran's version of Islam was corrupt, while bolstering the Islamic credentials of Hussein's government, evidenced by his claim to be a descendant of Imam Ali and the Prophet Muhammad. In an additional measure to appeal to the Shia, Hussein made Imam Ali's birthday an Iraqi national holiday (Karsh and Rautsi 1991: 30). Even Iraq's Scud missiles were named after Imam Hussein and his brother Abbas (Baram 1991: 66).

To prevent Iran's messages from fomenting sedition among the Shia in the armed forces, Shia clerics had been co-opted by the state and dispatched to the front lines, to convince their followers that they had no common cause with the Iranian Shia in the trenches opposite them. These clerics would stress that their Iranian foes were crypto-Shia still practicing

their Zoroastrian beliefs, creating an image of Persians who "called themselves Muslims" but were in fact still "Magians" of the pre-Islamic era
(Chubin and Tripp 1988: 101). In doing so, the state attempted to ensure
that the loyalty of the Shia lay with the Iraqi state on ethnic lines, and
attempted to dilute possible Iraqi Shia affinity with the Iranian Shia. With
reference to the sectarian divide in Iraq, Hussein went further to stress the
country's unity in the face of Iranian threats to foment communal tensions.
The Iraqi leader declared in the state-owned *Al-Thawra* paper that while
there were "Sunnis, Shi'ites and other religions and sects in Iraq" it was
"the unified Iraqi people who were fighting the war" (Dawisha 1986: 29).

The Iraqi state also employed *tarhib* to ensure Shia support for the war
effort. The security services monitored the Shia religious establishments,
particularly sermons for seditious themes during the war and ensured no
subversive political activity took place. All mosques and schools were to be
controlled by the government and all Shia scholars were made salaried
employees of the state. The security services were particularly watchful of
the activities of the Iraqi Shia exile organizations such as the Dawa Party
and the Supreme Council for the Islamic Revolution in Iraq (SCIRI). Both
parties had called on the Shia in the armed forces to defect, with some
having communication facilities within Iraq to broadcast such messages.
Iran allowed SCIRI to open up an office in Hajj Umran, an Iraqi town in
the north captured by the Iranians. On January 5, 1984, SCIRI issued
a statement calling for a revolt among the Iraqi military, and stressed
the crimes suffered by the Muslim Shia and Kurds at the hands of
Saddam Hussein (Islamic Republic News Agency, January 5, 1987 in
BBC/SUB/ME, January 7, 1987: A/4). The affects of Iraq or Iran's propaganda campaigns directed to the Iraqi Shia is difficult to ascertain. One of
the factors that could explain Shia steadfastness in the ranks was coercion
from the state, where defection or desertion could mean an uncertain fate
for their families back home. For those Shia who deserted, the only option
was to hide in the marshes of southern Iraq, with some joining Iraqi
opposition forces.

As the war seemed to unfold as a victory for Iraq in the first year, there
was little need for Hussein to abandon his politicized management of the
Iraqi military. However, as the Iraqi offensive began to lose momentum
and eventually collapsed under an Iranian counter-attack, it became clear
that freedom of action to commanders on the battlefield would have to be
granted. With the Iranian offensives into Iraq it became evident that the
political leadership's direct interference in dictating war strategy was ham-
pering the military's efforts. The de-politicization of the military began as
Hussein begrudgingly granted freedoms to the generals to prosecute the
war with autonomy, but took years to unfold as the leadership experi-
mented with balancing military effectiveness with political reliability.

8 The reassertion of the Iraqi officers 1984–1988

The Baathist de-politicization of the military

As the conflict transformed into a war of attrition, the officers wished to communicate to the leadership in the most subtle of manners that in order to defend the nation they should be given the freedom to prosecute the war based on military considerations as opposed to political dictates. Rather than maintaining static defense lines, the officers wanted to adopt a more aggressive strategy to defeat Iran. The leadership eventually fostered military professionalism at the expense of political loyalty, but the de-politicization of the armed forces was a gradual process that would continue until the final years of the war. Hussein had worked from 1968 to create a totalitarian military, and he was not about to undo his work overnight.

The gradual changes began with rewarding professional competence on the battlefield, by praising officers for their performance, rare in a system that only glorified Saddam Hussein as the "struggler-leader" and a "military genius." Hussein declared that both the state and the Party were grateful to the Army and praised its historical continuity as an institution that contributed to the political and socio-economic development of Iraq. The domestic media in Iraq devoted more coverage to the Iraqi commanders at the front. The mostly civilian political leadership who planned the war strategy allowed career officers into their meetings of the National Defense Council, a body second in importance to the RCC. General Khalil Abd Al-Jabbar Al-Shanshal, the former Chief of Staff who devised the initial invasion plan, was promoted to Minister of State for Military Affairs, as a concession to allow more career officers in the government (Baram 1989: 459).

While he granted greater autonomy, Saddam Hussein still presided over an intrusive network that maintained political control over the armed forces. Political guidance officers were pervasive in the military units at the front, although their role in objecting to the Army's decision in the field was reduced. His attempts to patronize personal loyalties among officers from selected tribes and clans also continued unabated. One development that Hussein did not factor into his planning was that the continued fighting would forge a professional identity and enhanced solidarity among the officer corps that would transcend parallel military networks based on competing tribes and clans within the armed forces. The solidarity among the officers developed as Iraq fought for its survival, and after a string of military defeats this common corporate identity would prove strong enough to challenge Hussein's interference in military planning.

Reforming the Popular Army

The anti-armies that were bolstered during the war included the Popular Army and the Republican Guards. As part of the totalitarian structure, the Popular Army had been created to provide military training to Baath Party members, but after the war it was open to all men of fighting age, ranging from eighteen to forty-five. The Army had close to 250,000 members at the beginning of the Iran–Iraq War and by February 1982 the Popular Army's numbers would reach 400,000 (Abbas 1989: 218). However it was largely ineffective as a combat force and its numbers remained constant at 500,000.

During the first year of the war, it provided civilian defense support duties such as manning checkpoints, escorting prominent Baathist official VIPs, aiding crowds to reach shelters during air raids and protecting strategic installations to free up the regular military for combat. As the war seemed to continue indefinitely, by 1981 the Popular Army was dispatched to the battlefield to counter Iran's numerical superiority in infantry. The Popular Army on the ideological level had been compared by some sources to the Iranian Revolutionary Guards. Both emerged as volunteer paramilitary militias designed to protect their respective ideological parties. The Popular Army in Iraq was the military of the Baath, and the Iranian Revolutionary Guard was the army of the Islamic Republican Party, a short-lived organization that supported Khomeini and the formation of the Islamic Republic. However a more accurate analogy can be drawn between the Popular Army and the Basij, a mass mobilization army, but the Iraqi version lacked the zeal and devotion of both Iran's Revolutionary Guards and the Basij.

Part of the Popular Army's poor performance on the front could be attributed to their lack of training. Training was limited to two months out of every year, providing lessons on the ideology of the Party as well as instructions on small arms use and low-intensity warfare (Kamrava 2000: 85). The Popular Army formations, easy to identify due to their special unit numbers, became the favorite targets of the Iranian Revolutionary Guards (Cordesman and Wagner 1990: 130). Popular Army units were usually deployed in between regular Army formations, and Iranians strategists learned early in the war that they were the weakest link in the Iraqi defenses. With the lack of professional military leadership, or heavy weapons or combined-arms skills, they proved no match for the infantry forces of the Iranians. When faced with human-wave attacks from the Basij, the Popular Army, and the regular Army units for that matter, could decimate the first wave of unfortunate combatants, but the subsequent waves would overrun the exhausted Iraqi positions. The difference between the regular Army and the Popular Army was that the latter was more prone to panic and flee the front lines. The collapse of the Popular Army's positions left the regular Army exposed, allowing the Iranian forces to push through gaps and outflank Iraqi Army units. To make matters worse, surrendering Popular Army units provided a large number of prisoners to Iran, eroding Iraqi morale. For the career officers, further resentment brewed towards the civilian leadership that placed the Popular Army units in such critical positions in the first place. Hussein was aware of such resentment and even blamed the defeats like Khorramshahr on the Popular Army, calling them a "burden to the regular army" (Chubin and Tripp 1988: 59).

Hussein would seek to reduce the Popular Army's role in the war by reforming its leadership and expanding the Republican Guard. The Baath removed inexperienced political leaders from positions as commanders in the Popular Army and replaced them with experienced officers. The Popular Army was no longer committed to the front lines where the Iranian military could take advantage of their weaknesses, but the leadership still pressured young men and eventually women to join for civil defense duties. The Popular Army was initially designed as a military of the Party, comprising loyal Baathist civilians as opposed to professional soldiers. As the war progressed, *tarhib* press ganged young men into its ranks. During the war the President was particularly critical of those who tried to abandon their service in the Popular Army, stressing that it was a "national duty" and anyone failing to enlist would be dragged out of their home. Those who resented joining this force referred to it as the "Unpopular Army" (*Al-Jaysh Al-la Sha'bi*) (Bengio 1998: 151). In March 1984, armed militiamen sealed off working class neighborhoods in Baghdad to take men into the Popular Army. On the road from Basra to Baghdad, military checkpoints were established to check the IDs of Iraqis old enough to be drafted. One account describes how Iraqis began flee from their cars as they approached the checkpoints for fear of being drafted or found out that they had deserted. Those who fled were often shot on the spot (Farouk-Sluglett *et al.* 1984: 27).

Reforming the Republican Guard

According to Quinlivan, a ruler creates parallel militaries to counterweight the regular armed forces that can turn against the regime through a coup. Second, this military dualism allows the leadership to expand a much larger regular army to project its power abroad with greater confidence.

Since the primary duty of the secondary military, a praetorian guard, is to protect the leadership, this force is usually bound to the leader through an exclusive loyalty based on kin, regional origins or common religious belonging. The loyalty between the political leadership and the praetorian guard must be guaranteed by exclusive perks, so it defends the system in which the ruler has given it a privileged status.

Since they serve as the "bodyguards" for the inner core, the parallel military does not have to recruit as many men as the regular army. Nor does it have necessarily to be capable of defeating the regular army in a drawn-out civil war. However, the leadership must also instill into the parallel military a sense of superiority and confidence that it can defeat the regular military during a potential showdown. This parallel military must possess a technological advantage over any given unit in the regular army. Doing so will make any regular army unit think twice about engaging the praetorian guard in a battle for the capital for example. Quinlivan (1999) stressed that such a military unit should be deployed in the regime's center of gravity so as to prevent any disloyal forces engaging in a coup from seizing the vestiges of power. Finally, such an elite force should report to the ruler through a chain of command that bypasses the conventional military hierarchy (ibid.: 135).

In Iraq's case, Baghdad was this center whose critical targets included the radio stations, the bases around the capital, the Presidential Palace or the Ministry of Defense. Hussein perhaps had envisioned that the Popular Army could serve the role of a parallel military force that could defend its regime at its darkest hour. During the Iran–Iraq War the Popular Army proved that it could not even stand up to untrained Iranian men charging against them on the front lines, never mind in a conflict with renegade elements of the Iraqi military. While the Popular Army did allow Hussein the ability to expand a much larger regular army to project its power abroad in the direction of Iran, it was doubtful that this militia could protect the leadership. While the Popular Army was bound to the leadership as a Baath military force, that tie was not based on the more powerful bond of blood or regional origins.

The Republican Guard (*Al-Haris Al-Jamhuri*) on the other hand had been created as a praetorian force based in Baghdad to protect the military officers in Arif's ruler regime from the military itself. This force inherited from the Arif regime allowed Hussein to develop an existing institution into his elite parallel military, serving as a screen between the Iraqi Army and Baghdad. It reported directly to Hussein, bypassing the military chain of command. While its small numbers did not necessarily mean it could defeat the regular Army in a drawn-out conflict, Hussein did invest the Guard with a sense of superiority and a vast array of superior weaponry to prove it could defeat a single regular unit during a coup attempt. The loyalty between Hussein and the Guard was ensured through the common regional origins and sectarian belonging of its men, predominantly Sunni

Arabs from the north of Baghdad. The Guard had been recruited primarily from members of Arif's Al-Jumayla, but the Baathists were able to win over even those officers who came from that tribe.

At the outbreak of the Iran–Iraq War, the Republican Guards consisted of a single brigade that did not take part in the initial offensive into Khuzestan or Qasr-e Shirin in 1980. The Guards' primary duty at that time was to protect Hussein, thus they were stationed within the confines of the capital (Huggins 1994: 31). The Guard first participated in the fighting a month after the war during the battle for Khorramshahr. A brigade from the Iraqi Special Forces and the Republican Guards brigade were given a crash course in urban warfare and then dispatched to the front where they helped take the town by October 24, 1980. Once they completed this mission, the Republican Guard returned to Baghdad in order to continue protecting the leadership (Quinlivan 1999: 145). However, as the regular Army's performance deteriorated on the battlefield, Hussein would eventually have to institute another military transformation by expanding the Guard and eventually deploying them to the front.

The war of attrition

The war evolved into a *harb al-istinzaf*, or "a war of attrition," as Iraq's defense rested in its ability to field an army and sustain casualties from the advancing Iranian forces. The Iraqi military was tasked with maintaining a defensive war that would inflict enough casualties on enemy forces and destroying its economic structure to force Iran to accept a ceasefire. During these battles, the armed forces were to prevent the Iranian military from seizing any further Iraqi territory in the south and the north and blocking the offensives campaigns to take the city of Basra. However, this was precisely the kind of war that was ultimately to the advantage of Iran due to its larger population base.

In order to break the stalemate, in early 1984, Iran launched the Val Fajr campaigns, which attempted to split the Iraqi forces on the war front. The northern areas around Kirkuk were defended by the First Army Corps, and the approach to Baghdad was guarded by the Second Army Corps, whose strength was increased to ten divisions or 100,000 troops. Most of the intense fighting of the Val Fajr campaigns occurred in the southern theater. The Fourth Army Corps guarded the areas between Qurna and Amara. The Corps had ten divisions, protecting the periphery of the marshes as well as the Basra–Baghdad road, and was commanded by Hisham Sabah Al-Fakhri. The Third Army Corps guarded the rear areas around Basra and was commanded by Mahir Abd Al-Rashid, the former commander of the First Corps in the north (O'Ballance 1988: 142–4). Abd Al-Rashid's rotation demonstrated one of Hussein's tactics of preventing officers from remaining in command of military units for extended periods to prevent them from cultivating a power base.

The Iranian thrusts brought their forces within range of Basra, while they opened up another front in shallow marshes where the Tigris and Euphrates rivers meet. On February 22, 1984, Iraqi positions were struck north of the Huwayza Marshes. The Iraqis had not manned these positions as they thought that the Iranians were unable to launch a large scale attack through the swampy terrain, but the Iranian forces used thousands of small boats to move through the marshes and disembarked onto dry land near the town of Baida (Pellitiere and Douglas 1990: 14–17). However, the ability of the Iranians to launch surprise attacks like the aforementioned assault would become more challenging after the restoration of Iraq–US diplomatic ties in 1984. Afterwards the US shared intelligence with the Iraqi armed forces on Iranian military deployments, depriving the latter of the element of surprise in selected battles. Information from Airborne Warning and Control aircraft (AWACs) based in Saudi Arabia and US satellites allowed the Iraqis to detect the movements of Iranian warplanes and prepare for Iranian human-wave assaults (Ra'iss Tousi 1997: 54). For example, during the most significant fighting in March 1984 when Iranian forces attempted to cross once again the Huwayza Marshes, the Iraqi forces were waiting for them due to the intelligence information they had received.

Hisham Al-Fakhri of the Fourth Corps led the Iraqi forces to repulse this Iranian offensive, as did Abd Al-Rashid when the Third Corps came under fire. The Iranian military withdrew to the Iraqi Majnun Islands, the location of undeveloped oilfields and were successful in holding them. In this instance political considerations hindered the course of combat. Rather than ordering the generals to move against the Islands, the political leadership halted the fighting to prevent more Iraqi casualties, a constant factor preoccupying Hussein. The Battle of Majnun resulted in 9,000 Iraqi casualties, but yielded close to 40,000 Iranian casualties (Cordesman and Wagner 1990: 514). In April 1984, the Iraqi President, believing that the Iraqi military demonstrated that it can withstand any Iranian offensive, repeated his offer to negotiate with the Iranians, but was rebuffed. By the end of 1984, the Iraqi military had lost control of the Majnun Islands, as well as a few swaths of territory (ibid.: 202).

A renewed Iranian offensive began the following year on March 11, 1985 with forces approaching the Baghdad–Basra road, threatening to cut the country in half. The Iraqis prepared a counter-attack planned by General Sultan Hashim and General Abd Al-Jawad Dhanun, the Army Chief of Staff. General Hisham Sabah Al-Fakhri, promoted to Assistant Army Chief of Staff for Operations, was responsible for the northern flank of the battlefield, while General Saadi Tuma Abbas Al-Jaburi, Assistant Army Chief of Staff for Training was delegated to the south. Further political interference emerged during this campaign as the counter-attack was only implemented after it met the approval of Saddam Hussein (O'Ballance 1988: 162). The Iraqis were successful in blunting the attack and

Table 8.1 The Iraqi military high command 1985

Post	Name
Commander-in-Chief of the armed forces	Field-Marshal Saddam Hussein
Defense Minister	Gen. Adnan Khayrallah Talfa
Minister of State for Military Affairs	Gen. Abd Al-Jabbar Shanshal
The Chief of Staff	Lt. Gen. Nizar Al-Khazraji
Armed forces Assistant Chief of Staff for Training	Lt. Gen. Saadi Tuma Abbas Al-Jaburi
Armed forces Assistant Chief of Staff for Operations	Lt. Gen. Thabit Sultan Ahmad
Armed forces Assistant Chief of Staff for Administration and Supplies	Lt. Gen. Abd Al-Sattar Al-Muini
Commander of the Republican Guard	Maj. Gen. Iyad Futayyih Khalifa Al-Rawi
Head of political guidance in the Defense Ministry	Maj. Gen. Abd Al-Jabbar Muhsin
Supervisor of military industries	Col. Husayn Kamil Al-Majid
Head of the President's bodyguard unit	Lt. Gen. Sabah Mirza
Air Force and air defense commander	Lt. Gen. Hamid Shaaban Al-Takriti
Commander of the Naval and Coastal Defense Forces	Maj. Gen. Abd Muhammad Abdallah
Commander of the First Special Army Corps (*"Allah Akbar Forces"*)	Lt. Gen. Kamal Jamil Abbud
Commander of the First Army Corps	Lt. Gen. Husayn Rashid Wandawi Al-Takriti
Commander of the Second Army Corps	Lt. Gen. Shawkat Ahmad Atta
Commander of the Third Army Corps	Maj. Gen. Dia Al-Din Jamal
Commander of the Fourth Army Corps	Maj. Gen. Muhammad Abd Al-Qadir
Commander of the Fifth Army Corps	Maj. Gen. Abd Al-Aziz Ibrahim Al-Hadithi
Commander of the Sixth Army Corps	Maj. Gen. Sultan Hashim Ahmad
Commander of the Seventh Corps	Lt. Gen. Mahir Abd Al-Rashid

Source: Bengio (1987: 455).

inflicting massive casualties on the Iranians. The counter-attack was deemed the Battle of Badr, named after the victory of the Prophet Muhammad's army over his enemies, and Hussein used this battle to bolster his own military credentials.

The expanded role of the Air Force, ballistic missiles and weapons of mass destruction (WMDs)

Hussein's limited role for the Air Force factored in his fear of dissension within this branch. The Air Force had played a significant role in most of Iraq's coups, and just one dissident pilot strafing the Presidential Palace during war time could have served as a signal for the military to revolt. A number of officers in the Air Force were not from his network of loyal clans and tribes and were not politically reliable (Tripp 2000: 242). In September 1983 for example, reports from diplomatic sources revealed that a coup was purportedly attempted by a group within the Air Force resulting in the execution of four officers (O'Ballance 1988: 123).

Due to these considerations, Hussein discouraged inter-service cooperation so that the Air Force and the Army could not coordinate a coup. On the battlefield, this arrangement resulted in the ground forces failing to work effectively with the Iraqi Air Force. By the time information from ground commanders on the battlefield filtered through the various political circles to the Air Force, it would be too late for them to perform in an effective manner. An example of such failures occurred during the battle in the Marshes in 1984 when the Iranian military was able to build a massive 17 kilometer pontoon bridge without Iraqi aircraft taking any actions to disrupt this effort (Heller 1994: 46). The Iraqi Air Force for the most part failed to achieve air superiority over Iran and failed to provide air support for Iraqi forces on the front lines.

Part of Iraq's war strategy after 1984 included the expanded use of its Air Force, long range ballistic missiles and battlefield chemical weapons to force Iran to accept a ceasefire. While the Air Force's performance during combined-arms operations in combat was lackluster, it was entrusted with destroying Iran's economic infrastructure. In March 1984, the Air Force utilized newly delivered French aircraft and the anti-ship Exocet missiles and targeted a Greek tanker, attacking a civilian ship for the first time in the Gulf. In April 1984, Iran retaliated by attacking an Indian freighter destined for Iraq and a Kuwaiti and Saudi tanker in May for their support of the Iraqi war cause, and Iraq escalated by conducting air raids on oil facilities on Iran's Kharg Island in 1984 and August 1985 (Nonneman 2004: 179). The Iraqi Air Force later acquired the capability of mid-air refueling, allowing them to strike facilities on southern Iranian islands of Sirri and Larak. The continued attacks eventually cut Iranian oil exports by 50 percent and the Air Force continued to attack targets related to Iran's oil industry to cripple its economy.

Iraq employed unconventional means of warfare to sap the morale of Iran. Iraq acquired Soviet Scud ballistic missiles to strike at Iranian cities beginning in 1985 in what was termed the "war of the cities," resulting in Iranian retaliation with similar attacks against Iraqi cities. The missile attacks were often inaccurate and failed to destroy anything of military value, serving as psychological warfare to break the morale of the other side. The Iraqi military first deployed chemical weapons in 1983, and expanded their use in 1984. The use of chemical weapons in 1983 was preceded by a warning from the Iraqi high command that it would employ "modern weapons" and warned Iranians "if you execute the orders of Khomeini's regime ... your death will be certain because this time we will use a weapon that will destroy any moving creature on the fronts" (BBC/SWB/ME, April 14, 1983: A/7–8). As the military historian Richard Holmes wrote in his work, *Acts of War*, chemical weapons are "great fear producers" and during World War I they, "inspired a fear that was all out of proportion to the damage done" (Holmes 2004: 212). During the Iran–Iraq War these weapons had little tactical value, and at times the munitions would fly back in the Iraqis' direction. Like the Scud missiles these weapons were psychological, wreaking collective panic and havoc among the Iranian forces as they disfigured their victims, causing a break-down of morale.

Iran's final offensives against Iraq 1986–1987

The battles for Faw and Mehran

Through the use of static defenses, the Iraqi military had been able to repulse the continuous Iranian offensives and inflict casualties on their forces. However, in February 1986, Iraqi Popular Army units, notorious for their unreliability in combat, were overcome by a surprise amphibious assault. The Iranians had rafted across the Shatt on the night of February 10, 1986 during a rainstorm, and the Iraqi commander, perhaps out of fear of punishment, or believing that he could repulse the attack, failed to report promptly to Baghdad that the Iranians had secured a beachhead. Once the news reached political headquarters, Iranian forces had begun to fortify their position on the Peninsula they had just captured, giving them control over the Shatt Al-Arab waterway.

The dynamics within the totalitarian military manifested themselves after this capture. Hussein's initial response to the loss of Faw was a polit-ical one, as the Peninsula was insignificant according to military comman-ders, however it did represent the symbolic loss of Iraqi territory. On February 22, twelve days after Faw fell, the Iraqis had gathered three division-strength columns, each one commanded by one of Iraq's best corps commanders: Hisham Al-Fakhri, Mahir Abd Al-Rashid and Saadi Tuma Abbas Al-Jaburi (Pollack 2002: 218). All three had taken part in

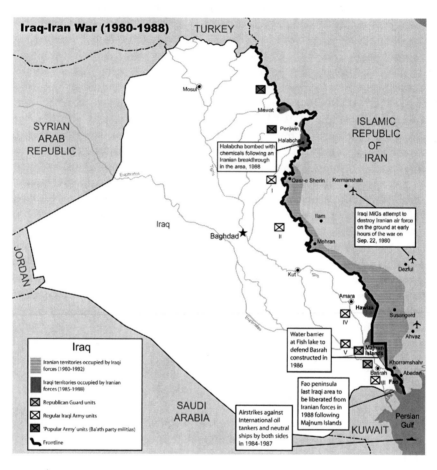

Iraq–Iran War (1980–1988)   TURKEY

SYRIAN
ARAB
REPUBLIC

ISLAMIC
REPUBLIC
OF
IRAN

Mosul

Mawat

Penjwin

Halabcha

Halabcha bombed with
chemicals following an
Iranian breakthrough
in the area, 1988

Qasr-e Sherin   Kermanshah

Ilam

Iraq

Baghdad

Mehran

Iraqi MiGs attempt to
destroy Iranian air force
on the ground at early
hours of the war on
Sep. 22, 1980

JORDAN

Kut

Dezful

Amara

Hawiza

Susangerd

Ahvaz

Water barrier
at Fish lake to
defend Basrah
constructed in
1986

Majnun
Islands

Khorramshahr

Abadan

Basrah

Fao

Fao peninsula
last Iraqi area to
be liberated from
Iranian forces in
1988 following
Majnum Islands

Iraq

Iranian territories occupied by Iraqi
forces (1980–1982)

Iraqi territories occupied by Iranian
forces (1985–1988)

Republican Guard units

Regular Iraqi Army units

'Popular Army' units (Ba'ath party militias)

Frontline

SAUDI
ARABIA

Airstrikes against
International oil
tankers and neutral
ships by both sides
in 1984–1987

KUWAIT

Persian
Gulf

Map 8.1 The Iran–Iraq War.

repulsing the Iranian offensive during the Battle of Badr. On the following day the Iraqi President personally ordered General Rashid to take command of the central column, with some detachments of the Republican Guard dispatched from the capital (O'Ballance 1988: 178). As the Guard moved towards the Peninsula, flood conditions made it harder for their tanks to advance, which were mauled by Iranian artillery on their side of the Shatt. The counter-attack successfully pinned down the Iranians on the Peninsula and prevented them from moving north to take any more territory. However, the battle proved to be a fiasco for the Iraqi forces due to their losses. Out of the three Republican Guards brigades that took part in the offensive, one was nearly eliminated (Huggins 1994: 31).

The entire battle from the counter-attack to its cessation was planned factoring in political pressure from the central leadership. Hussein forbade the commanders to send their men into hand-to-hand combat with the Iranians as they would incur excessive casualties. The political gain of Faw could not have been offset against the political loss of high casualties, resulting in further loss of morale in the Iraqi public. Hussein made a similar call when he failed to permit the Iraqis from retaking the Majnun Islands. As soldiers came back from the front, news of the defeat could not be hidden from the public. The setbacks challenged Hussein's public persona as a "military tactician." The further loss of Iraqi territory raised the specter of the military and the public's lack of confidence in Hussein's ability to defend Iraq. The Faw success demonstrated that the political leadership's strategy of remaining on the defensive in order to bring Iran to the negotiating table was futile.

On the international level, the failure to recapture to Faw was covered extensively in the media, with one source describing the coverage similar to the affect it had after the Tet Offensive against US forces in Vietnam, portraying the loss as more disastrous than was warranted (Pellitiere and Douglas 1990: 30). After the string of defeats there was speculation in Western circles that the Iraqi military was on the verge of collapsing. This collapse may have been imminent were it not for a series of military reforms after Iraq's defeat in the battle for Mehran.

The defeat at Faw further strained relations between Hussein and the Iraqi officers. Hussein's orders to prevent Mahir Abd al-Rashid from continuing the advance against the Iranian forces in Faw led to an apparent confrontation between the Iraqi President and the Major General. Abd Al-Rashid's rise can be evidenced from his origins, a Takriti whose daughter married the Iraqi leader's youngest son Qusay. Abd Al-Rashid's insider status allowed him to be brazen enough to tell international journalists that it was Hussein who prevented him from prosecuting the attack against Iranian forces in Faw. This admission followed a pattern where Abd Al-Rashid used the foreign and domestic media to boost his military reputation. He had made it a point to highlight his personal contribution in leading the Third Corps in blunting the Iranian offensives in 1984 that forced them to fall back onto the Majnun Islands. (Later in the war he would go on to recapture the Islands emerging as a national hero.) When a delegation of Kuwaiti parliamentarians visited Iraq after the Faw battle, the General admitted that it was a debacle where the Iraqis had suffered "huge casualties," which Hussein had forbidden any of his military commanders from doing publically. Abd Al-Rashid also admitted that political intervention had prevented his forces from marching further onto Iranian forces lodged in the Peninsula stating that he was waiting "until the Iraqi leadership allowed him to begin the liberation" (Chubin and Tripp 1988: 118–19). He also stated to his audience that they, "like the Iraqis, had the right to wonder why the final onslaught was delayed." The Kuwaitis present heaped praises on the General, angering Hussein who sought to depict only himself as the military genius behind the war. To prevent an alternative popular war hero from emerging, the Iraqi President had called Abd Al-Rashid from the front to Baghdad with the hope of disgracing him. However, in one of the most prominent incidents of the soldiers questioning Hussein's military judgment, the officers under General Abd al-Rashid's command threatened to what nearly amounted to a mutiny in the Third Corps. The President allowed Abd Al-Rashid to keep his position even though he must have felt threatened by the General's growing popularity, as he was from the inner core of Hussein's regime and a talented military commander. Abd Al-Rashid's "punishment" would have to come later after the conclusion of the war.

In order to reassert his military prowess, on May 12 Hussein ordered his military units to invade the Iranian border town of Mehran near the Iraqi central front in the hope that the Iranians would be willing to exchange it for Faw (Chubin and Tripp 1988: 118). The attack was described as a "bold new strategy" and "a daring expression of the Iraqi leadership's political decision" (ibid.: 64). This attack was the first offensive into Iranian territory since their defeat in 1982. Even though Iraqi commanders were hesitant about the strategic value of such an attack, Hussein used the capture of the town to portray himself as a military genius in the Iraqi media.

Major General Adin Tawfiq, Commander of the Second Army Corps, realized that his troops in Mehran could be exposed to Iranian armed forces deploying on the strategic heights surrounding the town and sought to take those positions. However, Tawfiq's units were heavy in armor and did not have the infantry to fight in mountainous terrain. Saddam Hussein, in another demonstration of political considerations interfering with military operations, rejected his plan as it would have required using several extra brigades from the strategic reserves (Cordesman and Wagner 1990: 28). On June 10, the forces under Tawfiq's command came under attack and requested air support. Hussein's policy of prohibiting generals from communicating directly with the Air Force as one of his pillars of coup-proofing resulted in the request for air support at Mehran being routed through Baghdad. The political leadership belatedly gave its approval for the Iraqi Air Force to deploy, but the Iraqi ground forces had already retreated from the town. After the loss of Mehran, Hussein blamed the army commanders for this defeat, particularly Major General Adin Tawfiq, who was recalled from the front to the capital and presumably executed (Abbas 1989: 223). A government communiqué declared that the battle had ended because "our brave armed forces have decided to evacuate the Mehran area" (quoted in Al-Khafaji 1988: 36). However, these communications had little effect on the officers who realized that the responsibility for the losses at Faw and Mehran lay with the political leadership.

The July 1986 Baath Conference and the reorganization of the military

After the string of losses, Hussein realized that he would have to abandon his micro-management of the battlefield and allow the military more freedom in conducting the war. Throughout the first six years of the war Hussein had cultivated patron–client relationships within the various armed forces, allowing him to control and subordinate branches such as the regular Army, the Popular Army, the Republican Guard and Military Intelligence. The loss of Faw and Mehran had political ramifications that would alter the relationship between the political authority and the military. The taste of defeat by senior officers in the Republican Guard compelled them to sympathize with the officers in the regular Army. The solidarity of the officers across two parallel military institutions undermined Hussein's divide and conquer tactics among the services of the armed forces. The disenchanted officers, including members from Hussein's own clan and tribe, challenged the conduct of the war according to political concerns. As the Iranian threat loomed on the battlefield, a sense of corporate professionalism developed among the Iraqi officers, a network that challenged or overlapped with the rival network established by Hussein based on patronage and kin relationships. The Faw defeat resulted in the loss of one-third of the Guards' forces, further weakening Hussein's credibility as a military commander who could dictate tactics to his generals. Second, the casualties among the Guards targeted the insiders in Hussein's system, those closest to the regime recruited on common tribal, town and rural origins, and thus they found common cause with the regular Army.

The military had to find a way to articulate in diplomatic terms their collective interests without challenging Hussein in a way where he would perceive that they were conspiring against him. The Extraordinary Congress of the Baath convened in July 1986, with simultaneous discussions held with the Iraqi general staff, dealt with the military setbacks and gave the generals a venue to express their concerns. Rather than confronting the Iraqi leader in a hostile manner, the Congress provided an opportunity for the officers to renegotiate the implicit contract between the ruler and his commanders (Chubin and Tripp 1988: 118). This new contract was based on the officers being granted permission to conduct a war on their own terms to protect their nation and the leader, as well as a system from which they had benefitted materially.

The first task was to convince the Iraqi leader that a static, defensive war reacting against the Iranian offensives along the border was ineffective and that the Iraqis would need to take the initiative by engaging in a more aggressive mobile strategy. After the losses in the summer of 1986, the Iranians would certainly conduct an all-out attack on Basra during January or February 1987, when the rains of winter limited the mobility of Iraq's armor and visibility of their aircraft. Pre-empting the Iranian offensive would require a change in strategy where the military would not merely content itself with holding the Iranian forces back, but inflicting a serious tactical defeat on the enemy. Such a shift required a transformation of the Iraqi military, which had primarily relied on armored units, to one that could effectively deploy mechanized infantry as well. At the Congress, the officers asked for a call-up of additional conscripts that could fill the ranks of the mechanized infantry units. Hussein, due to his political priority of insulating the Iraqi public from huge losses in lives on the front, had discouraged infantry operations as they were too costly in terms of personnel. However, the Iraqi armored forces were at a disadvantage when fighting Iran's lightly armed infantry, some of whom were willing to give up their lives to take out Iraqi tanks (Pellitiere 1992: 106–7). Combining bomber aircraft, helicopters, tanks, infantry and artillery, the officers argued they could strike a decisive blow against the Iranian military. In the past, such combined-arms operations were discouraged due to political reasons. Hussein had encouraged rivalry among the services of the military to prevent a corporate sense of identity that could turn against him in a potential coup. To conduct these combined-arms tactics, the officers had to convince Hussein to allow cooperation between the military services and devolve command and control authority to the commanders on the field.

In the Iraqi President's calculations, an Iranian victory seemed a more imminent threat to his personal rule as opposed to a military coup. Hussein ultimately surrendered operational control, depriving him of the ability to orchestrate the war from the capital. He gave in to all of their demands. The officers were allowed to concentrate on their professional task of defeating the Iranian military, with the ability to make independent decisions on the front. They were promised access to funds and armaments as they needed to prosecute the war. The practice of constant rotations of senior officers to prevent them from establishing a power base would be curtailed. The leadership in Baghdad also removed the political commissars who had been formerly assigned to all Iraqi units above battalion strength. Initiative on the battlefield was rewarded over political loyalty or blood relations to Hussein, and incompetent officers who were friends or relatives were purged. The Iraqi Air Force, which Hussein feared could be used in a coup against him, was allowed to take part in fighting on the war front in coordination with the ground forces (Axelgard 1988: 54).

While Hussein relinquished military decision-making powers to the generals, they still operated in a totalitarian-penetration system where he maintained an intricate system of control. The hands-off approach of the political leadership, resulted in a fair degree of de-politicization of the military, but Hussein still retained some of the elements he used to protect his leadership. The security apparatus continued to monitor the armed forces for any hint of political subversion. Parallel military institutionalism still existed and in fact, the Republican Guards was expanded, increasing from six to sixteen brigades, with close to 25,000 men to serve a more prominent role on the front (Chubin and Tripp 1988: 118). Furthermore, Hussein still cultivated patronage networks through the armed forces.

With these changes, several personalities emerged to prominence within the military. Defense Minister General Adnan Khayrallah Talfa served as the de facto representative of the military within the political leadership. He was the only member of the nine-person Revolutionary Command Council (RCC) to have served in the armed forces as a former tank officer. As a cousin, brother-in-law and childhood friend of Hussein, his power was connected to the political leadership through blood. In the RCC, Talfa encouraged his colleagues to respond positively to the military's requests, emerging as a liaison between the armed forces and the Party civilians. He also served as a convenient scapegoat, since if the reforms failed to produce any positive results on the front, Hussein could blame Talfa who had more or less directed these changes.

Additionally, senior officers were given posts on the National Defense Council a powerful body only subordinate to the RCC (McKnight 1991: 95). Iraq's Deputy Chief of Staff for Operations, General Husayn Rashid Wandawi Al-Takriti (a Kurd from Takrit) presided over a competent general staff. Senior field commanders such as Generals Hisham Al-Fakhri, Saadi Tuma Abbas Al-Jaburi, Mahir Abd Al-Rashid and Iyad Futayyih Al-Rawi also began to emerge to prominence. These generals began the instruction of combined-arms tactics to their troops and encouraged junior commanders to be aggressive and react more quickly without political approval.

The expansion of the Republican Guard

While Hussein had expanded the regular Army in 1975, he only did so with an opposing force, the Popular Army, to keep its power in check. The Popular Army however proved too weak to counter the Army particularly during the formers' spectacular defeats on the battlefield in the early 1980s. The Republican Guards, at the size of one brigade was developed into a force could take part in the war effort. By 1986 it had expanded from one brigade into seven. The expansion of the Republican Guard as a parallel military was characterized by better weapons, pay and training, resulting in a force with greater confidence and a collective self-esteem. Members of the regular Army became aware of their older weapons, less pay and training, and tended to feel inferior to the Republican Guard. However, the political dividends of increasing the strength of this parallel military outweighed the bruised egos among officers of the regular Army. Hussein had already relinquished a fair degree of operational freedom to the commanders on the battlefield and to counter this freedom of the regular Army, he needed a politically reliable force. Developing the elite Special Forces within the regular Army would only have strengthened the domestic balance of power in favor of the generals. The Guards however evolved as Hussein's personal praetorian guards. They were subordinated within the Iraqi leader's intelligence network, reporting to the Special Security Apparatus as opposed to the Ministry of Defense, ensuring that the Guards ultimately answered to Hussein. However, Hussein sought to project an image of the Guards as a force beyond mere bodyguards for the President. In one statement he said, "special guards who do not fight in defense of Iraq in Sulaymaniyya, Basra and the Misan borders, cannot defend the regime in the Presidential Palace" admitting that they would be delegated to defending both Iraq and the regime (BBC/SWB/ME, September 7, 1987: A/3–4).

After 1986, the Guard expanded from seven to twenty-five brigades organized into six divisions due to an increase in volunteers. With Hussein's approval, the general staff organized the Republican Guards into a corps formation, the Republican Guard Forces Command (RGFC). At the corps level, the Guards were fully integrated into the Army, while still serving its role of protecting the President when it was not deployed to the front. The General Staff, led by Deputy Chief of Staff for Operations General Husayn Rashid Wandawi Al-Takriti, had the best regular army divisions train the Guards in combined-arms operations and conducting large, corps-level offensive ground maneuvers. The leadership also lavished these units with the most advanced Soviet T-72 tanks and BMP-1 infantry fighting vehicles.

However these reforms would take a while before they would have any effect on the battlefield and by the close of 1986, the situation looked dire from the view of the political leadership. The Iraqi forces had continued to fortify the defenses around Basra and were able to prevent the city from falling to Iran's military, but the Iranian advances were relentless and the Iraqis could not strike a decisive blow to prevent the attacks. The situation in the north was equally distressing. While the Iraqi military was fighting the KDP and Iranian forces in the north, Jalal Talabani of the PUK had sought a settlement with the government in Baghdad. By January 1985, the negotiations had failed over the issue of control of security forces in the Kurdish autonomous region, control of the Kirkuk oilfields and the issue of financial autonomy. The PUK entered into an Iranian supported coalition comprising the KDP, leftist movements and Shia dissident militias. Iraqi military forces had to be diverted to pacify the Kurdish regions, but by the fall of 1986 the armed forces had lost control of the mountainous countryside to the KDP, who had occupied areas from Zakho to Barazan, and the PUK had taken over territories from Koy Sanjak to Qalat Diza, limiting the presence of Iraqi armed forces to the urban centers and oil facilities. The revolt in the north led to a crackdown on Kurds in the military who were systematically weeded out. The Shia were rewarded for their loyalty but towards 1987, all the commanders of the eight army corps and the Navy and Air Force were still in the hands of Sunni Arabs (Baram 1989: 466).

The Karbala campaigns and the second battle of Al-Basra

On January 9, 1987 Iran launched Operation Karbala Five to follow up its success at Faw with a massive assault against Basra, the largest offensive to take the city since 1982. Iranian forces had penetrated the first and second Iraqi defensive arcs and on January 12, Hussein visited the front and ordered more Republican Guard forces forward (O'Ballance 1988: 179). While it would appear that the leader was still seeking to portray himself as the supreme military commander, this was a rare visit to the front compared to his frequent visits during previous battles. The Operation was terminated by Iran on February 26 after failing to capture Basra. The Iraqi state continued to spin its defeats by declaring that the territory lost during this fighting was nothing more than "worthless pockets" of land (Al-Khafaji 1988: 36). However, the land that Iran held around eastern Basra, the Majnun Islands and the Faw Peninsula were hardly worthless, a fact not lost upon the Iraqi military. The setbacks were blamed on General Abd Al-Jawad Dhanun, the Iraqi Chief of Staff, who was dismissed. General Talia Khalil Duri, Commander of the Third Corps was also blamed for the setbacks and was replaced within a matter of days with Lieutenant General Dia Al-Din Jamal. Duri was transferred to the command of the Fifth Corps in the north (Cordesman and Wagner 1990: 320). This reshuffling demonstrated that Hussein's policy of constantly rotating officers had not been completely abandoned. A number of officers in the Third and Seventh Corps charged with defending Basra were either purged or even executed (ibid.: 252). While Hussein allowed a degree of freedom to the generals on the frontlines, the punitive measures for failure had not been removed.

The Iraqi forces dithered before conducting a counter-attack. Apparently debates emerged once again between the generals and the political leadership, with the latter concerned about the casualties a counter-attack would entail. Indicative of the reforms that had been implemented, the commanders were allowed to launch an offensive. On March 1 the attack began under the new commander of the Third Corps, Lieutenant General Dia Al-Din Jamal, in coordination with the commander of the Iraqi Air Force, Air Marshal Hamid Shaaban Al-Takriti, one of the most prominent examples of aircraft used in an aggressive support role since the war began. Furthermore, the military reforms allowed intelligence gathered from aircraft to be transferred rapidly to field commanders by reducing the bureaucratic barriers of the past (ibid.: 356). After the counter-attack, Iraqi forces had taken back one-third of the territory lost to Iran during the Karbala Five campaign (Axelgard 1988: 55). Just as in the battle of Faw however, the Iraqi Army could blunt the Iranian offensives, but took heavier losses. Nevertheless, the battle served as a victory for the Iraqis. Basra, Iraq's second largest city did not fall, and the generals, freed from political fetters, demonstrated that they could hold out against the waves of Iranian infantry. General Mahir Abd Al-Rashid as usual sought out the media's attention for his role in the fighting and claimed that the Iraqi forces under his command had inflicted a defeat against the Iranians or in his terms, "we harvested them." Just as after the battle of Faw, Abd Al-Rashid was bold enough to criticize indirectly the political leadership, hinting that it was holding him back from scoring a decisive victory (Pelli-tiere and Douglas 1990: 40).

In the north, the Iranian Karbala Six and Seven offensives in March 1987 pushed back elements of Iraq's First Army Corps, bringing the Iranian military forces within 100 kilometers of Kirkuk. The Iraqi Kurds continued with their attacks forcing the Iraqis to bring in more troops to stem further Iranian advances. In the same month Ali Hassan Al-Majid was given the position of commander of the Baath Party Northern Command. His appointment heralded the Anfal Campaign, a systematic effort by the state to eliminate the Kurdish opposition through sustained, institutionalized repression against the Kurds, both combatants and civilians. Al-Majid's appointment demonstrated that one of the totalitarian-penetration tactics of the state, political dominance over military affairs, had not been dismantled completely. With Iraqi forces barely able to repulse Iranian advances in the south and with the continued failure to retake Faw, the Anfal Campaign provided an opportunity to demonstrate to the military that Hussein could still bring about success on the battle-field. In this case the Iraqi military returned to its historic rule of maintaining internal security, albeit in an unprecedented brutal fashion. Al-Majid was not only Hussein's cousin, but also a member of the Regional Command of the Baath Party. Hussein's orders placed all military forces in the north out of the jurisdiction of the Ministry of Defense and into the hands of a Party organization. Al-Majid, as their commander, reported directly to the Iraqi President, thus bypassing any military chain of command. His appointment also demonstrated how kin networks and loyalty to the Party were important criteria for directing the military campaigns in the north. This period witnessed the mass destruction of villages, the disappearance of citizens, as well as the use of chemical weapons against pockets of Kurdish resistance, both combatants and civilians. In May 1987, as Iraqi forces managed to halt Iranian thrusts in the south, Iran launched Operation Karbala Ten in the north. The offensive was launched with Iranian units and Iraqi Kurdish militias where they made advances in the direction of Iraq's oil facilities in the vicinity of Kirkuk, but by mid-1987, Iraq's military had prevented any further Iranian gains.

During the fighting in 1987 aircraft were employed with more frequency against Iranian ground forces. While its losses were considerable, the Air Force did play an active role over the battlefield in checking Iranian offensives. Ironically, an action taken by the Iraqi Air Force in the Gulf would inadvertently aid the Iraqi war effort. On May 17, 1987, an Iraqi aircraft fired two Exocet missiles at the *USS Stark*, killing thirty-seven

American naval personnel on board. However, US President Reagan blamed Iran for escalating the tensions in the Gulf. The Iraqi President apologized for the incident and declared that the attack was accidental and would not affect US–Iraq relations. Iran argued that the attack on the *USS Stark* was not an accident but an Iraqi attempt to force the US to take a more active role in the Gulf. As a matter of fact, the attack had this very effect and Iraq had succeeded in bringing a superpower into the conflict.

Iraq's counteroffensive: 1988

After the Iranian offensive for Basra failed, the leadership realized that their foes had reached the end of their ability to continue their campaigns into Iraq. Saddam Hussein's goals expanded from ensuring the survival of his regime to seizing the initiative and driving the Iranian forces from Iraqi territory. Since 1984, the Iraqi armed forces had at their command superiority in technology and arms, in addition to an impressive logistics network. Nevertheless, it was not until 1988 that Iraq began to score decisive victories on the battlefield. In terms of arms, between 1986 and 1988 the Iraqi military received more than 2,000 tanks, including 800 of the most advanced Soviet model, the T-72, 300 fighter aircraft and close to 300 Scud missiles. By April 1988, the Iraqi armed forces was in a position to launch its offensive with 5,000 tanks, 4,500 armored fighting vehicles, 5,500 artillery pieces, 420 helicopters and 720 combat aircraft at its disposal (Mesbahi 1993: 89).

After defending Basra in early 1987, the Iraqi military began preparing to recapture all Iranian held Iraqi territory. In the desert behind Basra, these forces practiced rehearsal drills to seize areas such as the Faw Peninsula and the Majnun Islands. On April 17, 1988, the Iraqi military began the offensive to retake the Peninsula. Both the Iraqi Seventh Corps and the Republican Guard were involved in the attack. The Republican Guard Madina Al-Munawara Armored Division, Hammurabi Armored Division and the Baghdad Infantry Division attacked the Peninsula from the south, while the Seventh Infantry and Sixth Armored Divisions of the Seventh Corps led by General Abd Al-Rashid attacked from the north. During the battle, various services of the armed forces worked in tandem with fixed and rotary wing aircraft, armor, artillery and mechanized infantry, cooperating in a manner that was unprecedented due to Hussein's former policy of encouraging rivalries among the services. The Peninsula fell to the Iraqi forces within thirty-five hours, well short of the five days expected to retake Faw, a rapid success due to the military advancing without permission from the political headquarters in Baghdad.

By May 25 the Iraqi military began the first in a series of four offensives known as the *"Tawakalna Ala Allah"* (In God We Trust) Campaign to retake Iranian held Iraqi territory. Hussein had given the General Staff the necessary freedom to direct this campaign, where his praetorian guard closely fought together with the regular Army units. A month later, the Iraqi military launched an offensive against the Majnun Islands in the Hawayza Marshes. Just as in the battle for Faw, the Iraqi armed forces pounded the Iranian targets with a chemical weapons barrage. Both battles also saw the use of the Republican Guards Twenty-sixth Naval Infantry Brigade, which conducted amphibious assaults. Once they succeeded in controlling Majnun, military engineers constructed pontoon bridges to move Iraqi tanks onto the Islands. The Guards' Hammurabi and Madina Armored Divisions, which took part in the battle of Faw, had also fought in this engagement, supported by the Nebuchadnezzar Infantry Division (Pollack 2002: 227).

While Iraq secured victories in the south, it also used its military to strike at the Kurdish forces allied to Iran, often at horrific loss of civilian life. On March 16, 1988, Iraq fighter planes and helicopters used chemical weapons against the Kurdish town of Halabja in the north of Iraq killing close to 4,000 civilians. The Iraqi government justified the attack after the town had fallen to Iranian forces. By the end of August, Iraqi military forces had captured both the PUK and KDP headquarters securing the state's political control over the north. The Tawakalna campaigns recaptured all of Iraq's territory held by Iranian forces and they even took swaths of Iranian territory to pressure the Islamic Republic to end the war. While some commanders hoped to continue fighting to capture even more Iranian land, at this juncture Hussein intervened in order not to overextend the Iraqi forces (Hashim 2003a: 36).

The US tried to broker an end to the conflict through UN Security Council Resolution 598. Iran refused to accept the Resolution as it did not punish Iraq for initiating the conflict. On July 3, 1988 an American combat vessel in the Gulf, the *USS Vincennes* shot down an Iranian passenger plane killing all 290 people on board. While the US claimed that the plane had been mistaken for a warplane, Iran believed that America was staunchly behind the Iraqi war effort. Iran was faced with two difficult choices. It could either escalate a war that the US seemed to be intricately involved in or accept Resolution 598. It chose the latter. On August 20, 1988, Iran declared a ceasefire.

The Iranian acceptance of the Resolution provided a final opportunity for Saddam Hussein to spin the war as a victory to the Iraqi people and to the military. The Iraqi military had survived eight years of war and at the end held pockets of Iranian territory. Despite several conspiracies, the armed forces remained cohesive during the fighting. The political leadership had to devise some expression of thanks to the military for its role in defeating Iran, without creating war heroes that could later emerge to challenge the Party or take the credit for winning an eight year conflict that the Iraqi President sought to portray as his own victory. The chiefs of staff who devised the victorious campaign strategies at the end of the war were given scant media coverage. There were orchestrated tributes by the generals who paid homage to the "military genius" of Saddam Hussein and attributed the final victory to him. However, the media hungry General Mahir Abd Al-Rashid cultivated extensive media coverage during the post-war celebrations, but the political leadership sought to ensure that he would not emerge as prominent Iraqi hero after the close of the war. Al-Rashid, commander of the Seventh Corps, was put under house arrest in the fall of 1988. The fact that his daughter was married to Qusay Hussein, Saddam's younger son was not enough to save his position, and Qusay's marriage was annulled (Farouk-Sluglett and Sluglett 1990: 22).

While the war was depicted as a victory to domestic Iraq audiences, it ultimately led to Saddam Hussein's undoing. Iraq incurred a $80 billion dollar debt to European and Arab Gulf states. Iraq's oil industry had been destroyed and thus suffered from a decrease in revenue. Promises made by the Iraqi President of greater democratic freedoms after the war were never delivered. Finally, the Iraqi leader realized the difficulty in demobilizing his million man army into the Iraqi work force and could only "find work" for them by engaging in another foreign adventure.

9   Wars, coups, sanctions and collapse 1988–2003

The legacy of the Iran–Iraq War

The totalitarian military model carried over from the Iran–Iraq War and perpetuated itself through the 1991 Gulf War. Despite the reforms that gave greater freedoms to the Iraqi generals to conduct a more aggressive strategy during the last years of the Iran–Iraq War with minimal political interference, such changes had been rolled back during the 1991 and 2003 wars. The dominance of the Party, the numerous parallel militaries and the constant surveillance of multiple competing intelligence agencies that bore all the hallmarks of a totalitarian-penetration military were present during the Gulf Crisis and the 2003 Iraq War as they were prevalent during most of the Iran–Iraq War.

Military coups 1988–1990

The officers had led the military to victory and in the process had forged corporate solidarity through battle. Hussein had managed to control the military through neo-patrimonialism, but this system could be challenged by a defiant officer corps, which certainly came to realize that Hussein's survival during the war was dependent on their fighting ability. Hussein sought to shatter the institutional memory that could emerge in the armed forces and challenge his image as the supreme leader (Tripp 2000: 249). Hussein needed to present an image that their survival was dependent on his patronage and not the other way around.

Hussein sought to pre-empt a series of military coups both real and imagined that would emerge in the aftermath of the Iran–Iraq War. Military coups following the war would have made the Iraqi leader seem weak in the eyes of the regime insiders who were his core constituents. If this in-group saw weakness in his leadership, they could cooperate with a reinvigorated officer corps to overthrow him. To pre-empt such a scenario after the war, the vestiges of the totalitarian-penetration system that Hussein mastered began to re-emerge. Hussein reconsolidated control over the military, taking advantage of the officer corps' expansion as a result of eight years of war. It emerged as a large, heterogeneous force that precluded it from acting as a unified body that could articulate coherent political interests. Hussein used *targhib* and *tarhib* once again, employing patronage, discrimination and fear to manipulate the officers. Iraq's leader promoted certain officers, while demoting, purging and retiring others, and even executing some on even the suspicion that they were plotting against the political center.

Some war heroes were deemed as a threat by Hussein, like General Mahir Abd Al-Rashid, his son-in-law who was placed under house arrest. Abd Al-Rashid's brother, also a general, was killed by the regime. The removal of the two brothers broke their networks with the officers, and served as an example to other officers who sought to cultivate connections within the military. The removal of the generals convinced some officers to plan a coup before further purges would affect them. A plot within the military to assassinate Hussein unfolded in late 1988 and later resulted in the executions of dozens of complicit Republican Guard officers. In November 1988 a plan was discovered to shoot down Saddam Hussein's plane on his way to Egypt. A third coup attempt within the armed forces was discovered in September 1989 (Freedman and Karsh 1993: 29). The Special Security Service foiled a January 1990 coup attempt by elements of the Jabur tribe within the military who tried to assassinate the President (Baram 2002: 222). Each of the failed attempts was followed by a wave of purges and executions. Even Adnan Khayrallah Talfa, the Minister of Defense, who emerged as popular hero after the war, was deemed as a potential threat to Saddam Hussein. Talfa died in May 1989 in a helicopter crash. While it remains uncertain whether his accident was orchestrated by Saddam Hussein or that he had actually died in a sandstorm like Abd Al-Salam Arif, the Iraqi leader was in a position where another possible rival to his leadership had been removed.

The Iraqi leadership also faced difficulties in demobilizing the military after the eight year Iran–Iraq War. From an Iraqi military-centric perspective, the invasion of Kuwait was a tactic of the leadership to engage the Iraqi armed forces in another foreign policy adventure, deflecting the threat of a potential military uprising. Numerous sources have analyzed Hussein's motivations behind invading Kuwait, but there are a few accounts that attribute the action due to a failure to demobilize the military. Pellitiere and Douglas argued that the Iraqi economy had been devastated by the Iran–Iraq War and thus the state could not provide enough jobs for the soldiers. At the same time the economy would not revive until the Iraqi Army became demobilized. The Iraqi leadership saw itself trapped in a vicious dilemma. They wrote: "Taking all this into account, it seems obvious that Iraq invaded its neighbor because it was desperate. It had a million man army that it could not demobilize, because it had no jobs to send the men home to" (Pellitiere and Douglas 1990: 64). Thus invading its wealthy neighbor to the south offered the opportunity to occupy the military, in addition to eliminating Iraq's debts and resolving its economic crisis.

The work of the Iraqi scholar Faleh Abd Al-Jabar argued that the role of the military in internal Iraqi power dynamics was an important factor that led to the invasion (Jabar 1991: 27). The Iraqi government feared that the post-1988 Iraqi Army could turn into an "uncontrollable Leviathan" (Jabar 2003a: 118). The political leadership faced the dilemma of demobilizing the million man army and reintegrating them into Iraqi society as civilians. He cited two crises from the perspective of the ruling establishment: "In one, angry and hungry demobilized soldiers plagued civilian life, causing an upsurge in disorder and criminality. The second possible outcome envisaged an implosion of the army if they were kept under arms for any length of time" (ibid.: 119). In a study he conducted of the Iraqi war generation he gave evidence from an experiment where 50,000 soldiers were demobilized after the war. They found little opportunities returning to civilian life. The behavior was characterized by restiveness and uncontrollable violence, and once demobilized, the soldiers still exhibited a "clannish spirit" among themselves. Jabar wrote: "In the interim period, 1988–1990, the nation teetered on the verge of two options: reform and rehabilitation, or another military adventure" (Jabar 2004: 132). Mohamedou also supported the argument that the Iraqi military had to be taken into account as a reason for invading Kuwait. The invasion initially defused an internal threat by giving a mission to Iraq's million man army, which previously had nothing to do and perhaps could have turned their attention towards the Presidential Palace (Mohamedou 1998: 122). Jerry M. Long also stressed that the Iraqi leadership needed an external crisis to distract the potentially self-destructive energy of the military, in addition to other groups in Hussein's inner core (Long 2004: 9). The Kuwaiti invasion served as a diversion that allowed Hussein to consolidate his hold over the military, in addition to delaying promises of democratic reforms he promised during the Iran–Iraq War.

The Iraqi military's occupation of Kuwait

Prior to the invasion of Kuwait, Iraq had the largest military in the region, with 750,000 men, ground forces organized into ten corps and sixty-seven divisions. It had 5,800 tanks, 5,100 armored personnel carriers, 3,850 artillery, 650 aircraft and twenty-five naval vessels (Eisenstadt 1993: 43). Including the Popular Army and reserves, the Iraqi military became known as the "million man army."

At 2:00 A.M., August 2, 1990, Iraq invaded Kuwait under Lieutenant General Futayyih Al-Rawi's command, using four Republican Guard units: the Nebuchadnezzar, Hammurabi, Madina and Tawakalna divisions. The Iraqi Chief of Staff had not been informed of the invasion plan, demonstrating the lack of coordination between the Army and the Republican

Guard (Quinlivan 1999: 155–6). The Iraqi Special Forces entered Kuwait City directly with a helicopter and sea-borne attack. At 5:30 A.M., these forces had enveloped Kuwait City. The Kuwaiti military offered some resistance, but were overwhelmed by the number of Iraqi forces. By 2:00 P.M. the Iraqis were in full control and subsequently installed a provisional government replacing the Kuwaiti monarchy. The Iraqis justified the invasion in the name of supporting an internal Kuwaiti uprising against the royal family. Ala Husayn Ali, said to be a colonel in the Kuwaiti military, became the head of the newly formed Kuwaiti Republic established on 4 August (Bulloch and Morris 1991: 108). On the same day, security units under the supervision of Sabawi Ibrahim Al-Takriti, Director of General Intelligence, were flown in to control the Kuwait populace and to establish a security system similar to that of Iraq's.

By August 21, Iraqi Republican Guard units were moving to rear guard positions and were replaced by less well-equipped infantry forces of the Popular Army who were deployed on the southern Kuwait border, indicating that Hussein's priority was having his most trustworthy and battle hardened parallel military defending the capital and the leadership first, and Kuwait second. The relationship that would develop between the Iraqi political leadership and these forces deployed to Kuwait from 1990 to 1991 featured many similarities to the period of the Iran–Iraq War. In addition to the inherent government suspicion of the Iraqi military and its potential threat to its rule in Baghdad, during this specific period, the government viewed these Iraqi forces as a threat to its ambitions in Kuwait as well. The lack of discipline among the services stationed in Kuwait threatened the regime's efforts to turn the country into a fortress against an impending military confrontation with an international coalition. The Iraqi political authorities opted to monitor extensively the behavior of the Iraqi military to curb dissent, and at the same time to contain criminal acts among Iraqi soldiers in Kuwait. Soldiers caught looting for personal gain were punished, as "war spoils" from Kuwait were supposed to be handed over to the state. Simultaneously, the Baathist leadership used the Iraqi military to enforce its occupation of Kuwait through control of territory, and when necessary by carrying out brutal actions against Kuwaiti citizens who dared to oppose Iraq's presence in their Nineteenth Province.

During the Iraqi occupation of Kuwait the Iraqi military was monitored by virtually all intelligence organs including General Security (*Al-Amn Al-Amm*), General Intelligence (*Al-Mukhabarat al-Amma*), Military Intelligence (*Al-Istikhbarat Al-Askariyya*), Special Security (*Al-Amn Al-Khass*) and Baath representatives placed in every military unit. All these bodies provided detailed reports on the daily conduct of Iraqi military units and individual soldiers to the Iraqi leadership. The objective of this intensive monitoring of the Iraqi forces was twofold. First was the normal and daily surveillance over the activities of the military that the Baath routinely conducted to curb dissent and make sure that no entity within the Iraqi armed forces emerged as a threat to the regime. Second, the Baath leadership wanted to make sure that the military did not falter in the plan for the defense of Kuwait (Al-Marashi 2003d: 61).

The Iraqi Special Forces (*Al-Quwwat Al-Khassa*) was an elite military unit that served as shock troops usually transported by helicopter units and served as the first unit that conducted an armed attack on Kuwait City on August 2, 1990 (Mazarr *et al.* 1993: 46). They provided the Iraqi rulers of Kuwait, Ali Hassan Al-Majid and Sabawi Ibrahim with daily reports on the actions of their units. In particular the Iraqi Special Forces units in Kuwait fulfilled a counter-insurgency role of sorts, as it was delegated with carrying out most of the operations against "dissident" Kuwaitis, primarily reconnaissance and urban combat. The Iraqi Special Forces comprised ten brigades, with the Sixty-fifth, Sixty-sixth and Sixty-eighth Brigades stationed in Kuwait. It was these same units that were used in the north of Iraq during the Iran–Iraq War in the Anfal Campaign. Just as those units reported of their brutal tactics against the Kurds to Ali Hasan Al-Majid of the Baath Party, so too did they report to him in his capacity as the Baathist military governor of Kuwait. The leader of the Special Forces in Kuwait was General Bariq Abdallah al-Haj Hinta, also known as "Hero of al-Qadisiyya" (Al-Marashi 2003d: 70).

The Iraqi military's defense preparations

Prior to the onset of the Gulf War, the initial military strategy of the Baathist leadership was for Iraqi forces to "dig-in" inside Kuwait and along parts of the Saudi–Iraqi border and prepare for an imminent conflict with the United States-led Coalition. At the same time the leadership tried to thwart such an attack through various gestures, such as appealing to the Arab street to protest against their governments' cooperation with the US. The latter campaign is dealt with in a future volume by Ibrahim Al-Marashi, but this chapter specifically analyzes the military preparations for what the leadership believed would be an impending war. Hussein reasoned that a demonstration of a massive Iraqi defensive effort could serve as an important means of intimidating the US. The underlying assumption of the military defense plan for Kuwait was that the Americans were weak since the Vietnam War and would back off if they were to face a stiff resistance and incurred significant causalities. The leadership acknowledged that the Iraqi military would sustain large casualties in this confrontation and were not opposed to sacrificing a significant part of the Iraqi Army as part of this plan of inflicting heavy losses on Coalition forces.

Just as war populism was used by the political leadership to penetrate the military with a fighting ethos during the Iran–Iraq War, this tactic was also employed prior to the 1991 Gulf War. The successor to the symbolic "Qadisiyyat Saddam" was introduced on September 20, when the Iraqi Revolutionary Command Council stated that Iraq would not retreat from

Kuwait, and introduced Iraq's euphemistic term for the Gulf War, "the noble battle of the mother of all battles" (*al-munazala al-sharifa l-ma'rakat um al-ma'arik*), otherwise referred to as "the mother of all battles" (*umm kul al-ma'arik*) (Mazarr *et al*. 1993: 54). This title for the crisis revealed the Iraqi leader's emphasis on the scope and severity of an *impending* war with the United States. It also conveyed to his military the grave significance of the conflict and prepared them for a committed and involved entanglement. Nevertheless, the regime attempted to convince the armed forces that it would emerge victorious in such a battle. In a memo circulated among military units it states: "We are guaranteed victory because we are standing up to 30 nations, and that is a point of pride for us" (Al-Marashi 2003b: 2). This statement indicated that if only Iraqis survived the "mother of all battles," it would mean a victory no matter what happened on the battlefield itself.

By the end of September the Iraqi political leadership commanded the military to be prepared for an attack that could begin without any warning and to hold their positions in Iraq near the Saudi border and in Kuwait. From the years 1982 to 1987 during the Iran–Iraq War, the political leadership orchestrated a military strategy of holding the line without withdrawing unless ordered and inflicting massive casualties on the enemy. The Iraqi armed forces were ordered to conduct a similar strategy against the Coalition (ibid.).

On November 29, UN Security Council Resolution 678 set the deadline of January 15, 1991 for Iraq to withdraw from Kuwait (Weller 1992: 2). If Iraq failed to heed the deadline, Coalition forces were allowed to "use all necessary means" to compel Iraqi forces to withdraw (Roberts 1993: 144). The deadline posed a dilemma for Hussein and his relations with the military. A non-violent withdrawal from Kuwait would in fact be far worse than actual war because a withdrawal before the deadline would be much harder to portray as victory for the nation to the Iraqis and the military. Fighting the Coalition, a far more superior foe militarily seemed as the best option for Hussein: "Whilst there was still a chance to fight and even prevail against the US, Saddam had no intention of admitting to a premature defeat which would result in his personal humiliation and fall from power" (Dannreuther 1992: 45). A non-violent withdrawal from Kuwait would in fact have been worse than the actual war, as doing so could have been portrayed as a political defeat of the Iraqi military (Matthews 1993: 220). The logic behind such a rationale was that it would have been more difficult to spin a withdrawal before the deadline as a victory for Iraq to the military, whereas a brave military defeat was less humiliating (ibid.: 223). The leadership had invested heavily in a rhetorical campaign and in the incorporation of Kuwait to convince the Iraqis and the armed forces that they were defending the homeland. Such a withdrawal would have proven that Hussein's words were hollow and thus so was his regime. While the Coalition had superior firepower and the Iraqi Army suffered from a lack of morale and discipline, the regime hoped that the armed forces could be inspired to fight for their reunited nation and prove tenacious enough to cause casualties among enemy troops.

Conditions of the military during the air war

Prior to the Gulf War the Iraqi military was depicted as an ominous threat, with one million men under arms. The million man figure however failed to account for the divisions within the military due to Iraq's parallel military system. The Republican Guard consisted of twelve divisions. Seven of these divisions were deployed in the Kuwait theatre: the Hammurabi and Al-Madina Al-Munawwara armored divisions, the Tawakalna Ala Allah and Baghdad mechanized divisions, and the Al-Faw, Nebuchadnezzar and Adnan infantry divisions. The Al-Abid mechanized division and the Al-Mustafa, Al-Nida and Al-Quds infantry divisions were stationed in Iraq in order to maintain internal security. The regular Army had forty-five divisions. All six of its armored divisions and all three of its mechanized divisions were stationed in the Kuwait theater. Out of its forty-six infantry divisions, twenty-five were stationed in Kuwait, while the remainder was deployed to the borders with Iran, Syria and Turkey (Eisenstadt 1993: 84).

However, these vast Iraqi military assets seemed helpless as the Coalition began its sustained aerial bombardment in mid-January 1991. Over the next weeks, they sat out the bombardment and merely reported on the results of the attacks. The Coalition gained supremacy of the skies, destroying much of Iraq's Air Force, with the rest of Iraq's aircraft flown to its former enemy Iran for protection. As the air war continued, Saddam Hussein had withdrawn his elite Republican Guard from the Kuwait into the provinces closer to Baghdad in order to protect the regime itself. Unprepared elements of the regular Army and Popular Army were stationed in Kuwait with the task of inflicting casualties on the invading forces. It was in the Iraqi leadership's interest to precipitate the ground war as soon as possible, as the air raids were continuing to destroy Iraq's infrastructure and deplete its armed forces. In an attempt to force the allies into a conflict on land, the Iraqis occupied the coastal Saudi town of Khafji near the Kuwait border, on January 29, 1991, which resulted in the loss of twelve US Marines and many more Iraqi casualties (Gordon and Trainor 1995: 281).

The intense aerial attacks on Iraqi positions were taking a severe toll, resulting in casualties and desertions of Iraqi soldiers. The desertion phenomenon not only decreased the Iraqi military's fighting capability but demonstrated to the Coalition that their fighting ranks were collapsing as the air strikes continued. This trend was troublesome for the leadership since it proved to their enemy the effectiveness of their air war and would only delay their wish to engage the allied forces in a ground war. The political leadership was aware of the woeful state of the armed forces on the front lines of Kuwait and that they were left to face certain defeat (Dodge 2003b: 64). The Iraqi Army suffered from a lack of morale, inadequate training and failure to utilize their weapons to their full potential. The Hussein regime fought a conflict for goals that turned out to be less compelling to the Iraqi soldiers. On February 15, the RCC announced that Iraq would accept UN Security Council Resolution 660 and when the highest Iraqi authority declared its aim of seeking an "honorable and acceptable political solution to the crisis, including a withdrawal," this produced a worrisome reaction from the masses in Baghdad, who embraced and celebrated the news, demonstrating to the leadership what little support was left for the war (Litvak 1992: 422). While the Iraqi offer did nothing to hasten the end of the conflict its significance was that for the first time the seemingly irrevocable condition of the annexation of Kuwait had been reversed. As the Iraqi leadership's first strategy to cause the collapse of the Coalition failed, Hussein's only option left was to inflict enough casualties on the invading forces to bring about a ceasefire.

The ground war

On February 22, the Coalition issued an ultimatum to Iraq that it withdraw from Kuwait or face a ground assault within twenty-four hours. The Iraqis did not withdraw and on February 24 the ground war commenced. The Iraqi military had failed to expand their defenses along the entire Iraqi–Saudi border, a strategic miscalculation. The Iraqis believed that the Coalition could not carry out attacks in the vast Iraqi desert and failed to fortify completely the area west of Kuwait, leaving them vulnerable to the Coalition ground assault. Coalition forces feigned an amphibious assault off the Kuwaiti coast so that the Iraqi units would be distracted from the main thrust of the attack through the Iraqi desert coming directly from Saudi Arabia. This miscalculation led to the outflanking of Iraq's military on the front lines.

At this juncture, the war weary Iraqi troops surrendered en masse. The only sustained defense was put up by Republican Guard tank units to the west of Kuwait. On February 25, the Iraqis begin a hasty retreat from the Nineteenth Province. As they made their retreat on the Kuwait–Basra highway they faced an intense bombardment from hostile aircraft, which has been euphemistically referred to as the "highway of death." By February 26 Kuwait had been liberated and on February 28, a ceasefire was declared. The formal end of the war was declared on April 12, 1991.

During the air war, the Iraqi military was ordered to sit out the conflict and to defend itself with limited resources. Hussein closely controlled the military units during this period trying his utmost to encourage his forces not to be intimidated by the Coalitions' advanced war-making capability. Among the tactics Hussein used to inspire his forces were the Scud attacks on Israel as well as destroying Kuwait's oil facilities and the brief occupation of the Saudi town of Khafji. He coupled these actions with lengthy speeches to strengthen the resolve on the front line units. His greatest hope was that his forces would be capable of inflicting enough casualties on the enemy so that he could negotiate a suitable victory for the regime. Thus, the Iraqi defense during the war was not to protect the Nineteenth Province per se, but the leadership itself. This defensive strategy was his best bet for survival, and he was willing to pay the cost of the utter destruction of the Iraqi military to serve that end.

Nevertheless, Hussein was able to portray the massive defeat on the battlefield as a political victory. The destruction of the military units on the front line in Kuwait constituted a victory since the regime itself survived:

> They bore the stamp of a leadership which regarded the war as manageable, whatever the military outcome, as long as it was not permitted to touch on the underpinnings of the regime itself. The success, in the short-term at least, of this strategy on the internal front, despite its disastrous external consequences, is a testimony to the single mindedness of those who devised it.
>
> (Tripp 1993: 30)

Accordingly, since the regime had stood up to a coalition of thirty nations revealed that the Mother of All Battles was a victory no matter what happened on the battlefield itself (Bond 1998: 196). Essentially this basic strategy worked in 1991 to save Saddam Hussein. The regime portrayed the conflict as a conspiracy not to liberate Kuwait itself, but to unseat the government of Saddam Hussein. The fact that he survived this conspiracy was victory in and of itself (Glad 1993: 83). After the Gulf War, the Iraqi Republican Guard had internalized this discourse, evidenced by the following comment delivered at a military conference: "After the liberation of our land in Kuwait, and despite the fact that more than 30 countries headed by the occupation forces of the U.S. rushed madly upon our Republican Guard, our performance was heroic" (Woods 2006: 47). By this measure, the regime could well claim to have won the 1991 war.

The Iraqi uprising

The 1991 Gulf War left the Iraqi armed forces defeated and in disarray. At the outset of the war, Hussein feared that a military defeat might encourage dissident factions from within his regime to rebel. Yet as the war drew to a close, the challenge to his leadership did not surface from within the insiders but from elements of Shia and Kurdish communities who revolted in what has become known as the "Iraqi Uprising" (*Al-Intifada Al-'Iraqiyya*). The spark for this uprising was also partly ignited by US President Bush who called for the Iraqis to overthrow their leader but later failed

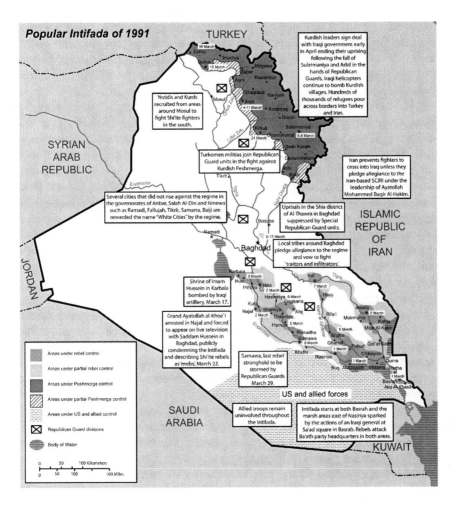

Map 9.1 The 1991 uprising.

to provide any support. For most of Iraq's fighting men, they were most certainly exhausted from taking part in an eight year war with Iran. Those soldiers deployed to the southern front had incurred massive casualties. In the lead up to the 1991 Gulf War Iraqi soldiers were not paid, fed or even armed adequately, so it came as no surprise that many of them felt an urge to take up arms against a government that left them to be killed at the hands of the Coalition fighting machine. Surviving soldiers who had retreated from the Kuwaiti frontlines into Basra around February 28 sparked the revolt by attacking portraits of the Iraqi leader a symbolic gesture unheard of in Saddam Hussein's Iraq (Jabar 2003a: 120). In the north close to 150,000 soldiers deserted their positions in the face of a Kurdish uprising.

These soldiers had become disillusioned with the Iraqi leader as Saddam Hussein's invasion of Kuwait had "humiliated" the military (ibid.). Other fighting men expressed the disillusionment felt by the regular Army towards the Iraqi President. One armored vehicle driver who took part in the Uprising said, "The Iraqi army cannot bear the responsibility of defeat because it did not fight. Saddam is responsible" (Jabar 1994: 107). For all of the leadership's correspondence emphasizing the "honor" in fighting the Coalition, the regime's rhetoric proved hollow. It was the honor of the soldier that was violated as they were left to be sacrificed on the front lines and through taking part in the Uprising, they sought to regain their honor against a leadership that had abandoned them. Nevertheless, the military units who took part in the revolt, or those who just stood by, did not have any sort of leader who could unite them and march onto Baghdad. The revolt that began in Basra spread throughout the south, including the Shia shrine cities of Najaf and Karbala. In March 1991, Kurdish rebels in northern Iraq seized buildings of the Iraqi secret services and the state Baath Party. The Kurdish militias were also in position to seize the oil rich city of Kirkuk in the north of Iraq. At its height, fifteen out of Iraq's eighteen provinces had revolted against the regime.

Hussein, in anticipation of a possible insurrection, had the Republican Guards withdrawn from Kuwait to the environs of Baghdad to protect the regime if Coalition forces were to move on to the capital. By withdrawing from Kuwait, most these units had escaped the brunt of the fighting and a ceasefire was declared before US General Norman Schwarzkopf could engage the Guards. These units, combined with the ability to use their helicopters would be the key element in putting down the Uprising, with minimal challenge provided by disorganized mutinous soldiers and armed civilians. Their role in crushing the insurrection was the first instance of the Guard taking on an internal security role. The Tawakalna, Madina and Hammurabi divisions that launched the invasion of Kuwait were ordered to suppress the twin uprisings. The Guards had better training and weapons, and even though weakened, it rallied behind the Iraqi leader. The Arab Sunni clan networks allied to Hussein were more prevalent in the Guard than in the regular military, and this uprising took on an ethnic and sectarian nature. The predominantly Arab Sunni soldiers were defending their privileged status in the Iraqi state, understandably expecting that Hussein's fall would be a tremendous loss for them as well. Their success demonstrated how at least one element of the Iraqi armed forces, while unable to ensure victory on the battlefield with the Coalition, excelled in its traditional role of suppressing internal insurrections, even an Uprising on two fronts. King Faysal feared that the Iraqi military was incapable of suppressing two simultaneous revolts within the south and north of Iraq. Decades later, the military had evolved where it proved its capacity of crushing two internal Iraqi revolts with the utmost brutality employed against fellow Iraqi citizens.

By the end of the 1991 Gulf War the Iraqi military had lost close to 2,633 tanks, 1,668 armored personnel carriers, 2,196 artillery pieces, 300 aircraft and its entire navy of twenty-five vessels. It was estimated that 200,000 to 300,000 Iraqi troops had become prisoners or had deserted. After the war, the Iraqi leadership sought to downsize the military, but it still remained as one of the largest military forces in the region with 400,000 men, the ground forces organized into six corps with close to thirty divisions. It still had approximately 2,200 tanks, 2,500 armored personnel carriers and 1,650 artillery pieces (Eisenstadt 1993: 44).

The reorganization of the military

Hussein set out reasserting control over the post-1991 military with the totalitarian-penetration tactics that served him successfully since his rise to power. The Iraqi leadership also attempted to improve morale in the military as he did in the Iran–Iraq War through raises in salaries, granting plots of land and cars to loyal military officers. Furthermore, he offered amnesties to deserters. In addition to this rhetoric of *targhib*, *tarhib* was also instilled through the RCC, the body that Hussein used to legitimize his commands. It issued a decree threatening soldiers who failed to maintain military "discipline" and "honor" with discharges, reduction in rank and withdrawal of pensions (ibid.). In an extreme manifestation of *tarhib*, the RCC issued a decree later where amputation would be implemented as a punishment for deserters.

Nevertheless, such symbolic gestures, coercive measures and material incentives did little to raise morale within the regular Army. It had endured nearly a decade of war, and with the sanctions on the import of military equipment, most of Iraq's inventory suffered poor maintenance and lack of spare parts. The Iraqi leader sought to reassert control over the regular military, which performed poorly with some of its ranks joining the Uprisings. The estrangement of the regular Army was not lost on the Iraqi leadership and it took several measures to ensure that it did not launch a coup, including creating additional security agencies and military units, as well as embarking on a new round of rotations of key military personnel.

Downsizing the military

The post-war Defense Minister Ali Hassan Al-Majid envisioned a "small but strongly built army for two basic duties." Those duties included playing "a nationalistic role" and to "defend Iraq's security and borders" from Iraq's three foes: moderate Arab countries, Israel and Iran (Eisenstadt 1993: 44). This "small but strongly built army" was exhausted from fighting for more than a decade, the defeat in the 1991 War and the meager resources that could be provided to the military, including ammunition, food and pay. The leadership had to deal with a regular armed force that was ever so distant, unwilling to fight and stayed on to merely collect a pay check. To control the military better, the leadership created new institutional mechanisms to monitor the armed forces and downsized the military to manage it better. In this effort to downsize the military, the Iraqi leadership no longer invested in the Popular Army and the National Defense Brigades (ibid.: 50). The latter had served as pro-government Kurdish militia units during the Iran–Iraq War, but elements from their ranks had joined the Kurdish uprising in the north after the 1991 Gulf War. A significant number of regular Army infantry divisions were also restructured or eliminated altogether. Many had provided little resistance during the Gulf conflict and large segments of their soldiers had either deserted or had been taken prisoner.

The Republican Guard proved its mettle during the war, providing the stiffest resistance to the Coalition attack and demonstrating its loyalty to the leadership during the 1991 Uprisings. As a predominantly Sunni Arab force, it proved that it could serve as a bulwark against threats from dissident Shia and Kurds. After the war, much of its equipment was left intact and it was downsized from twelve to seven divisions, with a total manpower estimated at approximately 60,000 (Cordesman and Hashim 1997: 237).

The regular Army was downsized from ten corps to five corps after the 1991 Gulf War, and forty-six infantry divisions were reduced to fifteen, a testimony to the casualties and desertions during the Gulf War. In the south, the Third Corps was based near Basra, and the Fourth Corps was based near Amara to counter the possibility of unrest among the Shia, as well as a growing insurgency in the marshes in the south. In the center, Baghdad was primarily defended by the Republican Guard and Special Republican Guard and indication that the government did not trust the regular Army to be based so close to the capital. In the north, the First Corps was stationed near Iraq's oil rich city of Kirkuk, while the Fifth Corps and the Second Corps were deployed near Mosul and Mansuriyya respectively, in positions outside of the Kurdish safe haven.

The Iraqi Air Force on the eve of the 1991 Gulf War Iraq had close to 650 Soviet and French-supplied combat aircraft (Cordesman and Hashim 1997: 263). After the conflict, that number was reduced to approximately 300. During the war, Iraq had sent its most advanced aircraft, such as the SU-24 and Mirage F-1Es to Iran, which later refused to give them back. The no-fly zones in the south and north of the country gave Iraq air limited space to continue training. Due to the UN sanctions, spare parts could not be imported into the country to maintain these aircraft. The Navy prior to the Gulf War consisted mostly of missile patrol boats, which were destroyed entirely during the war, and Iraq was unable to rebuild its navy as a result of the embargo

New anti-armies and military intelligence agencies

The efforts to bolster the Republican Guard during the Iran–Iraq War were part of the leadership's attempts to create a parallel military to prevent a coup from within the regular military. However, when coups would begin to emerge even within the Republican Guard, the government made further attempts to control this anti-army. In 1992 Hussein established Military Security (*Al-Amn Al-'Askari*) as an independent entity of the Military Intelligence Directorate, reporting directly to the Presidential Palace rather than the Ministry of Defense. Military Security grew out of the Special Bureau of Military Intelligence, after Saddam Hussein believed the latter failed to detect disturbances in the military. At the time of its creation, it was headed by Muhammad Nima Al-Takriti, the former head of Military Intelligence. The security agency was responsible for detecting and countering dissent, investigating corruption and embezzlement, and monitoring all formations and units in the armed forces. It was designed to infiltrate agents into every branch of the military, serving as the state's eyes and ears to ensure loyalty to the President and serving as a control mechanism in the military to restore discipline in the armed forces, similar to the political commissars of the Party (Al-Marashi 2002: 9). In this totalitarian-penetration system, intelligence services in addition to the Party had been tasked with overlapping duties in monitoring the military.

The Special Republican Guard (*Al-Haris Al-Jamhuri Al-Khas*) replaced the Republican Guards' former role as an elite praetorian guard, with Qusay serving as its commander. It provided protection for all presidential sites, including offices and personal residences. The Special Republican Guard provided further evidence of the institutionalized paranoia that characterized the totalitarian-penetration system. This anti-army was designed to counter another anti-army, the Republican Guard, which was created as a counter to the regular Army. Like the Republican Guard, the Special Republican Guard was not subordinated to the Ministry of Defense, but rather to the Special Security Service, which exercised operational control (ibid.: 10).

The Fidayin Saddam (also seen as Fidayeen or Fedayin) can be roughly translated "as those who sacrifice themselves for Saddam." A paramilitary militia with the strength of about 15,000 to 25,000 men, it was established October 25, 1995 and led by Saddam Hussein's oldest son Uday. Recruits joined out of fierce loyalty to Hussein, in addition to the benefits of higher salaries than regular Iraqi soldiers. Many of the fighters were from Hussein's hometown of Takrit or from his Al-Bu Nasir tribe, with no prior combat experience. They were usually paraded in the Iraqi media as masked men with all white or black uniforms. The Fidayin fighters were independent from the Iraqi Ministry of Defense and reported directly to Uday, serving as a counter to the Special Republican Guard led by Saddam Hussein's youngest son Qusay (Al-Marashi 2003b: 5).

The creation of anti-armies and military intelligence agencies to counter other anti-armies and military intelligence agencies that had originally been designed to thwart coups was a testimony to the nature of the Hydra that Hussein had created. Hussein's rule was characterized by a series of concentric circles where armed forces designed to protect his regime only led to the creation of counter armed forces to check the power of the praetorian guards tasked with guarding the leadership in the first place. The challenges to the structure Hussein had created began just a month after the conclusion of the Gulf War and would continue until the 2003 Iraq War. The failure of each of these coup attempts was a testament to the resilience of Hussein's coup-proof, totalitarian-penetration system that would only be dismantled by a foreign invasion of Iraq.

The Special Republican Guard had an opportunity to prove its role as a parallel military, thwarting a coup attempt within another parallel military – the Republican Guard – in June 1992 (Cordesman 1999: 25–6). In September 1993, Hussein ordered the execution of General Raji Abbas Al-Takriti, a former commander of the military medical service, and Saqr and Jasim Mukhlis for allegedly plotting a coup (Baram 2003: 97). Raji's only crime in fact was that he cracked a joke about the Iraqi leader in the presence of informants (Baram 2002: 221) It was Saqr's father and Jasim's uncle, Mawlud Mukhlis that had encouraged Hasan Al-Bakr to enter the military academy. Ironically, had it not been for the Mukhlis family, Saddam Hussein would have never been able to find a military patron in Al-Bakr that helped him become Vice-President in the first place. A further 100 to 150 officers were implicated in this plot including prominent military men from the Jabur and Ubayd tribes (Cordesman 1999: 26).

In May 1995, the Special Republican Guard quelled a revolt that erupted among the Dulaym tribe in Ramadi, 110 kilometers west of Baghdad, as a reaction to the execution of General Muhammad Madhlum Al-Dulaymi for his alleged involvement in a coup against Hussein (Baram 2002: 222). The Special Republican Guard also countered a coup in late June 1996 launched from within the Republican Guards. Air Force General Hamid Shaaban, the commander of the Iraqi Air Force was also suspected of taking part in this coup but was then released (Cordesman and Hashim 1997: 55). The fact that such a decorated war hero who played an important role in the battles for Basra in 1987 was even suspected of taking part in this plot demonstrated that distinguished careers defending the regime were not enough to sway suspicions of the leadership. Since trusted tribes like the Dur and Dulaym were involved in these coups, Hussein began to promote officers from the Al-Saadun clan from Basra, a Sunni Arab group that had enjoyed cordial relations with the Shia in the south (Baram 1997: 16). Reports of coup attempts also followed in the aftermath of the December 1998 American and British air strikes targeting suspected Iraqi WMD facilities. Following the strikes more shuffles occurred with a predominance of the Al-Duri and Al-Dulaymi tribesmen

Table 9.1 The military high command 1994

Post	Name
Commander-in-Chief of the Armed Forces	Field Marshal Saddam Hussein
Deputy Commander-in-Chief of the Armed Forces	Gen. Izzat Ibrahim Al-Duri
Defense Minister	Gen. Ali Hasan Al-Majid
Chief of Staff	Lt. Gen. Iyad Futayyih Khalifa Al-Rawi
Armed forces Assistant Chief of Staff for Administration	Lt. Gen. Ahmad Ibrahim Hammash Al-Muhaydi Al-Takriti
Armed forces Assistant Chief of Staff for Operations	Lt. Gen. Sultan Hashim Ahmad Al-Tai
Air Force Commander	Lt. Gen. Muzahim Saab Al-Nasiri
Army Air Corps Commander	Lt. Gen. Hasan Ali Hasan Al-Takriti
Armed forces Assistant Chief of Staff for Supplies	Lt. Gen. Iyad Khalil Zaki
Chief of Political Guidance	Gen. Jabbar Rajab Haddushi
Commander of the Republican Guard	Lt. Gen. Ibrahim Abd Al-Sattar Muhammad
Commander of Naval and Coastal Defense Forces	Brig. Gen. Khalid Bakr Khadr
Commander of Air Defense	Maj. Gen. Mahdi Salih Fathi
Commander of the First Army Corps	Maj. Gen. Mahmud Fayzi Muhammad Al-Hazza Al-Nasiri
Commander of the Second Army Corps	Maj. Gen. Yasin Fulayh Khalaf Salim Al-Muini
Commander of the Third Army Corps	Lt. Gen. Sabah Nuri Alwan Hammud Al-Ujayli
Commander of the Fourth Army Corps	Lt. Gen. Tariq Sadiq Abd Al-Husayn
Commander of the Fifth Army Corps	Lt. Gen. Nasir Said Tawfiq Abd Al-Ghafur Al-Nasiri

Source: Bengio (1997: 363).

Table 9.2 Select list of various officers purged, arrested or executed during the totalitarian military 1968–2003

Name of officer	Date of removal	Sectarian affiliation	Ethnic affiliation	Political affiliation	Tribe/clan	Manner of removal
Abd Al-Razzaq Al-Nayif	July 30 1968	Sunni	Arab	Independent	Al-Jumayla	Exiled to Spain
Ibrahim Al-Daud	July 30 1968	Sunni	Arab	Independent		Exiled to Jordan
Faysal Al-Ansari	Dec. 1968					Dismissed, then arrested
Jawad Abd Al-Majid	April 1969					Accused of spying for Iran
Saadun Husayn	June 1969					Executed
Said Hammu	June 1969					Executed
Muhammad Nuri Al-Khalil	Oct. 1969					Suspicious car accident
Ali Rajab	Oct. 1969					Suspicious heart attack
Abd al-Aziz Uqayli	1969	Sunni	Arab			Executed
Abd Al-Ghani Al-Rawi	Jan. 1970	Sunni	Arab			Fled to Iran after failed coup
Hardan Al-Takriti	Oct. 1970	Sunni	Arab	Baathist		Exiled to Algeria, assassinated in Kuwait
Salih Mahdi Ammash	Sept. 1970	Sunni	Arab	Baathist		Exiled through a diplomatic post
Nadhim Kazzar	June 1973	Shia	Arab/Kurd	Baathist		Executed
Muhammad Fadhil	June 1973					Executed
Adin Tawfiq	July 1986					Assumed to be executed
Mahir Abd Al-Rashid	Aug./Sept. 1988	Sunni	Arab			Placed under house arrest
Raji Abbas Al-Takriti	Sept. 1993	Sunni	Arab			Executed for coup attempt
Muhammad Madhlum Al-Dulaymi	May 1995	Sunni	Arab		Dulaym	Executed

Source: Makiya (1998: 292–6). Other information provided by the authors.

Note
This list is by no means exhaustive but mentions the officers referred to in the text.

staffing the highest military posts, indicating that the two groups had reha-
bilitated themselves in the eyes of the leadership (Al-Marashi 2003a: 203).

The internal dynamics during these years of failed coups against
Saddam Hussein reveal several trends. Relations to Saddam Hussein or
coming from certain tribes could only protect regime insiders to a certain
extent. Hussein's suspicion of a hint of disloyalty spelt the end of one's
career or one's life in the inner circle. Despite the execution of prominent
members of Hussein's family, fellow Takritis or Al-Dulaymis, Al-Duris or
Ubaydis, the other members of these social groups within the military still
stayed loyal to Hussein, a testament to the viability of the Iraqi leader's
patronage network. In fact these groups often went out of their way to
demonstrate their loyalty when a "black sheep" in the family had erred.
Even the Al-Dulaym who took part in a tribal revolt made efforts to reha-
bilitate themselves in the eyes of the leader. All of these groups simply had
grown used to enjoying the largesse of the state and a further coup would
not only undermine their well being, but their "being" altogether. The fear
of the regime's punishment ultimately induced cooperation. Divide and
rule tactics took advantage of the tensions between the different tribes,
clans and families that formed the backbone of the military. Even the
rivalry between his own sons, who controlled various military units and
militias, were used to strengthen the President's grip on Iraq's armed
forces. Hussein managed to survive a decade of sanctions and attempted
military coups, while using these cleavages in the military to his advantage,
preventing any one military unit, or one of his own relatives for that
matter, to attain the necessary strength to challenge his rule.

Preparations for the 2003 Iraq War

Prior to the 2003 war, the armed forces were cut down to 400,000 men.
The regular Army was reduced to seventeen divisions (three armored divisions, three mechanized divisions and eleven infantry divisions), but still
remained as the largest part of the ground forces (Jabar 2003a: 123).

On November 25, 2002, UN weapons inspections in Iraq resumed after
four years when the former UN team left Iraq in 1998 (Keegan 2004:
110–11). As the US and the UK were pursuing the case for war against
Iraq, Saddam Hussein was preparing his nation for an impending war
regardless of the outcome of the UN inspections. Prior to the war Hussein
continued to infiltrate the higher echelons of the military with fellow clansmen and Takritis. In 2000 the Chief of Staff position had been given to
General Ibrahim Abd Al-Sattar Muhammad Al-Takriti. Prior to the 2003
Iraq War, two of the five army corps commanders were Takritis, including
Sulayman Yusif Twayni, commander of the First Army Corps in the north,
and General Raad Abd Al-Majid Faysal, commander of the Third Corps in
the south (Baram 2003: 98). Hussein continued to patronize key tribes,
giving the position of Minister of Defense to a non-Takriti, Sultan Hashim

Table 9.3 Iraqi land forces in 2002

	HQ	Divisions	Brigades	Manpower
General Headquarters	1	–	–	30,000
Corps HQ	7	–	–	7,000
Republican Guard				
Armored divisions	–	2	–	30,000
Mechanized divisions	–	3	–	30,000
Infantry divisions	–	3	–	20,000
Special Republican Guards	–	–	6	26,000
Other Army formations				
Armored divisions	–	3	–	25,000
Mechanized divisions	–	3	–	25,000
Infantry divisions	–	11	–	80,000
Commando units	–	–	8	24,000
Special Forces	–	–	2	6,000
Total regular land forces	7	25	16	303,000
Recalled reserves	–	–	–	100,000
Total land forces in late 2002	7	25	16	403,000
First line reserves not recalled	–	40	–	500,000
Paramilitary forces				
Border Guards	–	–	6	30,000
Saddam Fidayin	–	–	7	20,000
Militia				
People's Army	–	19	–	50,000
National Defense Battalions	–	–	1	1,000
Total	7	84	45	1,054,000

Source: *Jane's World Armies*, October 29, 2002. Online, available at: jwar.janes.com/public/jwar/index.shtml (accessed 7 July 2007).

from the Al-Tai tribe in Mosul, breaking with the tradition of granting this post solely to relatives or fellow clansmen of the Iraqi President.

The military defense plan was designed within a totalitarian-penetration system. Saddam Hussein, in his honorific capacity of Commander-in-Chief of the armed forces, not the Minister of Defense, was the highest military authority in Iraq. Given the nature of the system he established, his active and direct control was absolutely necessary for ensuring the loyalty of the Iraqi armed forces. Military officers interviewed after the 2003 Iraq War complained that all tactical military orders essentially came from Saddam Hussein or his youngest son, Qusay (Woods 2006: 64).

The 2003 Iraq War

The 2003 Iraq War began on March 19, 2003, with a "decapitation" air strike against a structure believed to be a meeting place of Iraq's top leadership. Subsequently, American and British ground forces began the invasion by moving to seize the port of Um Qasr as well the oilfields in the south. Iraq launched a variety of missiles toward the bases of the invading forces in Kuwait, as one of the few offensive aspects of the Iraqi military's strategy. Besides the missile attack, an air offensive never materialized. The Iraqis had scattered its fighter aircraft with no intent on using them during combat, perhaps learning from the 1991 war that their pilots could not survive aerial engagement with the American and British forces.

The beginning of the ground war on the first day had caught the Iraqi military unprepared as they were not expecting to confront ground forces early in the war. The leadership had prepared the Iraqi military to sit out a long aerial bombardment as preceded the ground war in 1991. Iraqi forces were engaged in defending the port town of Um Qasr, and British forces also began to deploy to the southern Iraqi city of Basra, yet could not take the town due to Iraqi resistance. From the town of Al-Nasiriyya Iraqi forces were able to attack the American advance, inflicting some of the first enemy casualties on their march to the capital (Keegan 2004: 144). While the Iraqi armed forces put up little resistance in the first three days of the war, they defended Al-Nasiriyya in earnest, as units of the Fidayin had been deployed in the town. An ambush resulted in the deaths and capture of US prisoners of war (POWs) on March 23. The Iraqi state TV station broadcasted the images of four dead US soldiers, using them as a media ploy reminiscent of its display of captured POWs in the first Gulf War.

The Fidayin employed guerrilla tactics to inflict as many casualties as possible in the south. A battle outside Najaf, 130 kilometers south of Baghdad, had been one of the fiercest encounters of the Iraqi military forces. On March 24, elements of the Republican Guard Madina division engaged the Third Infantry Division outside the city of Karbala, placing US forces within eighty kilometers of the Iraqi capital. The next day, powerful sandstorms began and continued for two days delaying the US advance in the south of the country, providing a natural defense for the Iraqi division, although US aircraft were still capable of striking Republican Guard positions. The fighting outside of Karbala lasted for a couple of days, as well as battles outside of Najaf between Iraqi and US forces, but the Guards were weakened from aerial bombardment.

By the end of March, the Fourth Corps of the Iraqi regular Army in the south had been damaged heavily by air attacks but maintained some forces outside of Al-Kut and Al-Hilla to challenge the Marine's advance, while other units had been deployed near Karbala and Al-Najaf to engage the US Third Infantry Division. By this juncture in the battle, the headquarters of the Third Corps of the regular Army in Al-Nasiryya had fallen (Cordesman 2003: 85). The Iraqi military strategy of using the regular Army in the south faltered partly due to the fact that these units remained immobile. The totalitarian-penetration system that Hussein had fostered became unraveled. The regular Army, which had a history of fighting in Kurdish uprisings, a war with the UK, Arab–Israeli wars, the Iran–Iraq War, the 1991 Gulf War and finally the 2003 Iraq War, was slowly collapsing in the face of a foreign invasion.

At this point three Republican Guard divisions were deployed to defend the approaches to the capital (Murray and Scales 2003: 83). The Madina Division was deployed at the Karbala Gap on March 31, blocking the US Third Infantry Division's advance to Baghdad. However the Iraqi forces failed to take advantage of the narrow geography to make a concerted stand and the US division pushed through on April 2 with little resistance. The Iraqi forces had left major areas of the Gap undefended and at that point, many of Iraq's Republican Guards had been destroyed or had deserted their ranks (Cordesman 2003: 479). Other Republican Guard forces engaged the second prong of the invasion led by the First Marine Expeditionary Forces. On April 1, the Baghdad Division stationed outside of Kut took heavy losses and could not prevent the loss of a bridge on the Tigris River allowing US forces to proceed north to the Iraqi capital. Remnants of the Republican Guard were stationed to protect the south-east corner of Baghdad as the Marines continued their advance. The Guards at this juncture were mauled as they exposed themselves to the two-pronged American assault and suffered the brunt of air power as they redeployed (Hawkins 2003: 61). Deploying this parallel military in the south may have been part of Hussein's strategy to use the most effective forces to inflict enough US casualties to affect American public opinion. However, such actions led to the Guards' demise at the hands of the American air force and land units, weakening them to the point where they failed to maintain a cohesive defense of the Iraqi capital. The Republican Guard forces defending the outskirts of Baghdad began to collapse, spelling the end of the anti-army created in 1968 as a tool to protect Abd Al-Salam Arif's military ruler regime from the military itself. What had emerged as a praetorian guard in the totalitarian-penetration system, protecting Hussein from internal threats and the Iranian military, had wavered in the face of overwhelming American military force.

The American's defeat of the Republican Guard units defending the Karbala Gap opened up the approaches to Baghdad before the Iraqis could redeploy forces to defend the capital and by April 4 the US Third Infantry Division had captured Saddam Hussein International Airport (renamed Baghdad International Airport). Elements of the Iraqi Special Republican Guard on April 7 engaged US forces from the Third Infantry Division as they pushed into downtown Baghdad seizing some of Hussein's palaces. However, most of the elements defending Baghdad seemed to have melted away into the city or their hometowns. They were perhaps demoralized, thus weakening the leadership's tenuous control over the remaining elements of the Iraqi security forces, and the massive urban battle, consisting of house-to-house fighting for Baghdad never materialized.

By April 8 the First Marine Expeditionary Division moved through

Baghdad from the east to rendezvous with the Third Infantry Division already in the center of the capital. US military forces seized control of most of Baghdad and a tall statue of Saddam Hussein came down in the Firdaws Square in the center of the city, symbolically ending the Baath era in Iraq as the spectacle was broadcasted on international airwaves.

The divisions and political tensions between various elements of the Iraqi armed forces severely limited the leadership's ability to use its armed forces in the defense of the nation and the capital. The Special Republican Guards, the Republican Guards and the security services failed to maintain a cohesive defense of the capital, as every Iraqi force element pursued its own goals, power and survival. The more the US advanced, the more survival became the key goal, and the more the various Special Republican Guard, Republican Guard and security service elements that might have led the defense lost the will to fight and deserted.

In the north, the Iraqi First Corps headquartered in Kirkuk came under attack and on March 27, withdrew from areas around Kirkuk, allowing Kurdish forces to seize the positions around the city. As of a result of the air attacks most of these regular Army units were believed to have been immobilized by April 9 (Cordesman 2003: 115). Iraq's third largest city Mosul was defended by the Iraqi Fifth Corps. While the US was conducting air strikes against the Fifth Corps, attempts were also made to establish communication with its leadership. After lengthy talks, on April 11 an American commander accepted a ceasefire from the commander of the Fifth Corps. Some Iraqi soldiers left the battle for the city, leaving their equipment and uniforms to proceed with life as civilians (ibid.: 120). By April 14, the last of Iraq's defenses collapsed around Takrit. Saddam Hussein's silence combined with the apparent breakdown in Iraq's command and control and weeks of Coalition air strikes seemed to have broken the morale of the remaining Iraqi forces. They had little political or psychological incentives to continue the fight.

The lessons from the military defense strategies of 1991 and 2003 had some ramifications for the insurgency in Iraq. The Baathist leadership hoped that America's weakness, in other words its Vietnam Syndrome, would compel the United States to stop fighting once it incurred heavy casualties. Since this weakness had been exploited by the insurgents, it would appear that Saddam Hussein had developed some sort of grand plan for an insurgency to force the United States out through a campaign of guerrilla warfare. However, no documentary evidence of a prolonged post-war insurgency plan has been found. Also, if such a plan existed, then orders would have been given by the Baathist leadership to the Iraqi forces to take their arms, wait out the battle and then begin an insurgency at a later date. Such a plan would have admitted defeat before the 2003 war had even started and would have weakened morale on the Iraqi war front. The documents found after the conflict suggest that Hussein thought his war strategy would have succeeded in bringing about a collapse in

American morale during the fighting of the war itself. Insurgent groups, especially those loyal to the former Iraqi government began to emerge in the summer of 2003 and operated on an *ad hoc* basis, thus suggesting that their actions were improvisations rather than a preordained plan for a low-intensity guerrilla war. Nevertheless, the insurgency provided an opportunity to put Saddam Hussein's full military plans, which never materialized in 1991 and 2003, into effect. Mounting American casualties, a drawn-out war, and the United States losing its patience to fight did not materialize in 1991, nor in 2003, but ironically in a battle that followed the downfall of Saddam himself.

Part IV
The mandate army redux

10 The US and the Iraqi Army

I am a Muslim and Islamic law lays down that no infidel shall rule over me ... and because I am an Arab and Arabism forbids a foreign army to corrupt my country.

(Bengio 1998: 130)

This statement sounds like an Iraqi insurgent communiqué after the 2003 Iraq War. However, the quote belonged to Salah Al-Din Al-Sabbagh, the Arab nationalist leader of the Four Colonels junta that dominated Iraqi political life from 1937 to 1941. The "foreign army" that he was referring to was the UK's. In his words: "I detest Britain and all those who help it to enslave my people" (ibid.). Al-Sabbagh as a Muslim had opposed "infidel" British rule in a Muslim land. As an Arab nationalist, he rejected a foreign Western nation ruling Arab soil. He perceived the British mandate and Britain's interference in Iraqi affairs after its independence as an extension of imperialism at a time when the UK controlled the future destinies of most of the Muslim Arab lands, particularly the Palestine mandate. Hemphill wrote that Al-Sabbagh viewed the events in the Middle East as a continuation of a greater clash between Islam and Christianity: "The historical struggle between Christendom and Islam had never really ended, but was being fought on different battlefields and with different weapons" (Hemphill 1979: 103). Al-Sabbagh's vision of a new Crusade resonated with the neo-Crusader themes that proliferate the discourse of Al-Qaida in Iraq, in addition to a variety of Iraqi nationalist groups in opposition to the US role in their country (Al-Marashi 2006: 219). Finally, the Colonel was a proud soldier, who had served in the Ottoman military fighting the British and its allies. He would resent taking orders from British advisors in the Iraqi Army.

Al-Sabbagh's views were no different than the soldiers and officers who had found that their Army had been disbanded after the 2003 Iraq War. Various military men viewed the US role in Iraq similar to Al-Sabbagh and his colleagues' view of the UK. A good number of them had fought in a war with the US either in 1991 or 2003. They regarded the American decision to dissolve the Iraqi Army, the largest military force in the Arab world, as a means of keeping Iraq weak and strengthening Israel. These disenfranchised soldiers would join anti-American insurgent groups for the same reasons that motivated Al-Sabbagh. As Muslims they were opposed to "infidel rule" and many of them were ethnically Arabs who opposed American occupation of Arab soil. Finally, like Al-Sabbagh, they were proud soldiers who did not want to join an Army where they would have to take orders from Americans.

This chapter does not delve into the technical military details of the post-2003 Iraq armed forces, which could be found in Cordesman's (2006a) *Iraq Security Forces*. Rather it compares the circumstances surrounding the creation of the new Iraqi military in 2003, with the British efforts in 1921. In the early chapters, the "mandate army" was defined as a form of the "colonial army." The mandate system allowed the British to maintain indirect colonial control over Iraq and its military affairs. The American influence in Iraqi military affairs is analogous to the British experience, and hence the "mandate army" has returned to Iraq. The relationship between Iraq, after it was granted sovereignty in June 2004, its new military and the US resembled the situation in Iraq after it became independent in 1932. Despite the formal independence of Iraq, the nature, structure, size and mission of the Iraqi Army was ultimately determined in London (post-1932) or in Washington (post-2004). Like the UK, the US was ultimately responsible for training the new Iraqi Army, while in the meantime the Iraqi state depended on foreign troops to protect a nascent government. The UK and the US's primary concern was to train the Iraqi Army to deal with what they had termed the "insurgents."

Both the UK and the US were the dominant actors in Iraqi politics in both stages. Both envisioned a new Iraqi Army that could incorporate Iraq's various communities into a single, national institution that would transcend ethnic, religious and sectarian differences. However in both cases the Army's officer corps would be dominated by regional, ethnic or sectarian groups that tended to exclude the other. After 1932 the Iraqi officer corps was recruited primarily among Arab Sunnis and after 2004 this body consisted of mostly Shia and Kurdish officers. Ultimately the composition of the officer corps was determined by which political elites were working with the dominant foreign power at the time. These recruitment patterns also led to ethnic and sectarian cleavages inhibiting professional corporate ties in both newly formed armed forces.

British policy post-World War I and American policy in post-Baathist Iraq sought to create an Iraqi military that would safeguard the strategic interests of both London and Washington, but were often seen as "imperialist" interference in domestic affairs by Iraqi nationalists. The military emerged as a symbol in the context of a critical discourse of the British or American role in controlling Iraq's destiny. During the British period, the Iraqi aspirations for complete independence were projected on to the

Army, and the Army emerged as the guardian of what it perceived to be Iraq's interests. The Army asserted itself against a monarchy deemed too subservient to British interests – the same interests that the Iraqi Army was supposed to protect. An examination of how Iraqis view the armed forces after 2004 indicates that they are following the same nationalist trajectory that it embarked on several decades ago.

Disbanding the Iraqi military

The assessment that history is repeating itself in Iraq begins with the nation's wars with foreign powers. The UK engaged in a month long war with Iraq in 1941 to conduct a regime change as the US did in 2003. However there was a significant difference between how the victorious powers dealt with the Iraqi military. The chapter on dismantling the military moderator regime documented how the British did not disband the Iraqi Army, which had just fought a war with the UK, but rather purged it of nationalist officers loyal to Al-Sabbagh's Four Colonels junta. By doing so gradually, the Iraqi Army was still intact to maintain internal security, particularly during a Kurdish uprising that erupted in the 1940s.

Jay Garner, as head of the short-lived US Office for Reconstruction and Humanitarian Assistance (ORHA) declared his intention to use the Iraqi regular Army to "help rebuild their own country" and "not to demobilize it immediately and put a lot of unemployed people on the street." At his first news conference Garner expressed the foresight that the Army needed to be kept intact. "We'd continue to pay them," Garner told reporters, "to do things like engineering, road construction, work on bridges, remove rubble, de-mine, pick up unexploded ordnance, construction work" (Fineman *et al.*, *Los Angeles Times*, 2003: 1). Hashim, an expert on Iraqi military affairs wrote, "Garner's plan would disappear into the dustbin of history, with catastrophic consequences" (Hashim 2006: 92). Hashim's reference to "history" expressed the long-term ramifications of Coalition Provisional Authority (CPA) chief Paul Bremer's decision to disband the Iraqi Army in May 2003.

The CPA resembled the institution of the British High Commissioner in Iraq, both the highest authority in Iraq during its transition to independence. Despite the similarities, there hardly seems to be a sweeping action taken by the High Commissioner that resembles the CPA's disbandment order. Bremer has incurred numerous critiques for disbanding the Army. The focus on his action denies the role that powerful US civilian politicians in Washington had in deciding to disband the military, since it is doubtful that Bremer could have made such a monumental decree without the approval of his superiors. The dissolution order revealed early on how American administrators and Iraqi nationalists had two diverging views on Iraq's future and its past. A document prepared by the CPA entitled

"An Historic Review of CPA Accomplishments" merely devoted one line to this "accomplishment" writing: "Iraqi Army formally dissolved May 23, 2003" (Coalition Provisional Authority: 11). The failure to elaborate further on this act seemed as an indirect acknowledgement of the severity of the CPA's action. The CPA was correct in that for a "Historic Review," their action would certainly affect Iraq's future history. It also revealed the battle between the US and the Iraqis over a contested history. The US had envisioned Iraq embarking on a new linear history, abandoning the legacy of its past, which it conflated with Saddam Hussein's rule. Iraqis held a cyclical view of history, where a foreign power similar to the British mandatory authority sought to subjugate Iraq for "imperial" interests by dismantling the nation's shield – its Army.

Bremer justified his decision based on the argument that Saddam Hussein had oppressed Iraq's Shia and Kurds and since the military served the Iraqi President, therefore the Iraqi Shia and Kurds would embrace the decision to disband the Iraqi Army. Upon criticisms of his decision, Paul Bremer stated that the CPA decree was partly meant to appease the Kurds and the Shia. As for the Kurds, Bremer argued that the disbandment decree was a concession to their parties so that they would not secede from Iraq (Sharp 2005: 2). Under Saddam Hussein's presidency, the Kurds had suffered the climax of brute military repression. Yet at the same time this history also documented Kurdish officers who remained loyal to the Iraqi military. Even during the Kurdish revolts, Kurdish officers were allowed to rise through the ranks. During the Iran–Iraq War the commander of the Republican Guard was a Kurdish tank commander who received promotions based on his talent as a field officer. Kurds also served in paramilitary units that worked in tandem with the Iraqi military. Such military units were referred to as the "Knights," the National Defense Battalions or the *Jahash*, literally meaning "little donkey," the derogatory term to refer to Kurdish collaborators with the Iraqi military. Even the PUK had sided with the Iraqi government and the military during the initial years of the Iran–Iraq War and the KDP allied with the Republican Guard during fighting with the PUK in Irbil in 1997.

In his memoirs, Bremer wrote, "And in early meetings, Kurdish leaders Jalal Talabani and Masud Barzani made it clear to me that the Kurds would 'never' accept a formula to reconstitute and re-arm units of the former Iraqi army" (Bremer 2006: 55). While this statement may have been true, Bremer could have argued that the Kurds already had their *peshmerga* or militias in place to maintain security in the north and that an Iraqi Army would be needed to keep security in the center and south of the country. He could have offered a *peshmerga* force to be reconstituted in a security structure where a regional Army of the north would exist alongside federal army units, which had become a de facto reality by 2007 anyway. However, Jalal Talabani, then the leader of the PUK who became Iraq's President in 2006, declared that disbanding the military was a wise decision which "struck at the roots of the Arab nationalist militarism that plagued Iraq even before Saddam" (Hashim 2006: 94). This history of the Iraqi military documented the nexus between militarism and Arab nationalism during the British involvement in Iraqi affairs. The connection between militarism and nationalism was cemented as a response to foreign intervention in Iraq, and thus follows that an American decision to disband the Iraqi Army would only serve to increase the militarism and Arab nationalism in post-war Iraq to which Talabani had such an aversion.

Bremer also wrote that the Shia of Iraq also opposed the Iraqi military:

> The distrust the Shia population and leaders felt for the old army was, if anything, even deeper. They remembered the slaughter carried out by Saddam's army after the Gulf War, and many Shia felt lingering anger that America had not intervened to stop the killing.
>
> (Bremer 2006: 55)

Bremer, by referring to "Saddam's army" conflated the Saddam Hussein government with the regular Army, even though the latter existed well before he came to power in 1968. As stated in the introduction, the "Iraqi military," referred to the armed forces of Iraq that constituted the regular Army, Air Force and Navy, subordinated to the Ministry of Defense, in addition to the parallel militaries Saddam Hussein fostered such as the expanded Republican Guard, the Special Republican Guard, the Popular Army and the Fidayin Saddam. Bremer was correct in that the Republican Guard suppressed the post-Gulf War uprising with banners on their tanks that said, "No Shia [will be left] after today." Yet during this Uprising, the Republican Guard fought against members of the regular Army who were in revolt against the Saddam Hussein government. To see the Iraqi Army as a monolithic unit as Bremer did when he disbanded it revealed a lack of knowledge of the tensions within the Iraqi armed forces.

It also revealed Bremer's simplistic notions of Iraq's ethno-sectarian divide, ignoring the cleavages within Iraq's communities. Sentiments towards the Iraqi Army varied and they were by no means uniform within various Iraqi sectarian or ethnic communities. The CPA view of the Army along ethnic and sectarian lines did not factor in more visible fault lines in the Iraqi military, such as class, rural–urban, religious–secular and tribal divisions within the armed forces.

Some Shia regarded the military as an institution responsible for brutal domestic repression and discrimination in favor of the Sunni Arabs, but other Shia were loyal to this institution and even took part in Shia repression against fellow Shia. The Baath government could not have survived as long as it did without Shia and Kurds taking part in security forces to repress other "rebellious" Shia and Kurds. Regarding the ethno-sectarian divide in the Iraqi Army, Hashim wrote:

> While the history of Iraqi army has not been covered with marital glory, the vast majority of Iraqis take pride in their army. I noted this even among Shi'a and Kurdish officers who had served in the former army and had been purged, retired or imprisoned by the former regime, and were now serving in the new army.
>
> (Hashim 2006: 95)

The history of the Iraqi military may have been dominated by Arab Sunnis, but there were distinguished members of the Iraqi military that cut across the nation's ethno-sectarian mosaic. Saadi Abbas Al-Jaburi, a Shia, and Rashid Husayn Wandawi Al-Takriti, a Kurd, were respected generals who remained loyal to Hussein throughout the Iran–Iraq War. Officers from the Shahwani family served as prominent Turkmens in the military and the family suffered from taking part in a post-1991 coup. The authors even came across prominent Iraqi Christian officers who served in elite units such as the Special Forces.

While Bremer argued that his decision was intended to placate Shia and Kurdish demands, it alienated members of the Sunni Arab community. Towns and cities like Mosul, Takrit, Rawa, Ana, Haditha, Falluja, Samarra and Baquba were characterized by a strong military tradition. Mosul for example was known as "the city with a million officers" (International Crisis Group (ICG) 2003: 13). Most of the smaller towns were impoverished in the 1920s and 1930s and the Army offered a chance for upward mobility for disadvantaged Arab Sunnis. Decades later, the military still employed Iraqis from this area. When the military was disbanded, a significant proportion of the male population of these urban centers lost their livelihood. It was no wonder that this area became known as the restive Arab Sunni Triangle after the 2003 war. Hatim Jasim Mukhlis, leader of the Iraqi National Movement, brought up a point neglected when discussing the Arab Sunnis. Bremer, as well as many outside analysts of Iraq, observed that the majority of the officers in the Iraqi Army were Arab Sunni and concluded that this community was the most supportive of the Saddam Hussein government. However, Mukhlis stated that it had been forgotten that most of all the coup attempts against Saddam Hussein were led by Arab Sunni officers (ibid.: 17). If there was one group that suffered during the history of Iraq from repeated executions, particularly under Saddam Hussein's rule, it was the Arab Sunni officers.

Bremer also defended his decision in his memoirs, writing that the Army disbanded itself during the 2003 Iraq War (Bremer 2006: 55). The former Director of National Security and Defense in the CPA Walter Slocombe told the International Crisis Group: "To dismantle the army was simply to recognise an established fact" (ICG 2003: 6). However, even critics within the US government disputed Bremer and Slocombe's argument. A US government official who wished to be remain anonymous told the ICG: "Many of these soldiers felt there was an implicit bargain – they stopped fighting and we would treat them fairly. The decision to dismantle the army was viewed as a betrayal and sent the wrong message at the wrong time" (ibid.: 7). Another critic in the US government said, "My Iraqi friends tell me that this decision was what really spurred the nationalists to join the infant insurgency. We had advertised ourselves as liberators and turned on these people without so much as a second thought" (Fallows, *Atlantic Monthly*, 2005: 66). Hashim also wrote that even if the Iraqi Army melted away during the war that did not mean the institution dissolved itself: "The officers and men merely went home" (Hashim 2006: 92).

Rather than reconstituting the Iraqi Army in the power vacuum created after the war, the dissolution exacerbated the ongoing looting, organized crime and political violence. It is difficult to say with the benefit of hindsight that if the Iraqi Army had remained intact, all the crime, looting and violence in Iraq could have been avoided. Perhaps the Iraqi Army could have prevented these phenomena to a greater extent. What is more significant is that a belief had become ingrained in post-war Iraqi society that the US decision to disband the Iraqi military could have prevented the post-war chaos. The decree provided Iraqis with more rhetorical ammunition to criticize the US and the CPA. Even the Defense Minister Hazim Al-Shaalan, who was cooperating with the US and interim Iraqi government, declared that following the dissolution of the Iraqi Army, the problems of "anarchy" and "lawless behavior" were exacerbated: "Through this lawlessness, certain groups built dens of deceit, crime, and corruption. Had the Iraqi Army remained, these things would not have happened" ("Al-Sha'lan," *Al-Sharqiyya*, January 25, 2005). Shaalan's statements were made on the Iraqi channel *Al-Sharqiyya*, which had been characterized as a medium sympathetic of the former Baath Party at times (Al-Marashi 2007: 83). His critiques were broadcast on a channel that was widely watched in Iraq. The interview further reinforced the belief that the CPA decree fuelled Iraq's post-war chaos and further cultivated in the Iraqi public the notion that America's "liberation" was emerging into a nightmarish occupation.

"History" and the former Iraqi military

In a further defense of the disbandment decree Bremer wrote: "Any army needs barracks, bases, and equipment. But when Saddam's military melted away, barracks and bases had been demolished, stripped not only of all usable arms and equipment, but down to the wiring and plumbing, even the bricks themselves" (Bremer 2006: 55). Many of Iraq's ministries were also looted bare, but most of them were not disbanded. The CPA and political circles in Washington failed to appreciate that even if the facilities of the Army were looted or the soldiers merely went home, it still existed as a symbolic institution in the historical imaginary of the Iraqis.

Within the span of thirty years Iraqi society had undergone several collective traumas ranging from the Iran–Iraq War, the 1991 Gulf War, the decade of sanctions and the 2003 Iraq War, followed by the post-war chaos. The Iraqi Army served as one of the institutions that could have secured the nation after these traumatic events. The disbandment only aggravated this endless string of cataclysmic trials. In light of these traumas, the Iraqis searched for continuity with their past through institutions like the Army at a time when America was trying to rewrite a new future for the nation.

While the statue of Saddam Hussein coming down in Firdaws Square in April 2003 was a staged event for media consumption, some Iraqis expressed to the authors their regret that it was not an Iraqi Army unit bringing it down. In fact, one of the only statues to survive the post-war chaos was that of General Adnan Khayrallah Talfa (ICG 2003: 3). Talfa, the former Minister of Defense during the Iran–Iraq War, was related to Saddam Hussein through marriage and was his childhood friend and cousin. Despite his close ties to Hussein, Iraqis communicated to the author that they still believed his death in a helicopter crash was orchestrated by Hussein. While most of Hussein's statues were dismantled, the memory of Talfa, and his image even in a statue survived in post-war Iraq as he embodied a patriotic Iraqi Army. Even the feared Uday and Qusay, Hussein's sons and commanders of the Fidayin and Special Republican Guards respectively were treated with some reverence by the Iraqis. After the corpses were shown on TV to prove that they were in fact dead, Iraqis expressed to us that, "They were devils, but they were our devils and should not have been paraded on TV." The American attempt to change the Iraqi flag by commissioning an Iraqi exile to do so also caused an uproar in Iraq as it resembled the Israeli flag and was seen as another foreign attempt to break the Iraqis' link with their past. While the Iraqi Army had committed crimes throughout its history against its own population, as well as against Iranians and Kuwaitis, Iraqis expressed to the authors that it should have been their decision as to its fate, rather than that of a foreign occupying power. The sentiments of Iraqi pride felt towards the Army can be summed up by a schoolteacher who said, "regardless of the *crimes* the army may have committed, it belongs to the people and remains the symbol of national unity" (emphasis added) (ibid.: 4). The CPA had an opportunity to punish the perpetrators of the crimes in the military or use of truth and reconciliation committees rather than imposing a collective punishment on the entire Army, depriving Iraq of a historical institution and a force that could have maintained order in the post-war chaos.

The respect the Iraqi Army garnered as a national institution was evident in post-Baathist Iraq as Iraqi Army Day was still celebrated on January 6, as it had been in Iraq since the military's foundation. On January 6, 2004, during the Eighty-third celebration of Iraqi Army Day, the Baghdad-based newspaper *Al-Manar* held an interview with former Staff Major General Najib Al-Salihi. Al-Salihi served in post-Baathist Iraq as Secretary General of the Free Officers and Civilians Movement, a group of former Iraqi officers who were opposed to Saddam Hussein's government. When asked what Iraqi Army Day meant to him as a military leader he replied: "To Iraqis and to us military men, January 6 represents a history full of glories, heroics, and great deeds of manhood, as well as constant readiness for sacrifice. The army is a symbol of national sovereignty and independence" ("Party leaders," *Al-Manar*, January 6, 2004: 1, 4). Salihi's repeated invocation of the "history" of the Iraqi Army sought to create a link between an uncertain future with a past that he deemed glorious.

During the Army Day celebrations a year later held at Al-Taji base, former Interim Prime Minister Iyad Allawi also echoed previous sentiments of pride in the history of the Iraqi Army: "Since the day of its establishment and throughout its history, our army has been an army for Iraq and a shield to safeguard its borders, land, waters, and skies." He further referred to the history of the institution by saying: "Despite Saddam's attempts to put out the candle of the army and suppress its spirit, he has failed to destroy and alter the history of the establishment of our army, the army of Iraq" ("Allawi" *Al-Sabah al-Jadid*, January 8, 2005: 4). In the lead up to the Iraqi national elections, in December 2005 Allawi campaigned on the premise of restoring the dignity of the Iraqi Army as a political platform. Allawi, as head of the National Iraqi List coalition, addressed a group of former Iraqi Army officers, depicting the former Iraqi Army as an integral part of the nation's history: "In fact you are aware more than others that this army played an important role in the history of Iraq." He also declared that the institution was an "anchor" for the nation, incorporating all of its communities in its ranks: "You in the Iraqi Armed Forces are aware that the Army was composed of all strata of the Iraqi society and from all colors and forms. That is Iraq. It includes Shiites, Sunnis, Christians, Turkomans, Kurds, and Arabs" ("Allawi," *Al-Sharqiyya*, December 1, 2005). His statement was reminiscent of King Faysal and Jaafar Al-Askari's desire to create an Iraqi Army that would unite all of the nation's communities and Allawi's final statement resembled the King's assessment written in 1933 that Iraq could not survive without a strong army. Allawi concluded: "Iraq would never have stability unless there is a capable army that is able to defend Iraq's borders and the people of Iraq" (ibid.).

Allawi represented the Iraqi state at that time, but opposition parties also used the Army as a symbol to rally behind. During the same Army Day celebrations that Allawi spoke at, Harith Sulayman Al-Dari, the secretary general of the Association of Muslim Scholars (AMS) served as an opposition organization at that time, representing the interests of Sunni Arabs. Al-Dari lamented the dissolution of the Iraqi Army and argued that only those who were ignorant of the Army's history would have blamed it for Saddam Hussein's actions. He wrote of the Army in the pro-AMS daily, *Al-Basair* that the Iraqi Army was exploited to protect "personal, partisan, and factional" interests that erupted in coups, acknowledging "dark periods" in Iraq's history. Furthermore he argued that the Saddam Hussein government turned it into "a private army," and he blamed Hussein for entangling "the army in adventures, such as the eight-year war with Iran and the invasion of Kuwait at a cost of great life to the military." In his words, such diversions of the Army prevented it from becoming the "army of the people and the homeland and the *Arab nation*" (emphasis added) ("Iraqi Muslim scholars leader," *Al-Basa'ir*, January 12, 2005: 12). Not only did Dari refer to the history of the Army but invoked an Arab nationalist discourse prevalent during the era of the Four Colonels.

The Iraqi Defense Minister Al-Shaalan in his interview with *Al-Sharqiyya* reminded his audience of what happened after every change in government: "During the coups de etats in the past, the Iraqi Army remained as it was; namely, that police work and security were maintained. Only the command used to change" ("Al-Sha'lan," *Al-Sharqiyya*, January 25, 2005). Abd Al-Muhsin Shalash, secretary general of the Free Iraqi Society Party also made a statement similar to Al-Shaalan's in the paper *Al-Manar*: "In the case of a change of regime anywhere in the world the regular army remains intact, as it has nothing to do with political changes" ("Party leaders," *Al-Manar* January 6, 2004: 1, 4). The aforementioned points made by Al-Shaalan and Shalash were conveyed to the authors by former members of the Iraqi military on repeated occasions. When discussing the dissolution of the Iraqi military, they would routinely delve into the history of Iraq's past coups; any new Iraqi administration would purge the Army of its opponents but keep the institution intact.

Shalash also reverted to a former trend in Iraqi history when stating how the Iraqi Army sought to emulate the Turkish Army. He said of the Iraqi Army: "It remains a neutral party and a faithful guardian of the country, as in the liberal countries. Such examples are the Turkish army and the Iraqi Army under the monarchy." While some circles in Turkey would disagree with Shalash that the Turkish Army is "a neutral party," especially prior to the July 2007 Turkish elections, nonetheless he followed a tradition in Iraq's past where Al-Sabbagh, Hikmat Sulayman, Sami Shawkat and Abd Al-Karim Qasim admired the military's role in Turkey and hoped that the Iraqi Army could play the same role. Shalash concluded his statements by invoking the historical legacy of the Iraqi Army: "We hope that 6 January would remain the official day of the Iraqi Army, as it is undoubtedly a historical fact" (ibid.).

During an interview with the independent Baghdad daily *Al-Dustur* (*The Constitution*) Staff General Amir Bakr Al-Hashimi, the former Chief of Staff of the new Iraqi Army reiterated the importance of historical legacy: "In preparing for the new army we must benefit from the previous experiences because our army is an old army, which was formed in 1921, and it has high experiences" ("New Iraqi army chief," *Al-Dustur*, May 30, 2004: 1). Thus, even though he held the highest rank in the new Iraqi Army, Al-Hashimi still felt the need to remember the tradition inherited from the former Iraqi military.

The history of the Iraqi Army was also characterized by episodes of internal repression that were hardly glorious, nevertheless it became an institution whose history was revised in light of Bremer's disbandment decree. As it was the only institution left that symbolized Iraq's sovereignty at the time, Iraqis went back in time to revive the image of the Iraqi Army and distance it from the politicians of the past, most notably Saddam Hussein.

Humiliation and the former Iraqi military

Ahmed Hashim, when analyzing Iraqi motivations for joining the insurgency quoted Isaiah Berlin who wrote: "Nationalism is an inflamed condition of national consciousness which can be and has occasion been tolerant and peaceful. It usually seems to be caused by wounds, some form of collective *humiliation*" (emphasis added) (Berlin 1972: 17). To further his point, Hashim then quoted a former Army officer who joined the insurgency due to the "shame and humiliation at the dissolution of the army" (Hashim 2006: 98). The notion of humiliation after the disbandment of the Iraqi military emerged on numerous occasions and often in different contexts. For example one of the banners held by former Iraqi soldiers and officers protesting outside of the CPA after its decree read: "Dissolving the Iraqi army is a humiliation to the dignity of the nation" (Fineman *et al.*, *Los Angeles Times*, 2003: 1). In late January 2005, Iraq's former Defense Minister Al-Shaalan spoke of the dissolution of the Iraqi Army as follows: "It implied humiliation and belittlement of the Iraqi Army. Frankly speaking, we could not tolerate this" ("Al-Sha'lan," *Al-Sharqiyya* January 25, 2005). In a nation where honor (*sharaf*) often serves as a commodity more valuable than money itself, the disbandment decree was viewed as an insult to the honor of the oldest institution in Iraq and by extension to the Iraqi population at large, and finally a violation of the honor of the individual Iraqi soldier.

In defending the disbandment decree, Slocombe told the ICG, "[I] can't see why a conquered and vanquished army should expect to be nurtured and paid for nothing" (ICG 2003: 7). However, even paying them for "nothing" would have been a better alternative than depriving soldiers of immediate employment, motivating them to join the insurgency and sectarian militias. The fact that they were "conquered and vanquished" was humiliating enough for the soldiers, but disbanding their armed forces further aggravated these former military men and motivated them to join what they would regard as an honorable national resistance movement against an occupation.

The notions of humiliation, disempowerment and despair from a lack of livelihood were expressed during interviews with former Iraqi military personnel. For example, Colonel Ali Sadiq said in September 2003: "I served in the army for some 18 years. I am an officer and I have a family and kids to feed. I shouldn't be forced to pay for Saddam's ouster" (ibid.: 11). Another officer said, "If they don't pay us, if they make our children suffer, they'll hear from us." Couched in this officer's implicit threat is the notion of humiliation as former officers were forced to accept degrading employment to survive: "They take jobs that do not befit army officers, such as selling vegetables or sweets" (Hashim 2006: 96). Staff Brigadier General Nabil Khalil reiterated their sense of desperation: "The Americans dissolved the army and then they decreed they would not give us a cent, precisely in order to make us understand that we were a *vanquished* army" (emphasis added) (ICG 2003: 12). Khalil's use of the term "vanquished," as was employed by Slocombe, underlined the notion of humility felt by the former Iraqi military as well as the Iraqi perception that the decree was a power play. The General gave further evidence of what he perceived as the CPA's attempts to manipulate the former members of the armed forces: "Then, all of a sudden, in July, Mr. Bremer decided to be magnanimous: he paid us in advance three months' worth of our pay. How can one account for such a cavalier attitude?" (ibid.: 13). Ultimately the CPA's decree led to 400,000 men with military training without work. According to the ICG, every soldier provided on average for a family of four and thus the CPA decree meant that approximately 1.6 million Iraqis were deprived of an income (ibid.). Furthermore the CPA did not make any sustained effort to help these former soldiers with their transition to civilian life. Even Saddam Hussein acknowledged the challenges of demobilization and the consequences for failing to do so. In this volume, this fear is attributed as one of the reasons that led to the invasion of Kuwait.

Rebuilding the new Iraqi Army

The CPA ordered the creation of a new Iraqi Army with the aim of recruiting twenty-seven battalions or 40,000 men, a further indication that the 400,000 men that were left unemployed after the disbandment decree had little numerical chances of joining the new force. The CPA made no provisions for the Iraqi armed forces to have an air force, as the US military would provide air support in the near future, as the UK had done for the Iraqi Army during the mandate. The new Iraqi Army was envisioned by the CPA to function as a light infantry force, to maintain internal security without a strong logistics component or heavy armor, thus reassuring its neighbors that the new Iraqi Army would be incapable of invading a country outside of its borders. In Bremer's memoirs he said, "Shortly after arriving, I had told General Abizaid and McKiernan that the President wanted an Iraqi military adequate for national defense. But we would not countenance a huge, unrepresentative force that repressed Iraq's citizens and threatened her neighbors" (Bremer 2006: 56). These decisions made by the Americans are eerily similar to how the British made decisions about Iraq's mandate army in 1921. Just as the CPA hoped that the Iraqi Army could assume America's military role in Iraq, at the Cairo conference in 1921 the British also envisioned an Iraqi mandate army without an air force and thus dependent on the UK for air support, while the Iraqis would take over responsibility for internal order (Dodge 2003a: 135–6). Until the Iraqi mandate army would be strong enough to defend Iraq, British forces would stay in the country as the military grew. Both the British in 1921 and the US in 2003 set out a number of how many Iraqi troops they envisioned would be sufficient for defending Iraq, thus allowing the British and American troops to withdraw. Just as the British underestimated how many Iraqi soldiers would be needed to achieve this task, so did the US. The Americans realized that number of 40,000 was woefully inadequate and that an armed force of over of 200,000 troops would be required with an air force and navy and an army outfitted with artillery and tanks to bring stability to Iraq.

The post-war Iraqi security structure

While the new Iraqi Army was to be trained, a series of parallel militaries emerged similar to the vast array of armies created during the Saddam Hussein era. The Facilities Protection Service (FPS) defended targets of political and economic value, largely in a static defense role (Hashim 2003a: 42). It was primarily tasked with defending the Iraqi ministries and oil pipelines from insurgent attacks. The FPS reported to the Ministry of the Interior under the Iraqi Governing Council (IGC), the caretaker body that was to serve as an Iraqi liaison with the CPA. The Department of Border Enforcement (DBE) also reported to the same Ministry when the IGC existed. Their mission was to guard Iraq's porous borders with Syria, Saudi Arabia and Iran, as they allowed for the infiltration of fighters into Iraq. Finally the other parallel military force was not even Iraqi, but consisted of CPA-funded US private security companies that guarded key infrastructure and officials. The presence of the private security companies caused resentment among the Iraqis, similar to the resentment in the 1930s to the Assyrian Levies. The Iraqis then considered the Levies as private British mercenaries (Longrigg 1953: 197). Decades later the Iraqis regarded the private security companies in the same vein.

On September 3, 2003, during the CPA/military occupation phase in Iraq, the CPA issued Order Number 28, "Establishment of the Iraqi Civil Defense Corps," or the ICDC. These temporary paramilitary units were controlled directly by the US (Hashim 2003a: 41). Organized into battalions, each unit received an intensive two week training course by US instructors. The ICDC assumed a security role beyond that of the Iraqi police, serving at checkpoints and carrying out joint patrols with Coalition forces.

However problems began to plague the ICDC. First the units were pen-etrated by recruits belonging to insurgent groups, as would happen later with the new Iraqi Army. The ICDC needed to recruit members in a rushed manner, and the enlistment procedure often failed to vet former loyalists of the Saddam Hussein government. In a reference to another group extremely loyal to Hussein, the ICDC was referred to by Iraqis as "Bremer's Fedayeen" (ICG 2003: 21). The third deficiency within the ICDC was a pattern common to the armed forces of Iraq since their incep-tion: the prevalence of patronage networks. Political party leaders sought to infiltrate their followers, some of them members of the *peshmerga* and Shia militias, within the ranks of the ICDC.

There were also critiques of America's control of the ICDC which was to follow guidelines and rules established by the US Department of Defense. An article in the Baghdad based *Al-Basa'ir*, the paper of the AMS. was critical of the regulations imposed on its soldiers. It argument that the ICDC served the interests of the US resonated with the perception that the Iraqi Army in the 1920s was a mandate army of the British. In one article, Imad Al-Qaysi a writer for *Al-Basa'ir* blasted this relationship: "This means that the enlisted person, according to Article 5, is obliged at all times to obey all the war laws, including all the orders and policies issued by the US Defense Department, and not the Iraqi Defense Min-istry." The question of sovereignty of Iraq's military was questioned in this article as it was in the early 1920s: "The name of Iraq was jammed in at the end of this paragraph, but on condition that the United States allows it to practice such a right. Where, then, is the sovereignty in all this?" The author of the report concluded, "On top of all this, they call the corps the Iraqi Civil Defense Corps, but it would have been better to call it the US Civil Defense Corps in Iraq" ("Iraqi Civil Defense Corps," *Al-Basa'ir*, August 26, 2004: 5). By July 2004, after the transfer of sovereignty to an interim Iraqi government, the Iraq Civil Defense Corps was converted into the National Guard (Dodge 2005: 22). The name had changed but its duties were the same. In January 2005 all Iraqi National Guard units in Iraq were subsumed into the new Iraqi Army.

Iraqi sovereignty and the military

In its initial phases in the 1920s and 1930s, the Iraqi mandate army was designed as a force to maintain internal security, while the British took care of Iraq's external defense, similar to the situation in Iraq in 2007, where the US was concerned that the Iraqi military at least be able to deal with internal security from threats such as the insurgency and sectarian militias. In Iraq's mandate era and post-1932 independence period, Iraqis were irritated over what they perceived as foreign infringement on Iraqi sovereignty by dictating affairs relating to the military. Staff Brigadier General Khalil Nabil even made this historical analogy in an interview. When criticizing the CPA's control over the Iraqi military he said, "Are we going to revert to the disastrous formula of the British mandate, when there were two chains of command – an Iraqi one that served merely as a go-between and a foreign one that made all the decisions?" (ICG 2003: 17). The British Military Mission in Iraq established under the 1922 Treaty of Alliance resembled the post-2003 Iraq War Multi National Transitional Security Command (MNTSC). Both institutions maintained considerable control over the Iraqi military and continued to do so after Iraq's independence. In both instances, foreign control over army divisions and the influence of the UK or US military advisors stirred resentment among the Iraqi officers.

After 2003, debates emerged over how Iraq could establish stable institutions of state without a strong military to protect them. For example, Lieutenant Majid al-Azzawi, declared his concern over the absence of a sovereign army to defend Iraq, saying, "There can be no state without an army and without a national defense. If tomorrow the U.S. decides for purely electoral and domestic reasons to withdraw, who will defend our 3,000 km-long borders?" (ibid.: 12). This concern was also expressed by Jaafar Al-Askari in the paper he wrote on the situation in Iraq in 1932: "It would be utterly foolhardy of us to plan the establishment of government, industrial and agricultural industries without putting in place sufficient security forces to preserve the system" (Facey and Shawkat 2003: 243). Like the Iraqi military that was formed after the 2003 Iraq War, Al-Askari stressed that the Army had to deal decisively with internal security, enforce the rule of law and collect weapons held by civilians. Al-Askari realized that Iraq would have to depend on the UK for its protection until the Iraqi Army was prepared to handle these tasks, just as the US would take charge of Iraq's external and internal defense until the new Iraqi Army could cope with the same threats that existed after Iraq's independence in 1932.

The challenges of recruitment and training

The problems with recruitment were not new to Iraq and the British faced the same difficulties in the 1920s. Despite the considerable dangers associated with military work in post-war Iraq, former officers and young men enlisted in the armed forces as it was one of the few sources of employment. The other challenge to recruitment was a result of the security situation. Suicide car bombers in post-Baathist Iraq targeted potential army recruits as they waited in line to enlist. Furthermore, if a recruit could enlist, he faced the daunting possibility of being killed on duty. The insurgency preyed upon inexperienced recruits, with insurgent gunmen often armed with more weaponry than the new Iraqi Army.

While much of the training and arms supply for the new Iraqi Army came from members of the Coalition, the new Iraqi Army also received some modest training and arms supply from other Arab countries. This was also a point of contention to some in Iraq who resented how a traditionally proud and strong nation like Iraq was reduced to a mere recipient of aid and training from smaller Arab countries. For example, the decision to send Iraqi officers for training in Jordan was criticized by former Iraqi officers. The Coalition had adopted the "train the trainer" approach where 700 Iraqi officers would receive seven-weeks' training at Jordan's Royal Military Academy. These trainees would return to Iraq and train other Iraqis. On January 3, 2004, Iraqi writer Imad Shaaban ridiculed the decision to train the Iraqi officers in Jordan in a commentary in the newspaper *Al-Ittijah al-Akhar*, owned by Mishan Al-Juburi, a politician who escaped from Iraq and founded the first insurgent satellite channel *Al-Zawra* (Al-Marashi 2007: 80). Shaaban wrote sarcastically: "I beg your pardon, has anyone heard about the expertise of the Jordanian Army or read about the lessons that it has gained in the field of battle?" The fact that the Jordanian Army perhaps performed better than any of the Arab armies in the 1948 Arab–Israeli War is forgotten by this author. However, Shaaban meant to criticize the recent experience of the Jordanian Army:

> So what has suddenly transpired that requires the officers of the fourth strongest army in the world to be trained by an army that was used only to suppress demonstrations and riots, crush the Palestinians, and protect the border with Israel?

He then evoked the humiliation frame that had been used by past Iraqi commentators on the state of the military: "What is happening is indeed humiliating," and in almost a formulaic manner used by other Iraqis, he reminded his audience of the past history of the Iraqi military: "The glories of the Iraqi Army cannot be erased so easily" ("Iraqi writer," *Al-Ittijah al-Akhar*, January 3, 2004: 5).

In a fashion reminiscent of Iraqi criticism of the British in the 1920s this writer also echoed similar sentiments when referring to Bremer: "He is the High Commissioner and the absolute ruler," a disparaging analogy used to link the CPA to the highest authority in the British mandate of Iraq. Finally he concluded with a statement similar to the language employed in the 1920s and 1930s in Iraq. Shaaban wrote, "Every Iraqi minister has an American officer that makes decisions on his behalf and from whom he takes his instructions. Even the Iraqi ministers know this fact" (ibid.). The reference to American advisors in the Iraqi ministries in this article resembles one of the Iraqi poets in the 1930s, who referred to British control over the Iraqi ministries in the same manner, lamenting, "He who enters the Ministries will find that they are shackled with the chains of foreign advisers" (quoted in Tarbush 1982: 40).

During the March 1921 Cairo conference it was agreed that an Iraqi Army would be created along British lines, with training and equipment provided by the UK. The Iraqis also criticized US efforts to train the Iraqi Army on American lines. In August 2006, the speaker of the Iraqi Parliament Mahmud Mashhadani argued that American training was not raising the performance level of Iraqi troops and was damaging the legitimacy of the Iraqi Army among the Iraqi populace. He said: "The training is done on the American way and in accordance with the American mentality, which the Iraqi people hate. Thus, the Iraqi people view this Iraqi security force as one to protect the Americans" ("Iraqi speaker," *Al-Zaman*, August 13, 2006: 5). His statements corroborated Cordesman's assessment that one of the greatest problems the US faced was that an Iraqi Army it trained and armed would be seen by Iraqis as a paramilitary force that served the interests of an occupier (ICG 2003: 16). Essentially Mashhadani was criticizing what he perceived as a mandate army protecting "imperial interests" of the US. The US found itself in a no win situation in post-Baathist Iraq. The Iraqi Army could not survive without American training and arms, yet its support of the Iraqi military hurt the latter's legitimacy in the eyes of the Iraqis.

Iraq's first military academy in the mandate was based on the model of the Royal Military College at Sandhurst in the UK. In this case, continuity with the British past remained, when this school at Al-Rustamiyya had reopened after the 2003 war. Even the British in the 1920s admitted that the school had been handicapped as they rushed to train the Iraqis, often in an improvised way (FO 371/10095, Report, Iraqi Administration, April 1922 to March 1923: 112). The rushed training for the new Iraqi Army organized by the Coalition Military Assistance Training Team had also produced similar results. During the mandate talented graduates from the Iraqi military schools were given the opportunity to pursue their studies, including flight training in the UK (FO 371/8998, Report, High Commissioner, October 1, 1920 to March 31, 1922: 37). In a bimonthly publication of the MNTSC called the *Advisor*, it detailed the training efforts of the new Iraqi military. Just as the UK trained Iraq's first pilots on British soil, one article described how a future Iraqi Air Force pilot would study in the United States Air Force Academy (*Advisor*, July 7, 2007: 10).

Ethno-sectarian cleavages in the Iraqi military

Debates surrounding Iraq in the years after 2003 questioned whether the country was in a state of civil war, a particular concern among US policy makers. This question was not new to Iraq as it was expressed in the 1930s, when the British ambassador to Iraq, Edmonds, described the situation in Iraq "drifting into something not far off civil war' (FO 371/20795, December 23, 1936). In the 1930s, with their own arsenals at their disposal, the tribes and militias had been able to carve out para-states of their own in the south and north, just as the Iraqi insurgents in post-Baathist Iraq had been able to carve out their own states within a state in the Al-Anbar and Diyala provinces and in neighborhoods of Baghdad.

Ethno-sectarian alliances have challenged the cohesiveness of the new Iraqi military and comparisons have been made with the Lebanese Army prior to 1975. In the initial years of the Lebanese civil war, soldiers often joined forces with their respective sectarian militias. Iraqis such as Ali Dabbagh, the representative of Ayatollah Sistani (who later became spokesman for the Iraqi Prime Minister Nuri al-Maliki) compared Iraq's situation to Lebanon when stating, "we risk witnessing a Lebanonisation of the situation with every Iraqi fighting over every street corner" (ICG 2003: 19). Creating a multi-ethnic force where national loyalty transcended the primordial had proved daunting for the new Iraqi Army, as it was for the former Iraqi Army after its creation in 1921.

The totalitarian military under Saddam Hussein consisted of numerous parallel militaries, whether it was the regular Army balanced by the Popular Army, or the Republican Guard countered by the Special Republican Guard. In post-Baathist Iraq, the armed forces were characterized by unofficial parallel militaries such as the Shia Mahdi Army and the Badr Brigade of the Supreme Council for the Islamic Revolution in Iraq (SCIRI), and predominantly Arab Sunni forces such as the Islamic Army in Iraq. These groups had infiltrated the various branches of Iraq's military with the aim of furthering their sectarian agendas. Members of insurgent groups, sectarian and ethnic militias could join the military with relative ease. Iraqis hostile to the US and new Iraqi government took advantage of aggressive military recruitment and rudimentary background checks to acquire training and arms. Off duty soldiers sympathetic to the insurgency would cooperate with these groups, providing them with sensitive operational information. For example, in the summer of 2004 a staff member of General Amir Bakr Al-Hashimi, the first Chief of Staff in the new Iraqi Army gave information to insurgents that they used to assassinate another army officer (Sharp 2005: 5). The breach of security ultimately led to the dismissal of General Al-Hashimi.

Members of the Shia and Kurdish militias filled the ranks of military units, particularly those stationed in the south and north respectively. According to the KDP's military bureau, the *peshmerga* had evolved into a regular and disciplined "Army of Kurdistan" in their words and thus argued were no longer a "militia." The Kurdistan Regional Government (KRG) administered its own military academies in Sulaymaniyya, operated by the PUK, and another in Zakho run by the KDP (ICG 2003: 18). Two divisions of the new Iraqi Army, the Second and Third, each made up of 15,000 soldiers, have Kurdish commanders and its ranks are more than 50 percent Kurdish (Cordesman 2006b: 35). The KRG has proved reluctant to forming multi-ethnic military units in the area they administer. A

Kurdish Colonel in the Iraqi Army opposed the central Iraqi government efforts to "dilute" the Kurdish constituency of his brigade:

> The ministry of Defense recently sent me 150 Arab soldiers from the south. After two weeks of service, we sent them away. We did not accept them. We will not let them carry through with their plans to bring more Arab soldiers here.
>
> (ibid.: 61)

A similar view was expressed by a member of the PUK who said, "No Arab soldier should be assigned to Kurdistan and no Kurdish soldier should be assigned to the Arab regions. Soldiers from Ramadi ought to patrol the border with Saudi Arabia. And the North is too cold for Arab soldiers" (ICG 2003: 17). The aforementioned tensions between Arabs and Kurds in the military had their historical precedents. Similar problems plagued the Army in 1930 according to a British report:

> The Arabs consider the Kurds treacherous and say they never know whether they will not be shot in the back by the Kurds in action. They treat the Kurdish soldiers with opprobrium. This the Kurds resent in their turn and the whole force is full of mutual jealousy and hatred and mistrust.
>
> (Air 23/120/, 1/BD/56, July 17, 1930)

In the mandate armies of both periods, ethno-sectarian cleavages affected its overall cohesiveness. The KDP and PUK have been reluctant to let Arabs join Iraqi military units in the north and Kurdish soldiers have also refused to serve outside the KRG. The first battalion that underwent training by the US faltered due to ethno-sectarian differences as Kurds objected to serving in any of the Arab provinces (ICG 2003: 18).

Both the British and American mandate armies suffered from troops deserting while training was in progress. A total of 900 men started training for the first battalion of the new Army, but close to 480 quit due to the working conditions, low salaries and their perceived humiliation (ibid.: 15). The same crisis occurred when the British trained the Iraqis during the mandate. The Iraqis then joined the military out of economic need, rather than a sense of loyalty to the newly formed Iraqi state. In the 1920s Iraqi troops were discontent with their working conditions and some wanted to quit to join the army of the newly formed Republic of Turkey (CO 730/1, Intelligence Report, no. 11, April 15, 1921). In post-Baathist Iraq, soldiers that managed to pass the training, deserted after receiving orders to deploy in areas far from their home or to insecure provinces where the insurgency ranged, such as the volatile "Arab Sunni triangle" (ICG 2003: 15). During a graduation parade in the Al-Habbaniyya military base west of Baghdad, about 1,000 new Iraqi soldiers protested, some of them taking off their shirts, throwing them away in rage and threatened to not carry out their military service at all after being informed that they would serve outside their hometowns ("Iraqi soldiers," *Al-Sharqiyya*, May 1, 2006). Iraqi troops in the new Army have proved reluctant to forgo ethnic and sectarian loyalties and adhere to the commands of the central government. In certain cases, they refuse to combat ethno-sectarian militias whose members could include friends, neighbors and family members. During the fighting in Falluja in April 2004, US forces sent an Iraqi fighting unit comprising mostly Sunni Arabs to suppress a revolt led mostly by Sunni Arabs. The Americans were frustrated as this military unit went into Falluja, disbanded and sided with the rebels.

This phenomenon was not new to Iraq, serving as a problem the British and Iraqi government faced in the 1930s. A British report in 1935 described a similar situation as follows: "Many of the officers are believed to be in sympathy with the Government's opponents, and the majority of the rank and file, being Shi'ah ... some few officers actually refused to proceed to the front" (FO 371/18945, March 21, 1935). Conscription resulted then in a military comprising troops recruited among the rural tribes in Iraq. When these conscripts were deployed to fight against their fellow tribesmen in revolt in 1935, their loyalty to the tribes was stronger than their loyalty to an army they were forced join.

The effectiveness of Iraqi military forces

The quality, mission and role of the new Iraqi Army in the years after its creation did not settle doubts as to whether it could provide security for Iraq in the case of an American withdrawal. In addition to high attrition rates and desertions during combat, the Iraqi Army's performance in the field had been lackluster. One source documented how American trainers referred to an Iraqi habit of "Inshallah firing" meaning if "God willed it," the soldier's bullets would hit their intended target (Fallows, *Atlantic Monthly*, 2005: 70). While such comments made the Iraqi military seem totally incompetent, one also has to realize that they were being trained for an entirely new mission. The Iraqi military often fought in trenches during the Iran–Iraq War or in wide spaces during the 1991 Gulf War and in some cases not at all during the 2003 Iraq War. While the military had been used for domestic repression in the past, bombing villages with artillery or haphazardly from the air, it rarely had a mission as an urban counter-insurgency force. The Iraqis were learning these tactics just in the way the American forces had to learn this style of warfare in Iraq after the end of the 2003 war.

In August 2006, Iraqi Parliament Speaker Mahmud Mashhadani declared, "Any armed group can defeat an Iraqi army brigade because it [the former] has sophisticated rockets and weapons" ("Iraqi speaker," *Al-Zaman*, August 13, 2006: 5). His assessment of the fragility of the armed forces also had a historical precedent. The British High Commissioner Henry Dobbs feared that Iraq's military in 1925 could be defeated by one of the armed Iraqi tribes (CO 730/82/24432, April 26, 1925). In terms of weapons Mashhadani also blamed the United States for intentionally providing the Iraqi Army with insufficient equipment for fear of creating a strong Iraqi Army that would be difficult to control: "The Americans have an obsession that if a strong Iraqi security force is established it may conspire against them. Therefore, the Iraqi forces are being armed and equipped with weapons that are not worth talking about" ("Iraqi speaker," *Al-Zaman*, August 13, 2006: 5). His sentiment was also expressed in the mandate and post-1932 independence era in Iraq. Iraqis were convinced then that the UK wanted to keep the mandate army strong enough to maintain internal order to secure British interests, including oil-fields and the overland route to India, while at the same time ensuring that this Army would not emerge strong enough with advanced weapons to challenge the British presence in Iraq. For example, the British feared that giving the Royal Iraqi Air Force additional aircraft could challenge the air superiority enjoyed by the British Royal Air Force stationed in Iraq.

By 2007 the Iraqi Air Force consisted of a mere fleet of helicopters and a few transport aircraft, hardly sufficient to support Iraqi ground forces in combat. In January 2007 a battle between the rather inexperienced Iraqi military and insurgents in the restive area of Haifa Street in Baghdad lasted for several hours. The insurgents lodged in a building proved tenacious during the battle, pinning down the Iraqi soldiers. In another battle during the same month, a beleaguered Iraqi military unit fought a pitched battle with an estimated 600 insurgents in the vicinity of the southern Iraqi town of Najaf. The decisive factor in both battles was American air support. An inexperienced military dependent on foreign air support had an historical precedent in Iraq. Despite the anti-Britishism in the Iraqi military, it was still dependent on the Royal Air Force in suppressing the Kurdish and tribal uprisings raging in the north and south respectively.

The US government stressed that despite these setbacks the new Iraqi Army continued to achieve levels of professionalism and proficiency. It argued that increasing numbers of Iraqi Army battalions were capable of coordinating, planning and executing security operations independent of Coalition forces in their own areas of responsibility, with the Coalition providing only logistical and intelligence support. However, critics doubted the successes claimed by the US government and accused it of embellishing actual Iraqi troop capability and combat readiness in its desperation to show progress.

The Maliki government and the military

On September 6, 2006, the US handed over control of the new Iraqi armed forces command to the government of Nuri Al-Maliki. Iraq's Prime

Minister, who is also the Commander-in-Chief of the armed forces, controlled the state's small Air Force and Navy, and the Iraqi Eighth Army Division, which the US claimed had an entirely indigenous, autonomous chain of command. American officials hailed this move as a crucial milestone in Iraq's path to independence, but the Iraqi security forces were hardly self-sufficient at that juncture and in no position to take over the security of the entire Iraq. The positive assessments were contradicted by a leaked assessment from the US National Security Advisor that accused the Al-Maliki government of seeding the military with Shia militia members and removing effective military commanders on an ethno-sectarian basis (Gordon, *New York Times*, 2006: 1). In June 2007 Al-Maliki appeared to address such criticisms in a speech to the Iraqi Army:

> I tell you in all frankness that the prerequisite of victory is making soldiers and officers patriots who care for nothing except Iraq, regardless of their affiliations. Focus on this doctrine, the doctrine of equality, the doctrine of the homeland, the doctrine that would spare the army sectarianism, confessionalism, and political partisanship. The army must not be involved in political partisanship and parliamentary life.
>
> ("Al-Maliki speech," *Al-Iraqiyya*, June 6, 2007)

He urged the army to remedy the trends of sectarianism that were crippling the armed forces, although Al-Maliki's government suffered from the same sectarian symptoms. Finally he also made a reference to a persistent trend in Iraq's history: "The army cannot be politicized as happened in the past" (ibid.). Essentially he asked the armed forces to appreciate the lessons from Iraq's tumultuous military history and ensure that history did not repeat itself. However, the speech and similar efforts could not placate Al-Maliki's opponents in the government. The predominantly Arab Sunni Tawafuq Front decided to withdraw its members from the Iraqi National Assembly in August 2007, after accusing Al-Maliki of failing to curtail the infiltration of Shia militia members in the military. The ethno-sectarian cleavages within the Iraqi armed forces seemed likely to handicap the Al-Maliki government for the rest of its tenure. Another challenge facing the Al-Maliki government was highlighted in a July 2007 US Government Accountability Office (GAD) report. The report stated that 190,000 AK-47 assault rifles and pistols given to Iraqi security forces in 2004 and 2005 were unaccounted for and most likely had fallen into the hands of insurgents (GAO 2007). One of King Faysal's fears was that the populace had more arms than the Iraqi Army and Jaafar Al-Askari stressed that the military's priority was to collect arms in the hands of civilians, the same problems Al-Maliki faced decades later.

History repeating itself in Iraq

"Alas, we Americans do not naturally look to history for cautionary lessons about the future. Had we done that, our post-Saddam expectations would have been different" (Peretz, *New Republic*, 2004: 25). The preceding statement by Martin Peretz proved to be a sad testament to the valuable history lessons that early Iraqi history could have provided to American policy makers, as well as the British, Australian, Italian and other members in the Coalition. While the authors described Iraq's post-2003 military as a mandate army to stress the historical relevance of the British experience in Iraq, the historian Keith Watenpaugh also made a similar analogy in his article "The *guiding principles* and the U.S. 'mandate' for Iraq" (Watenpaugh 2003). In a summer 2003 journal article by Judith Yaphe entitled, "War and occupation in Iraq: what went right? what could go wrong?," she offered specific lessons to learn from the British as they built up Iraq's military (Yaphe 2003: 396). A good number of her recommendations, particularly those relating to the military, were never heeded.

It is not just that the history of the Iraqi military that had begun to repeat itself in post-Baathist Iraq, but the overall political development of the nation as well. When commenting on the transfer of sovereignty to an interim Iraqi government, Haifa Zangana wrote an article entitled, "Iraqis have lived this lie before." She also sought to analyze the events in Iraq as a repeat of the mandate era:

> In Iraq we don't just read history at school – we carry it within ourselves. It's no wonder, then, that we view what is happening in Iraq now of "liberation-mandate-nominal sovereignty" as a replay of what took place in the 1920s and afterwards.
>
> (Zangana, *Guardian*, 2004: 20)

Furthermore, in a journal article entitled "History Matters," the scholar Eric Davis stressed the need to understand Iraq's past if one wanted to make sense of Iraq's present. He wrote: "In the Middle East, history – or perhaps more precisely, historical memory – deeply informs the contemporary cultural and political consciousness of its peoples" (Davis 2005b: 229).

Granted, there were differences between Britain's mandate experience in Iraq and that of the US in post-Baathist Iraq. However, the comparisons between the British and American experiences shed light on how Iraqis could use their past to make sense of the present. Citing the similarities between the two periods emphasizes the significance of the past for Iraqi. What is achieved through this study is an attempt to understand how the Iraqis could utilize historical memory to criticize the American role in developing the Iraqi military. To understand the Iraqi discontent with the

US in Iraq, one only needs to look at the events that transpired in the 1920s and 1930s when Britain dominated Iraqi affairs, particularly those relating to its military.

The American domestic debates surrounding the withdrawal of American forces from Iraq focused on whether the Iraqi forces would be ready in the near future to secure their country. Domestic pressure to have troops withdraw from Iraq also had a historical precedent. In the March 1921 Cairo Conference, the dilemma of the British delegates would be the same that would face US officials decades later: how to reduce the exorbitant costs of deployments in Iraq, while at the same time not hurting Iraq's ability to defend itself, both externally, and more crucially, internally. Quincy Wright wrote of the domestic environment in the UK during the British mandate in 1926: "Incidentally, it may be noticed that the anxiety of the Parliament and British public opinion about the expense of the undertaking did not reduce the difficulties" (Wright 1926: 752). After 2003, the words "Parliament" and "British public opinion" could be substituted with "Congress" and "American public opinion." Just as Paul Bremer moved on to the lecture circuit after his role as civilian head of the CPA, his British equivalent, High Commissioner Henry Dobbs also gave a series of lectures, such as the one he delivered at the Royal Empire Society in 1933. Dobbs concluded his speech with a frank assessment, a sentiment echoed years later by various American officials involved in the war in Iraq. Dobbs said, "We have squandered blood, treasure and high ability. We have bound debts and taxes on the necks of generations of our descendents." He concluded, "You ask, For all this shall we have reward? I answer that I cannot say" (quoted in Salih 1996: 48).

The title of one article, "Iraq's Doubtful Future" featured in the London *Times* seems to describe Iraq's prospects after the 2003 war. The article dated September 1922 gave a skeptical assessment of Iraq's political destiny. Its subline, "Feisal bid for independence, British prestige in the balance," might very well have read after the 2003 Iraq War, "Prime Minister Maliki's bid for independence, American prestige in the balance." In the mandate army chapter a quote from the article stated: "Were the British to leave the country he [King Faysal] would find the problem of defence almost impossible of solution. Up to the present the Arab Army [Iraqi Army] has been but a little better than a farce" (*The Times*, September 12, 1922: 9). The doubt over whether Iraq's weak army could secure the country after a British withdrawal were key to the debates in the UK, as they were in the US from the years from 2007 to 2008. A British report in 1923 argued that certain factions in Iraq waited eagerly for the withdrawal of foreign troops:

> Those who have thought about it welcome the date for two reasons, the one because they have complete confidence in the army and look

forward to the time when they can use it as they wish, the other because they know the day of our departure spells collapse, the fall of Faisal and the return of the Turks.

(CO 730/40 33280, 20 June 1923)

The security concerns about a premature British reduction of forces threatening the stability of Iraq, and working to the benefit of Turkey is reminiscent of the debates in the US that withdrawal of US forces would strengthen Shia factions who would use the Army as they wished and would strengthen Iran's role in Iraq and the entire region.

The UK presence in independent Iraq was also represented by the presence of the two military bases in Habbaniyya and Shuayba. In fact, the Habbaniyya base was the first to be attacked during the 1941 Anglo-Iraqi war. The possibility of American bases in Iraq was also viewed by the Iraqi public as a violation of the military sovereignty of Iraq. This view was expressed by Adnan Al-Dulaymi, an Iraqi politician who formed his own party generally representing Sunni Arabs in Iraq. In an interview with a Jordanian paper, Al-Dulaymi declared that the Americans would stay in Iraq by confining themselves to specific bases, but would not remain in the streets of the cities like the British had done when they occupied Iraq in 1917. He said of the British, "In the early years they interfered in everything, and then they had advisors until 1954. They did not have armies. They had two bases, one in Basra, and Al-Habbaniyya. They had consulates in Basra, Mosul, and Baghdad." He argued that the Americans would do the same by establishing military bases just as they did in Japan, Italy and Germany ("Iraqi Sunni cleric," *Al-Ra'y*, August 25, 2005: 5).

On the state funded *Al-Iraqiyya* channel, a video clip showed in standing formation a group of men dressed in uniforms from the various branches of the new Iraqi armed forces. In an example of Iraqi militainment, after a few seconds into the video clip, beats from the traditional Iraqi *chawbiyya* folkloric dance begin whereupon these Iraqi troops started to dance. The state projecting an image of a military through a music form enjoyed by all Iraqis demonstrated its attempts to portray an armed force to defend all Iraqis regardless of ethnicity and sect. The historical similarities between the British mandate era efforts in training the Iraqi military and similar American efforts demonstrated a persistent dilemma facing both foreign powers in their respective experiences in Iraq. Both Iraqi armed forces at those times were dependent primarily on two foreign nations for technical military expertise and arms. In terms of legitimacy, dependence on foreign nations for training and weapons during an occupation created the image that both militaries were mandate armies created to serve the interests of Western powers. In the 1920s and 1930s the military had to prove its Iraqi nationalist credentials by revolting against what was deemed as a pro-British government. The question remains as to whether Iraq's future army would do the same. It is possible that the new

Iraqi Army can prove its nationalist credentials, demonstrating its independence from the US and emerging as the national embodiment of sovereignty. The Iraqi Army was able to demonstrate its independence from the British. This demonstration also took the Iraqi Army on a path of intervening in Iraqi political affairs, paving the way for the ultimate rise of Saddam Hussein and the eventual disbandment of the Army in 2003.

11 Conclusion

The Iraqi state in the 1920s and after 2003 had not developed the institutions where conflicting ideologies and nationalist trends could be articulated through a political process. Iraq's politics during the early decades of the monarchy were marked by conspiracies, intrigue, corruption and shifting personal agendas. Iraq's politicians took advantage of rivalries within the Army, serving as political patrons to client networks within the officers corps. In 1936 politicians, such as Hikmat Sulayman used the military to achieve power. His dependency on General Sidqi to launch a coup ultimately led to the rise of the military itself as the ultimate arbiter of power. Combined with personal ambition, these officers would turn on their patrons through further coups, proving that brute force was more effective than political debate and bargaining. From 1936 to 1941 Iraq's political destiny was determined and dictated by the military, with the officers serving as military patrons to the politician clients. The praetorians did not administer Iraq from positions of executive authority, but they did have the ultimate say on which governments remained and which would fall. The ex-Sharifian officers, particularly Nuri Al-Said witnessed the very institution he helped to develop, the anchor of royal policy, turn against him.

All of the coups in Iraq from 1936 to 1941 aimed at removing governments with which the officers did not agree. Only in three cases was violence used to overturn a government: Sidqi's coup of October 1936 that resulted in the death of Al-Askari, the August 1937 coup that resulted in the death of Sidqi and the conflict of April 1941. In the other four coups, the officers overturned these governments with the mere threat of violence. None of the coups resulted in overthrowing the monarchy, or changing the constitution and the parliamentary system of government. The officers as moderators, never needed a valid, detailed political program that they sought to implement, nor did they use a political organization to implement such an agenda. They lacked the institutions or vision for that matter to evolve into the military ruler regimes of 1958 to 1968. The officers after 1958 sought to change the governments by ruling directly, then violence was employed on numerous occasions and the entire political system, including the constitution, was changed according the interests of the military officers in power, and they generated subsequent coups in rapid succession.

Prior to 1936, the officers had served as clients of elite families involved in politics. After 1936 the officers, coming from the middle class, had become the rulers. It was the wealthy elite who had to become the clients of the officers. In the pursuit of power these officers had made enemies, and to lose power would ultimately result in exile, imprisonment or death. While some of the officers may have been motivated by ideology or obtaining wealth vis-à-vis their enhanced political power, their ultimate priority proved to be survival itself. These officers had aligned themselves with politicians who promised reforms during this period, but both the military men and their civilian allies were too preoccupied with their survival to implement the societal reforms that were later instituted under the military ruler regimes.

The 1936 and 1941 military coups also demonstrated the generational divisions within the ex-Sharifian officers. Most of all Iraq's military officers had studied at Ottoman military colleges, and were instructed by German officers. Some of the Iraqis admired how the disparate German states were unified under a strong military. The series of coups represented an assertion of power by the younger officers who served in the Ottoman Army, which Batatu classifies as the post-1918 Sharifian group. The pre-1918 Sharifian group had joined the Arab Revolt. The post-1918 group worked in the short-lived Arab Kingdom in Damascus. The moderator praetorians, Bakr Sidqi and Abd Al-Latif Nuri and the Four Colonels were ex-Sharifians from the post-1918 group (Batatu 1979: 337). While Sidqi and Nuri were Iraqi nationalists, the Four Colonels manifested pro-Arab nationalist tendencies. Thus, what appeared as superficial political infighting among the praetorians and politicians had also an undercurrent of ideological struggle among the officers themselves. The struggle was ultimately a contest to chart Iraq's relations with the region: whether it would be a pillar of British policy in the Middle East, the core of a resurgent Arab nation or an ally with the new regional powers of Iran and Turkey. The 1936 coup was led by Iraqi nationalists. Pan-Arabism imbued the coups of 1937, 1938 and 1941.

The endurance of the pan-Arab trend from the coups of 1937 until 1968 could be explained by the fact that a large group of the officers came from the predominantly Sunni Arab northern provinces, the same area that had suffered economically due to the severance of economic links with Syria, and thus prone to Arab nationalist tendencies. Most of Iraq's officers were Sunni Muslims, ethnically Kurdish, Turkish or Arab, or a mix of these cultures. However the officers that took part in the 1937 coups were predominantly Arab Sunni, as few Kurds were joining the Staff and Military College after the Barazani rebellion, and few Arab Shia joined as well. From 1921 to the present this ethno-sectarian heterogeneity led to an unstable dynamic in the military, a reflection of the dynamics in Iraq's society at the time. Ethnic and sectarian loyalties in the military ultimately threatened the cohesion and integration of Iraq's communities in the army, a dynamic that persisted throughout Iraq's history and which continues in the reformed Iraqi military in the aftermath of the 2003 Iraq War.

Al-Bakr's government represented a break with Iraq's moderator and ruler regime past. For most of the period since 1936 to 1968, Iraq had been either ruled by the military behind the scenes or ruled by the military directly. With the exception of the period from 1941 to 1958, the military always had a final say in political affairs. It seemed that a Baathist civilian government could not survive without the approval of the military. However, the Baathists after 1968 found a successful balance between civilian and military power. President Al-Bakr was an officer who enjoyed the support from the military, yet presided over a civilian government through the RCC and the Baath Party. Unlike the Qasim ruler regime, Al-Bakr did not declare himself as the "sole leader" as Qasim or the Arif brothers did and Al-Bakr had support among a political party, the Baath. Qasim failed to establish such a base and his ruler regime succumbed in 1963 to a rival faction in the military. Unlike the Arif military ruler regime in 1963, Al-Bakr did not subordinate civilian rule to military authority, but rather devolved power to civilian leaders, particularly Saddam Hussein, who shared the same familial origins.

Once Saddam Hussein became President of Iraq in 1979, the military had been subordinated under Baath authority, even though the armed forces were the key pillar in protecting the power of the Party. Since the Baathist takeover in 1968, the priority for the Party vis-à-vis the military was de-politicizing it to weaken its potential to emerge as a moderator or ruler regime, or from being a competitive interest group for that matter. At the same time, the military was to be re-politicized with the guidance of the Party. Thus, the military in this totalitarian-penetration system was designed to serve as an ideologically committed military of the Party.

During the era of the totalitarian military from 1968 to 2003 the Iraqi officers had to operate in a difficult environment. *Targhib* involved providing for the material well being of the officers. The officers also operated in an atmosphere of *tarhib* out of fear from purges or the fear of a negatively worded report written by the political spies within their ranks. There was little incentive for them to perform well on the battlefield if they knew that a promotion would be given to an officer who was less competent but shared kin ties with the President or was a Party faithful. At the same time failure to perform well could result in strict punitive measures. This problem was only compounded by the fact that the officers could not make independent decisions on the battlefield, which could also result in failure and strict punishments. An officer also did not want to perform too well on the battlefield and then emerge as a popular war hero, as that could be seen as a threat to Hussein's popularity and also result in dire consequences.

In the totalitarian-penetration system and during Iraq's wars from 1980 to 2003, professionalism was often the victim in an atmosphere where political loyalty trumped combat efficiency. Hussein's policy of maintaining control over the military during war time included placing his clansmen in key security positions, infiltrating the armed forces with Party faithful and intelligence agents, and creating overlapping and parallel military structures (such as the regular military, the Popular Army and Republican Guards). This system hindered military performance, as the officers from various clans and rival military institutions competed with each other on the battlefield, often mistrusted the other and could rarely coordinate their actions on the war front. The various armed units, such as the Republican Guard, the regular Army and the Popular Army often competed for battlefield successes. These arrangements ensured the regime's control over the armed forces, preventing it from launching a coup, but at the same time fostered incompetence on the battlefront due to petty rivalries.

While Hussein gave greater freedoms to the officers from 1984 to 1988, he reverted back to his old habits from 1991 to 2003. The Iraqi leader had molded an over-centralized, highly politicized chain of command structure that reported directly to the Iraqi President. This systematic politicization of the armed forces, led to officers referring all military decisions upwards out of fear of alienating the political center. This system made it easier for him to control and manipulate the armed forces as all military actions had to receive approval from his office. For commanders in the field, this rigid relationship meant that the momentum of operations and taking the initiative on the battlefield often stalled while awaiting orders from the capital. Under such circumstances, they often failed to exploit opportunities during battles and incurred more casualties in the meantime. At the same time, officers often exaggerated their successes on the battlefield and neglected to report their failures. The political subordination of the military resulted in an underlying strain between the commanders and the Iraqi President in this period. The micro-management on the President's part, further communicated to the officers that the Party still did not trust the military out of fear that they would plot a coup during the war. The politicization of the armed forces created a coup-proof system, but not a military that could stand up to the US on two separate occasions.

Assessing the history of the Iraqi military

The upcoming volume by Ibrahim Al-Marashi is based on Iraqi military sources themselves and deals with how the Iraqi military and security services fought in the 1991 and 2003 wars. This history of the Iraqi military was mostly based on secondary sources from scholars and analysts based in the US or Europe. The lessons to be drawn from Iraq's past were sitting in the libraries offering American officials in the Department of Defense,

CPA and all branches of the military a better understanding of the history of the Iraqi military.

As the authors of this volume, we decided to write the first history of the Iraqi military from its inception to its demise to demonstrate that disbanding the military eliminated the longest standing organization in Iraq's history. It was an institution that even preceded the formation of the monarchy. It did not appear that Paul Bremer and other American officials appreciated the history of the Iraqi Army, Air Force or Navy, and thus failed to take into account the deep rooted respect and appreciation that the Iraqi populace felt towards these services over numerous decades. Although certain Iraqis may have been opposed to the government of Saddam Hussein and his internal security services, it did not preclude them from a deep pride in the regular Iraqi Army. Iraqis viewed the regular Iraqi Army as a distinguished institution, a guardian of Iraq and of the Iraqi people.

One of the historical trends outlined in this volume is that Iraq's armed forces have been characterized by parallel militaries or anti-armies, otherwise referred to as dual-militarism or what we have termed "multimilitarism." Appreciation of this fact would seem to have logically led to disbanding the elite praetorian guards responsible for defending the leadership, such as the Republican Guard, the Special Republican Guard or the Fidayin Saddam, as well as the intelligence services affiliated with them such as the Special Security Service, the Baath Military Bureau, Military Intelligence and Military Security. It was primarily these organizations that were responsible for internal repression, such as the Republican Guard who quelled the twin uprisings. Bremer referred to "Saddam's army" but forgot that there was an Iraqi Army that predated the Special Republican Guard and the Fidayin. True, Saddam Hussein tried to transform the Army into his army as all of Iraq's leaders tried to do once they were in power. At the same time officers resisted Hussein leading to several failed coup attempts.

The second historical trend that characterized Iraq's politics and its military was that of patronage networks based on generational, tribal, clan and familial belonging. While most of these patronage networks in the military recruited Sunni Arabs, there were also prominent Shia and Kurds who rose through the ranks. Disbanding "Saddam's army" served as a collective punishment of an entire institution rather than focusing on the key tribal and clan members in the armed forces that were responsible for the military transgressions during the Baathist era.

Finally, the third trend under Saddam Hussein's rule was that the military was subjugated to civilian Baath authority through the infiltration of fear at all levels in the armed forces. In an interview, Colonel Abu Ali described how "at every moment, military commanders expected that a car belonging to the military intelligence (*istikhbarat*) would come to pick them up" (ICG 2003: 11). While the Iraqi Army may have been complicit

in crimes, one also has to take into account that Iraq's soldiers often operated out of fear of what would happen to them or to their families if they
failed to act on orders from the political center. One soldier interviewed in
this study told the authors;

> How could I have possibly refused orders when I knew that it would
> affect the fate of my family back home? It was only when they were
> able to get out of the country [Iraq] that I could desert my unit.

Nevertheless the decision to prosecute the political minders and military
intelligence operatives who were responsible for projecting this fear into
the fighting ranks never materialized. Rather a collective punishment was
enforced affecting the rank and file of the Iraqi armed forces.

By 1935 the Iraqi military crushed the internal rebellions or what the
British termed the "insurgency," meaning that Iraq's first episode of
internal political violence lasted close to fifteen years. Simon wrote, "The
result was an army able to achieve what was unthinkable some years
earlier without the massive help of the RAF and the Levies: the imposition
of the government's dominance over the provinces" (Lukitz 1995: 92).
Based on the past precedent it is conceivable that the post-2003 Iraqi military could attain the strength where it can suppress the insurgencies in
Iraq. However, the tenacity of the insurgency in Iraq post-2003 differed
from that which began in 1920. The insurgency of the 1920s and 1930s
was entirely an Iraqi phenomenon that took place in the rural plains of the
south or the mountains of the north. The insurgency post-2003 was mostly
an urban one with volunteers who are not entirely Iraqi and have no compunction about killing themselves and civilians with them to further their
cause. Combined with a political solution, an expanded Iraqi military with
a vast arsenal at its disposal could crush the insurgency in the long term as
long as disgruntled Iraqi civilians withdraw their support for the insurgents. However, in the 1930s an expanded military did not lead to stability
in Iraq's politics.

Coming back to our cycle, in 1921 the Iraqi Army was established in a
mandate with weak democratic institutions during its first insurgency. The
Iraqi public saw that their destiny was controlled by the British who they
believed sought to exploit its natural resources. As a nationalist backlash,
the public projected its aspirations for complete independence on the
growing Army. In order to achieve this independence, the military revolted
in a series of coups from 1936 to 1941 and ran government affairs, and
discovered that control of the state allowed the Army to strengthen its size,
armaments and rent seeking abilities within the nation. After a humiliating
defeat by the British in 1941, and a lackluster performance in the 1948
Arab–Israeli War, the Army became the government in 1958. Other pan-
Arabist and Baathist officers, jealous of the officers in power, realized that
their ambitions for wealth and power could also be achieved if they

launched a coup in 1963. Officers in the meantime tried to overthrow the Arif military government and failed until 1968, ending the era of contested military regimes, with officers constantly jostling for power through the coup d'état. Only the Baath under Saddam Hussein could end the chaos of constant military turnovers, by personally fostering a totalitarian system that was able to bring stability to civil–military relations. By 1975 Hussein was convinced that he created a coup-proof system preventing the possibility of a military coup, and launched a massive military expansion, engaging the armed forces in wars with Iran, Kuwait, the US and thirty other nations. As the literature on totalitarian states describes how only an external shock can bring about the collapse of such a system, it was the Anglo-American invasion of 2003 that undermined Saddam Hussein's regime. After 2003 the Americans re-established an army in a state with weak democratic institutions during a period of civil internal conflict, and eighty-two years later, the US controlled Iraq's destiny, bringing Iraq "back to the future" in 1921.

Political factions in the "new Iraq" have differing views of the future of Iraq's state. Some factions argue for an Islamic state, some for closer relations with Iran, while others support an Iraq integrated into the Arab world. Some supported a loose federal structure in Iraq while others supported a strong unitary state. The military found itself caught in the middle of the political battles in the 1930s and finally emerged as its referee, and ultimately ruling Iraq more than a decade later. The Iraqi military has the potential of not repeating its mistakes of the past. With American and NATO training, it could emerge as one of the most professional armed forces in the Middle East. It could also emerge as an integrated institution that stresses Iraqi nationalism as opposed to sectarian and ethnic agendas. However, there are no guarantees that the Iraqi military, if it survives as a cohesive body, will not follow the interventionist past of Iraq praetorians.

Appendices

Appendix A

Table A.1 List of selected coups; actual, attempted and alleged

Date	Leaders	Qualifications of the leaders and collaborators	Adversary	Method	Public reaction	Result	Objectives and outcome
Oct. 29, 1936	Bakr Sidqi	Acting Chief of Staff in collaboration with Al-Abali leaders	Constitutional monarchy	Unopposed military action	Passive	Success	Moderate reforms, not achieved Military patronage of civilian government
Aug. 11, 1937	Yamulki	Field officers	Military dictatorship	Assassination and revolt of army units	Passive	Success stability	Restitution of former regime and relative
Dec. 24, 1938	The Seven	Field officers with Nuri Said	Constitutional monarchy	Army alert and threat of action	Passive, unaware of events	Success Said	Appointment of Nuri
Apr. 5, 1939	The Seven	Field officers	Constitutional monarchy	Pressure and threats	Passive, unaware of events	Success	Appointment of Abd Al-Ilah to regency
Feb. 21, 1940	The Four Colonels	General and field officers	Constitutional monarchy and rival group of officers	Split in army and alarm for action	Passive, unaware of events	Success	Government of Nuri Said

Date	Leaders	Participants	Regime	Action	Popular Response	Outcome	Result
Feb. 1, 1941	The Four Colonels	General and field officers connected with the Mufti and Rashid Ali Al-Gaylani	Constitutional monarchy	Threat of army revolt	Passive	Success	New government dependent on military
Apr. 3, 1941	The Four Colonels and Rashid Ali Al-Gaylani	Army commanders and nationalists	Constitutional monarchy	Unopposed military revolt	Passive and favorable	Success	Government of Rashid Ali Al-Gaylani, war and defeat
Jul. 14, 1958	Qasim and Arif	Association of field officers	Constitutional monarchy	Violent military action	Demonstrations and killings	Success	Republic
Mar. 8, 1959	Shawwaf	General and field officers at Mosul	Rule of Qassim and the left	Military revolt aided by UAR	Riots in Mosul	Failure	Union with the UAR
Feb. 8, 1963	Abd Al-Salam Arif	Active and retired field officers and Baathists	Military dictatorship of Qassim	Violent military action	Violent riots	Success	Cooperation of officers and Baath, massacre of Communists
Nov. 13, 1963	Mundhir Wandawi	General and field officers National Guard and radical wing of Baath	Military dictatorship	Military revolt and demonstrations	Demonstrations	Failure	Rule of radical wing of Baath
Nov. 18, 1963	Abd Al-Salam Arif	Top level of military dictatorship	Baath Party and National Guard	Violent military action	Passive	Success	Elimination of political parties, Baath/military dictatorship
Sept. 16, 1965	Arif Abd Al-Razzaq	The Prime Minister and some general officers	Abd Al-Rahman Arif	Military action	Passive	Failure	Overthrow of Arif and union with Egypt
Jun. 30, 1966	Arif Abd Al-Razzaq	General and field officers	Abd Al-Rahman Arif	Military insurrection	Passive	Failure	Repetition of attempted coup of September 1965

continued

Table A.1 Continued

Date	Leaders	Qualifications of the leaders and collaborators	Adversary	Method	Public reaction	Result	Objectives and outcome
Jul. 17, 1968	Hasan Al-Bakr, Nayif Abd Al-Razzaq, Ibrahim Al-Daud	Field officers	Abd Al-Rahman Arif	Military action	Passive	Success	Baath takeover
Jul. 30, 1968	Hasan Al-Bakr Baathists	General and field officers	Nayif Abd Al-Razzaq, Ibrahim Al-Daud	Military action	Passive	Success	Baath consolidation
Jan. 20, 1971	Abd Al-Ghani Al-Rawi, Salih Al-Samarrai	Retired generals	Hasan Al-Bakr/ Baath government	Military action	Passive	Failure	Iranian backed coup, execution of plotters
Jun. 30, 1973	Nadhim Kazzar	General security service	Hasan Al-Bakr/ Baath government	General security revolt	Passive	Failure	Execution of Kazzar, reform of the security apparatus
Jan. 1990		Officers from Jabur tribe	Saddam Hussein government		Passive	Failure	Executions
Jun. 1992	Sabri Mahmud	Officers from the Republican Guard	Saddam Hussein government	Coup plotters intercepted at the Taji base	Passive	Failure	Executions
Sept. 1993	Raji Abbas Al-Takriti	Officers and prominent Takriti family	Saddam Hussein government		Passive	Failure	Executions
Jun. 1995	Muhammad Madhlum Al-Dulaymi	Members and officers of the Dulaymi and other tribes	Saddam Hussein government		Tribal revolts	Failure	Executions, fighting with tribes

Source for years 1936–1966 Be'eri (1970: 246–50), other coups compiled by authors.

Appendix B: Iraqi army units

hadhira	squad
fasil	platoon
ra'il	troop
sariyya	company
fawj	battalion
katiba	battalion
liwa	brigade
firqa	division
faylaq	corps
jahfal	group
jaysh	army

Appendix C: Iraqi military ranks

muhib	field marshal, general of the army
fariq awwal	general
fariq	lieutenant general
liwa	major general
'amid	brigadier general
'aqid	colonel
muqaddam	lieutenant colonel
raid	major
naqib	captain
mulazim awwal	first lieutenant
mulazim	second lieutenant
arif	sergeant
naib	corporal
jundi awwal	private first class
jundi	private

Glossary

Fayaliq Al-'Iqab   Punishment Corps.

Harb Al-Istinzaf   "A war of draining" or war of attrition.

Al-Haris Al-Jumhuri   "Republican Guards," elite combat units.

Intifada   "Uprising," referring to the uprising in 1952 and the twin uprisings that took place in northern and southern Iraq after the 1991 Gulf War.

Al-Istikhbarat   Shorter term usually referring to "Military Intelligence."

Al-Jaysh Al-Aqaidi   "Ideological Army."

Al-Jaysh Al-Sha'bi   "Popular Army."

Jihaz Al-Amn Al-Khas   "Special Security Apparatus."

Mudiriyyat Al-Amn Al-'Amma   "General Security Directorate."

Mudiriyyat Al-Istikhabrat Al-'Askariyya Al-'Amma   "General Military Intelligence Directorate."

Mudiriyyat Al-Tawjih Al-Siyasi   Directorate of Political Guidance.

Mukhabarat   "Intelligence agency" usually referring to the General Intelligence Service.

Peshmerga   From the Kurdish "*pesh*" meaning "towards" and "*merga*" meaning "death." Usually used as a collective term for the militias of the Kurdish parties. Still used to refer to Kurdish members of the post-2003 Iraqi military.

Al-Quwwat Al-Khassa   "The Special Forces."

Qadisiyya   The historic battle where the Arabs defeated the Iranian Sassanid army.

Qadisiyyat Saddam   Euphemistic term for the Iran–Iraq War.

Targhib   "Enticement."

Tarhib   "Intimidation."

Bibliography

Primary sources

Public Record Office, UK

Foreign Office Series FO 371
Foreign Office Series FO 406
Colonial Office Series CO 730
Air Ministry Files Air 23

Published official publications

"Report by His Britannic Majesty's Government on the Administration of Iraq for the period April 1923–December 1924," in R.L. Jarman (ed.) (1992) *Iraq: Administration Reports 1914–1932*, vol. 7, Slough: Archive Editions.

FO 371/8998 "Report by His Majesty's High Commissioner on the finances, administration and condition of the 'Iraq for the period from 1 October 1920 to 31 March 1922," in R.L. Jarman (ed.) (1992) *Iraq: Administration Reports 1914–1932*, vol. 7, Slough: Archive Editions.

FO 371/9004 "Report on Iraq administration, October 1920 to March 1922," in R.L. Jarman (ed.) (1992) *Iraq: Administration Reports 1914–1932*, vol. 7, Slough: Archive Editions.

FO 371/10095 "Report on Iraqi administration, April 1922–March 1923," in R.L. Jarman (ed.) (1992) *Iraq: Administration Reports 1914–1932*, vol. 7, Slough: Archive Editions.

"Report by His Britannic Majesty's Government in the United Kingdom of Great Britain and Northern Ireland to the Council of the League of Nations on the Administration of Iraq for the year 1928," in R.L. Jarman (ed.) (1992) *Iraq: Administration Reports 1914–1932*, vol. 9, Slough: Archive Editions.

"Special Report by His Majesty's Government in the United Kingdom of Great Britain and Northern Ireland to the Council of the League of Nations on the progress of 'Iraq during the period 1920–1931," in R.L. Jarman (ed.) (1992) *Iraq: Administration Reports 1914–1932*, vol. 10, Slough: Archive Editions.

Coalition Provisional Authority, *An Historic Review of CPA Accomplishments*, online, available at : cpa-iraq.org/# (accessed July 6, 2006).

United States Government Accountability Office, "Stabilizing Iraq: DOD cannot ensure that U.S.-funded equipment has reached Iraqi security forces," GAO–07–711, July 2007.

Articles

The Times *(London)*

(1940) "Iraq's doubtful future," September 12: 9.
(1940) "An Iraq crisis: the regent and the army," March 19: 9.
(1952) "Offices burnt in Baghdad riot, new cabinet under army chief," November 24: 6.
(1959) "New division for the Iraqi army," January 7: 9.
(1959) "Arms and the man," May 12: 11.
(1959) "Rearming of Iraq's forces," June 26: 12.
(1963) "Iraq again looks to west for military aid," May 24: 10.
(1969) "Iraq orders Arab guerillas to obey its commands," April 18: 5.
(1970) "Iraq army's uncertain loyalties," September 5: 12.
(1974) "Rebel Kurds faced by three army divisions," March 19: 7.
(1978) "Communists 'executed' by Iraqi Baathists," June 1: 6.

Other newspapers and periodicals

Fallows, J. (2005) "Why Iraq has no army," *Atlantic Monthly*, 296: December: 60–77.
Fineman, M, Vieth, W. and Wright, R. (2003) "Dissolving Iraqi army seen by many as costly move," *Los Angeles Times*, August 24: 1.
Gordon, M.R. (2006) "Bush adviser's memo cites doubts about Iraqi leader," *New York Times*, November 29: 1.
Hirst, D. (1971) "The terror from Tikrit," *Guardian*, November 26: 15.
Peretz, M. (2004) "History lesson: what we should have known," *New Republic*, 230: June 28: 25.
Zangana, H. (2004) "Iraqis have lived this lie before: the British transfer of sovereignty in the 20s was equally meaningless," *Guardian*, June 29: 20.
(1963) "First Proclamation," *Iraq*, 1: May: 1.
(1978) "Popular Army: its role in defending revolution," *Iraq Today*, 3: January 16–31: 4.
(2007) "Future Iraqi Air Force pilot studies in the United States," *Advisor*, July 7: 10.

Open Source Center (OSC) documents

(2004) "Iraqi writer ridicules decision to train Iraqi officers in Jordan," OSC Document GMP20040106000180, *Al-Ittijah al-Akhar*, January 3: 5.
(2004) "Party leaders hail Iraqi army day, call for exploiting ex-officers' experience," OSC Document GMP20040111000022, *Al-Manar*, January 6: 1, 4.
(2004) "New Iraqi army chief of staff on army divisions, training plans, US role," OSC Document GMP20040602000155, *Al-Dustur*, May 30: 1.
(2004) "Al-Sharqiyah talk show views NATO training of Iraqi army," OSC Document GMP20040710000168, *Al-Sharqiyya*, July 10.
(2004) "Report criticizes regulations of Iraqi Civil Defense Corps," OSC Document GMP20040829000084, *Al-Basa'ir*, August 26: 5.

(2004) "Defense ministry invites former officers to join new Iraqi army," OSC Document GMP20041005000132, *Al-Sharqiyya*, October 5.

(2005) "Iraqi prime minister Allawi addresses ceremony marking army day," OSC Document GMP20050125000041, *Al-Sabah al-Jadid*, January 8: 4.

(2005) "Iraqi Muslim scholars leader laments dissolution of Iraqi army on anniversary," OSC Document GMP20050113000243, *Al-Basa'ir*, January 12: 12.

(2005) "Al-Sha'lan on election security plan, ministry achievements, army pay raise," OSC Document GMP20050125000068, *Al-Sharqiyya*, January 25.

(2005) "Iraqi Sunni cleric interviewed on Iraq situation, constitution; opposes federalism," OSC Document GMP20050825538007, *Al-Ra'y*, August 25: 5.

(2005) "Iraqi figure says call on former officers to join army 'not serious,'" OSC Document GMP20051102537001, *Al-Jazira*, November 2.

(2005) "Iraq's Allawi addresses former Iraqi army officers, urges them to 'work' for Iraq," OSC Document GMP20051201540002, *Al-Sharqiyya*, December 1.

(2005) "Iraqi defense ministry reports rise in 'terrorist' operations after elections," OSC Document GMP20051227574003, *Al-Sharqiyya*, December 27.

(2006) "Iraqi soldiers protest against placement outside hometowns," OSC Document GMP20060501543002, *Al-Sharqiyya*, May 1.

(2006) "Iraqi speaker airs views on domestic security, US withdrawal, regional issues," OSC Document GMP20060814621002, *Al-Zaman*, August 13: 5.

(2007) "Iraq Al-Maliki speech to army commanders reported; political, security update," OSC Document GMP20070606634002, *Al-Iraqiyya*, June 6.

Books and journal articles (Arabic and English)

Abbas, A. (1989) "The Iraqi armed forces: past and present," in Committee Against Repression and for Democratic Rights in Iraq (ed.) *Saddam's Iraq: revolution or reaction?*, London: Zed Books: 203–28.

Abdulghani, J.M. (1984) *Iraq and Iran: the years of crisis*, London: Croom Helm.

Al-Arif, I. (1982) *Iraq Reborn: a firsthand account of the July 1958 revolution and after*, New York: Vantage Press.

Al-Hassani, A. (1940) *Tarikh al-Wizarat al-'Iraqiyya* [History of Iraqi Cabinets], vol. 3, Sayda, Lebanon: Matba'at al-'Irfan.

Al-Khafaji, I. (1988) "Iraq's seventh year: Saddam's quart d'huere', *Middle East Report*, 151: 35–9.

—— (2000) "War as a vehicle for the rise and demise of a state-controlled society: the case of Ba'thist Iraq," in S. Heydemann (ed.) *War, Institutions and Social Change in the Middle East*, Berkeley CA: University of California Press: 258–91.

Al-Marashi, I. (2002) "Iraq's security and intelligence network: a guide and analysis," *Middle East Review of International Affairs*, 6: 1–13.

—— (2003a) "The clan, tribal and family network of Saddam's intelligence apparatus," *International Journal of Intelligence and Counter Intelligence*, 16: 202–11.

—— (2003b) "The struggle for Iraq: understanding the defense strategy of Saddam Hussein," *Middle East Review of International Affairs*, 7: 1–10.

—— (2003c) "The mindset of Iraq's security apparatus," *Journal of Intelligence and National Security*, 18: 1–23.

—— (2003d) "Saddam's security apparatus during the invasion of Kuwait and the Kuwaiti resistance," *Journal of Intelligence History*, 4: 61–86.

—— (2006) "Iraq's 'cyber insurgency': the internet and the Iraqi resistance," in R. Berenger (ed.) *Cybermedia Go to War: role of non-traditional media in the 2003 Iraq war*, Spokane WA: Marquette Books: 213–31.

—— (2007) "The dynamics of Iraq's media: ethno-sectarian violence, political Islam, public advocacy, and globalization," in M. Price, D. Griffin and I. Al-Marashi (eds.) *Toward an Understanding of Media Policy and Media Systems in Iraq, Center for Global Communication Studies Occasional Paper no. 1*, Philadelphia: University of Pennsylvania: 67–101.

Al-Musawi, M. (2006) *Reading Iraq: culture and power in conflict*, London: I.B. Tauris.

Al-Qazzaz, A. (1985) "The changing patterns of the politics of the Iraqi army," in M. Janowitz and J. Van Doorn (eds.) *On Military Intervention*, Hants: Gower Publishing: 336–59.

Al-Sabbagh, Salah Al-Din (1956) *Fursan al-'Urubah fil-'Iraq* [The Knights of Arabism in Iraq], Damascus: n.p.

Al-Samir, F. (1981) "The role of the army in the national in the social and political development of Iraq," in C. Heller (ed.) *The Military as an Agent of Social Change*, Mexico DF: El Colegio De Mexico: 107–26.

Altinay, A.G. (2004) *The Myth of Military Nation: militarism, gender, and education in Turkey*, New York: Palgrave MacMillan.

Axelgard, F.W. (1988) *A New Iraq? the Gulf War and implications for U.S. policy*, New York: Praeger.

Baram, A. (1989) "The ruling political elite in Bathi Iraq, 1968–1986: the changing features of a collective profile," *International Journal of Middle East Studies*, 21: 447–93.

—— (1991) *Culture, History and Ideology in the Formation of Ba'thist Iraq, 1968–89*, London: MacMillan.

—— (1994) "Calculation and miscalculation in Baghdad," in A. Danchev and D. Keohane (eds.) *International Perspectives on the Gulf Conflict, 1990–91*, New York: Palgrave MacMillan: 23–52.

—— (1997) "Neo-tribalism in Iraq: Saddam Husayn's tribal policies: 1991–96," *International Journal of Middle East Studies*, 29: 1–31.

—— (1998) *Building towards Crisis: Saddam Hussein's strategy for survival*, Washington: Washington Institute for Near East Policy.

—— (2002) "Saddam Husayn, the Ba'th regime and the Iraqi officer corps," in B. Rubin and T. Keaney (eds.) *Armed Forces in the Middle East*, London: Frank Cass: 206–30.

—— (2003) "Saddam's power structure: the Tikritis before, during and after the war," in T. Dodge and S. Simon (eds.) *Iraq at the Crossroads: state and society in the shadow of regime change*, Oxford: Oxford University Press: 93–113.

Batatu, H. (1979) *The Old Social Classes and the Revolutionary Movements of Iraq: a study of Iraq's old landed and commercial classes and of its communists Baathists and free officers*, Princeton NJ: Princeton University Press.

—— (1982) "Iraq's underground Shi'i movements," *Middle East Report*, 102: 3–9.

Be'eri, E. (1970) *Army Officers in Arab Politics and Society*, London: Pall Mall Press.

Bengio, O. (1987) "Iraq," in A. Ayalon, B. Newson, I. Rabinovich and H. Shaked (eds.) *Middle East Contemporary Survey: 1985*, Boulder CO: Westview: 423–59.

—— (1997) "Iraq," in A. Ayalon, A. Liftman and B. Maddy-Weitzman (eds.) *Middle East Contemporary Survey, 1994*, Boulder CO: Westview: 320–68.

—— (1998) *Saddam's Word: political discourse in Iraq*, Oxford: Oxford University Press.

Berlin, I. (1972) "The bent twig: a note on nationalism," *Foreign Affairs*, 51: 11–30.

Bond, B. (1998) *The Pursuit of Victory: from Napoleon to Saddam Hussein*, Oxford: Clarendon.

Bourdillon, B.H. (1924) "The political situation in Iraq," *Journal of The British Institute of International Affairs*, 3: 273–87.

Bremer, L.P. (2006) *My Year in Iraq: the struggle to build a future of hope*, New York: Simon and Schuster.

Bulloch, J. and Morris, H. (1991) *Saddam's War: the origins of the Kuwait conflict and the international response*, London: Faber and Faber.

Chubin, S. and Tripp, C. (1988) *Iran and Iraq at War*, Boulder CO: Westview.

Cigar, N. (1992) "Iraq's strategic mindset and the Gulf War: blueprint for defeat," *Journal of Strategic Studies*, 15: 1–29.

—— (2004) *Saddam Husayn's Road to War: risk assessment, decisionmaking, and leadership in an authoritarian system*, Quantico VA: Marine Corps University Foundation.

Cleveland, W. L. (1971) *The Making of an Arab Nationalist: Ottomanism and Arabism in the life and thought of Sati' al-Husri*, Princeton NJ: Princeton University Press.

Cordesman, A.H. (1999) *Iraq and the War of Sanctions: conventional threats and weapons of mass destruction*, Westport CT: Praeger.

—— (2003) *The Iraq War: strategy, tactics, and military lessons*, Washington DC: Center for Strategic and International Studies Press.

—— (2006a) *Iraq Security Forces: a strategy for success*, Westport CT: Praeger.

—— (2006b) *Iraqi Force Development and the Challenge of Civil War*, Washington DC: Center for Strategic and International Studies.

—— and Hashim, A.S. (1997) *Iraq: sanctions and beyond*, Boulder CO: Westview.

—— and Wagner, A.R. (1990) *The Lessons of Modern War Volume II: the Iran-Iraq war*, Boulder CO: Westview.

Curtis, M. (2006) *Introduction to Comparative Government*, New York: Pearson Longman.

Dannreuther, R. (1992) *The Gulf Conflict: a political and strategic analysis*, London: International Institute for Strategic Studies.

Davis, E. (2005a) *Memories of State: politics, history and collective identity in modern Iraq*, Berkeley CA: University of California Press.

—— (2005b) "History matters: past as prologue in building democracy in Iraq," *Orbis*, 49: 229–44.

Dawisha, A. (1986) "The politics of war: presidential centrality, party power, political opposition," in F. Axelgard (ed.) *Iraq in Transition: a political, economic and strategic perspective*, Boulder CO: Westview: 21–32.

Dawood, H. (2003) "The 'state-ization' of the tribes and the tribalization of the state: the case of Iraq," in F.A. Jabar and H. Dawod (eds.) *Tribes and Power: nationalism and ethnicity in the Middle East*, London: Saqi: 110–35.

De Gaury, G. (1961) *Three Kings in Baghdad, 1921–1958*, London: Hutchinson.

Deringil, S. (1990) "The struggle against Shiism in Hamidian Iraq: a study in Ottoman counter propaganda," *Die Welt des Islams*, 30: 45–62.

Dodge, T. (2003a) *Inventing Iraq: the failure of nation building and a history denied*, London: Hurst and Company.

—— (2003b) "Cake walk, coup or urban warfare: the battle for Iraq," in T. Dodge and S. Simon (eds.) *Iraq at the Crossroads: state and society in the shadow of regime change*, Oxford: Oxford University Press: 59–76.

—— (2005) *Iraq's Future: the aftermath of regime change*, London: Routledge.

Durra, M. (1969) *Al-Harb Al-'Iraqiyya al-Britaniyya* [The Iraqi–British War], Beirut: Dar Al-Tali'a.

Eisenstadt, M. (1993) *Like a Phoenix from the Ashes: the future of Iraqi military power*, Washington DC: Washington Institute for Near East Policy.

Eppel, M. (1988) "The Hikmat Sulayman–Bakr Sidqi government in Iraq, 1936–37, and the Palestine Question," *Middle Eastern Studies*, 24: 25–41.

Facey, W. and Shawkat, N.F. (eds.) (2003) *A Soldier's Story: from Ottoman rule to independent Iraq, the memoirs of Jafar Pasha Al-Askari*, London: Arabian Publishing.

Farouk-Sluglett, M. and Sluglett, P. (1987) *Iraq since 1958: from dictatorship to revolution*, London and New York: I.B. Taurus.

—— (1990) "Iraq since 1986: the strengthening of Saddam," *Middle East Report*, 167: 19–24.

Farouk-Sluglett, M., Sluglett, P. and Stork, J. (1984) "Not quite armageddon: impact of the war on Iraq," *Middle East Report*, 125/126: 22–30.

Finer, S.E (1962) *The Man on Horseback: the role of the military in politics*, London: Pall Mall Press.

Freedman, L. and Karsh, E. (1993) *The Gulf Conflict, 1990–1991: diplomacy and war in the new world order*, Princeton NJ: Princeton University Press.

Furtig, H. (2000) "Iraq as a Golem: identity crises of a western creation', in K. Hafez (ed.) *Islamic World and the West: an introduction to political cultures and international relations*, Leiden: Brill: 204–16.

Galvani, J. (1972) "The Baathi revolution in Iraq," *Middle East Reports*, 12: 3–22.

Gause, G.F. (2002) "Iraq's decision to go to war, 1980 and 1990," *Middle East Journal*, 56: 47–70.

Ghareeb, E. (1982) *The Kurdish Question in Iraq*, Syracuse NY: Syracuse University Press.

Glad, B. (1993) "Figuring out Saddam Hussein," in M.L. Whicker, J.P. Pfifner and R.A. Moore (eds.) *The Presidency and the Persian Gulf war*, Westport CT: Praeger: 80–92.

Gongora, T. (1997) "War making and state power in the contemporary Middle East," *International Journal of Middle East Studies*, 29: 323–40.

Gordon M.R. and Trainor, B.E. (1995) *The Generals' War: the inside story of the conflict in the Gulf*, New York: Back Bay.

Haddad, G. (1971) *Revolutions and Military Rule in the Middle East: the Arab states*, New York: Robert Speller and Sons.

Hale, W. (1994) *Turkish Politics and the Military*, London: Routledge.

Hashim, A. (2003a) "Military power and state formation in modern Iraq," *Middle East Policy*, 10: 29–47.

—— (2003b) "Saddam Husayn and civil-military relations in Iraq: the quest for legitimacy and power," *Middle East Journal*, 57: 9–41.

—— (2006) *Insurgency and Counter-Insurgency in Iraq*, Ithaca, NY: Cornell University Press.

Hawkins, W.R. (2003) "Iraq: heavy forces and decisive warfare," *Parameters*, 33: 61–7.

Heller, M. (1977) "Politics and the military in Iraq and Jordan, 1920–1958: the British influence," *Armed Forces and Society*, 4: 75–97.

—— (1994) "Iraq's army: military weakness, political utility," in A. Baram and B. Rubin (eds.) *Iraq's Road to War*, New York: St. Martins Press: 37–50.

Helms, C.M. (1984) *Iraq: eastern flank of the Arab world*, Washington DC: Brookings Institution.

Hemphill, P. (1979) "The formation of the Iraqi army, 1921–33," in A. Kelidar (ed.) *The Integration of Modern Iraq*, New York: St. Martins Press: 88–110.

High Committee for the Celebrations of the 14th of July (1961) *The Iraqi Revolution in its Third Year*, Baghdad: Ministry of Guidance.

Hiro, D. (1992) *The Longest War: the Iran–Iraq military conflict*, New York: Routledge.

—— (2001) *Neighbors, Not Friends: Iraq and Iran after the Gulf wars*, London: Routledge.

Holmes, R. (2004) *Acts of War: the behaviour of men in battle*, London: Cassell.

Huggins, W.D. (1994) "The Republican Guards and Saddam Hussein's transformation of the Iraqi army," *Arab Studies Journal*, 2: 31–5.

Huntington, S.P. (1968) *Political Order in Changing Societies*, New Haven CT: Yale University Press.

Hurewitz, J.C. (1982) *Middle East Politics: the military dimension*, Boulder CO: Westview.

International Crisis Group (2003) "Iraq: building a new security structure," *Middle East Report*, 20: 1–34.

Iraqi Army Training Command (1985) *Ri'asat Arkan al-Jaish Mudiriyyat al-Tatwir al-Qitali, Dalil: Idarat al-Wihdah fi al-Selim* [Iraqi Army Traning Command, Manual: proper unit management, 2nd edn.], Baghdad: Military Press, March.

Jabar, F.A. (1991) "Roots of an adventure – the invasion of Kuwait: Iraqi political dynamics," in V. Brittain (ed.) *The Gulf Between Us: the Gulf War and beyond*, London: Virago: 27–41.

—— (1994) "Why the Intifada failed," in F. Hazelton (ed.) *Iraq since the Gulf War: prospects for democracy*, London: Zed Books: 97–117.

—— (2003a) "The Iraqi army and anti-army: some reflections on the role of the military," in T. Dodge and S. Simon (eds.) *Iraq at the Crossroads: state and society in the shadow of regime change*, Oxford: Oxford University Press: 115–30.

—— (2003b) "Sheikhs and ideologues: deconstruction and reconstruction of tribes under patrimonial totalitarianism in Iraq, 1968–1998," in F.A. Jabar and H. Dawod (eds.) *Tribes and Power: nationalism and ethnicity in the Middle East*, London: Saqi: 69–109.

—— (2004) "The war generation in Iraq: a case of failed etatist nationalism," in L.G. Potter (ed.) *Iran, Iraq, and the Legacies of War*, Gordonsville VA: Palgrave Macmillan: 121–50.

Janowitz, M. (1965) *The Military in the Political Development of New Nations*, Chicago: University of Chicago Press.

—— (1977) *Military Institutions and Coercion in the Developing Nations*, Chicago: University of Chicago Press.

Jawdat, A. (1976) *Dhikriyat 'Ali Jawdat 1900–1958* [The Memoirs of Ali Jawdat, 1900–1958], Beirut: Mataba'at al-Wafa.

Kamrava, M. (2000) "Military professionalism and civil–military relations in the Middle East," *Political Science Quarterly*, 115: 67–92.

Karsh, E. (1988) "Military power and foreign policy goals: the Iran–Iraq war revisited," *International Affairs*, 64: 83–95.

—— and Rautsi, I. (1991) *Saddam Hussein: a political biography*, New York: Macmillan.

Kedourie, E. (1970) *The Chatham House Version and Other Middle Eastern Studies*, London: Frank Cass.

Keegan, J. (2004) *The Iraq War*, London: Hutchinson.

Kelidar, A. (1975) *Iraq: The Search for Stability*, London: Institute for the Study of Conflict.

Khadduri, M. (1960) *Independent Iraq, 1932–1958*, 2nd edn., London: Oxford University Press.

—— (1963) "The role of the military in Iraqi society," in S. Fisher (ed.) *The Military in the Middle East: problems in society and government*, Columbus OH: Ohio State University: 41–51.

—— (1969a) *Republican Iraq*, Oxford: Oxford University Press.

—— (1969b), "Iraq, 1958 and 1963," in W. Andrews and U. Ra'anan (eds.) *The Politics of the Coup d'Etat: five case studies*, New York: Van Nostrand Reinhold Company: 65–88.

—— (1978) *Socialist Iraq: a study in Iraqi politics since 1968*, Washington DC: Middle East Institute.

Khuri, F.I. (1982) "The study of civil–military relations in modernizing societies in the Middle East: a critical assessment," in R. Kolkowicz and A. Korbonski (eds.) *Soldiers, Peasants, and Bureaucrats: civil–military relations in communist and modernizing societies*, London: George Allen & Unwin: 9–27.

Langley, M. (1936) "Iraq and her problems," *Contemporary Review*, 149: 52–60.

Lenczowski, G. (1965) "Iraq: seven years of revolution," *Current History*, 48: 281–9.

—— (1966) "Radical regimes in Egypt, Syria, and Iraq: some comparative observations on ideologies and practices," *Journal of Politics*, 28: 29–56.

Litvak, M. (1992) "Iraq," in A. Ayalon (ed.) *Middle East Contemporary Survey, 1991*, Boulder CO: Westview: 416–44.

Long, J.M. (2004) *Saddam's War of Words: politics, religion and the Iraqi invasion of Kuwait*, Austin TX: University of Texas Press.

Longrigg, S.H. (1953) *Iraq, 1900 to 1950: a political, social, and economic history*, London: Oxford University Press.

Lukitz, L. (1995) *Iraq: the search for national identity*, London: Frank Cass.

MacDowall, D. (1996) *A Modern History of the Kurds*, London: I.B. Tauris.

McKnight, S. (1991) "The forgotten war: the Iraqi army and the Iran–Iraq war," *Small Wars and Insurgencies*, 2: 91–102.

Makiya, K. (1998) *The Republic of Fear: the politics of modern Iraq*, Berkeley CA: University of California Press.

Marr, P.A. (1970) "Iraq's leadership dilemma: a study in leadership trends, 1948–1968," *Middle East Journal*, 24: 283–301.

—— (1985) *The Modern History of Iraq*, Boulder CO: Westview.

Matthews, K. (1993) *The Gulf Conflict and International Relations*, London: Routledge.

Mazarr, M.J., Snider, D.M. and Blackwell Jr. J.A. (1993) *Desert Storm: the Gulf War and what we learned*, Boulder CO: Westview.

Mesbahi, M. (1993) "The USSR and the Iran–Iraq War: from Brezhnev to Gorbachev" in F. Rajaee (ed.) *The Iran-Iraq War: the politics of aggression*, Gainesville FL: University Press of Florida: 69–102.

Middle East Research and Information Project (1973) "Iraqi Coup Attempt," *Middle East Reports*, 19: 15–16.

Mohamedou, M. (1998) *Iraq and the Second Gulf War: state building and leadership security*, San Francisco: Austin and Winfeld.

Muhsin, J., Harding G. and Hazelton, F. (1989) "Iraq in the Gulf War," in Committee Against Repression and for Democratic Rights in Iraq (ed.) *Saddam's Iraq: revolution or reaction?*, London: Zed Books: 229–41.

Murray, W. and Scales, R.H. (2003) *The Iraq War: a military history*, Cambridge: Belknap.

Nonneman, G. (2004) "The Gulf States and the Iran–Iraq War: pattern shifts and continuities," in L.G. Potter (ed.) *Iran, Iraq, and the Legacies of War*, Gordonsville VA: Palgrave MacMillan: 121–50.

Nordlinger, E.A. (1977) *Soldiers in Politics, Military Coups and Governments*, Englewood Cliff NJ: Prentice Hall.

O'Ballance, E. (1988) *The Gulf War*, London: Brasseys.

—— (1996) *The Kurdish Struggle, 1920–94*, New York: St. Martins Press.

O'Neil, P. (2004) *Essentials of Comparative Politics*, New York: WW Norton & Company.

Parasiliti, A. (2001) "Lessons learned: the Iraqi military in politics," in J. Kechichian (ed.) *Iran, Iraq, and the Arab Gulf States*, New York: Palgrave: 83–94.

—— and Antoon, S. (2000) "Friends in need, foes to heed: the Iraqi military in politics," *Middle East Policy*, 8: 131–40.

Pellitiere, S.C. (1992) *The Iran-Iraq War: chaos in a vacuum*, New York: Praeger.

—— and Douglas, D. (1990) *Lessons Learned: Iran-Iraq war*, Washington DC: United States Government Printing.

Perlmutter, A. (1977) *The Military and Politics in Modern Times: on professionals, praetorians, and revolutionary soldiers*, New Haven CT: Yale University Press.

Pollack, K. (2002) *Arabs at War: military effectiveness, 1948–1991*, Lincoln NE: University of Nebraska Press.

Quinlivan, J. (1999) "Coupproofing: its practice and consequences in the Middle East," *International Security*, 24: 131–65.

Ra'iss Tousi, R. (1997) "Containment and animosity: the United States and the war," in F. Rajaee (ed.) *Iranian Perspectives on the Iran–Iraq War*, Gainesville FL: University of Florida: 49–61.

Roberts, A. (1993) "The laws of war in the 1990–91 Gulf conflict," *International Security*, 18: 134–81.

Sajjadpur, K. (1997) "Neutral statements, committed practice: the USSR and the war," in F. Rajaee (ed.) *Iranian Perspectives on the Iran–Iraq War*, Gainesville FL: University of Florida Press: 29–38.

Sakai, K. (2003) "Tribalization as a tool of state control in Iraq: observations on the army, the cabinets and the national assembly," in F.A. Jabar and H. Dawood (eds.) *Tribes and Power: nationalism and ethnicity in the Middle East*, London: Saqi: 136–61.

Salih, K. (1996) *State-Making, Nation-Building and the Military: Iraq, 1941–1958*, Göteborg: Göteborg University Press.

Sariolghalam, M. (1997) "Decision-making inputs: Iraq's premises before the war," in F. Rajaee (ed.) *Iranian Perspectives on the Iran–Iraq War*, Gainesville FL: University of Florida Press: 104–10.

Segal, D. (1988) "The Iran–Iraq war: a military analysis," *Foreign Affairs*, 66: 946–63.

Sharp, J. (2005) "Iraq's new security forces: the challenge of sectarian and ethnic influences," Washington DC: Congressional Research Service.

Shawkat, S. (1939) *Hadhidhi Ahdafuna: Man aman biha fahwa minna* [These are Our Aims: Anyone who Believes in Them is Among Us], Baghdad: Wizarat al-Ma'rif.

Shwadran, B. (1960) *The Power Struggle in Iraq*, New York: Council For Middle Eastern Affairs Press.

Simon, R. (1986) *Iraq between the Wars: the creation and implementation of a nationalist ideology*, New York: Columbia University Press.

Sluglett, P. and Farouk-Sluglett, M. (1978) "Some reflections on the Sunni/Shi'i question in Iraq," *Bulletin of the British Society for Middle Eastern Studies*, 5: 79–87.

Stafford, R.S. (1925) *The Tragedy of the Assyrians*, London: George Allen & Unwin.

Sterner, M. (1984) "The Iran–Iraq war," *Foreign Affairs*, 63: 128–43.

Tarbush, M.A. (1982) *The Role of the Military in Politics: a case study of Iraq to 1941*, London: Kegan Paul International.

Trab-Zemzemi, A. (1986) *The Iran–Iraq War: Islam and nationalisms*, New York: United States Publishing.

Tripp, C. (1993) "Iraq and the War for Kuwait," in J. Gow (ed.) *Iraq, the Gulf Conflict and the World Community*, London: Brasseys.

—— (1996) "Symbol and strategy: Iraq and the war for Kuwait," in W.F. Danspeckgruber and C. Tripp (eds.) *The Iraqi Aggression against Kuwait: strategic lessons and implications for Europe*, Boulder CO: Westview.

—— (2000) *A History of Iraq*, Cambridge: Cambridge University Press.

Troutbeck, J. (1959) "The revolution in Iraq," *Current History*, 36: 81–5.

Wagner, J. (1979) "Iraq," in R. Gabriel (ed.) *Fighting Armies*, Westport CT: Praeger: 64–78.

Watenpaugh, K.D. (2003) "The *guiding principles* and the U.S. 'mandate' for Iraq: 20th century colonialism and America's new empire," *Logos*, 2: 26–37.

Weller, M. (1992) *Iraq and Kuwait: the hostilities and their aftermath*, Cambridge: Cambridge University Press.

Woods, K.M. (2006) *Iraqi Perspectives Project: a view of Operation Iraqi Freedom from Saddam's senior leadership*, Norfolk VA: Joint Center for Operational Analysis.

Workman, T.W. (1994) *The Social Origins of the Iran–Iraq War*, Boulder CO: Lynne Reiner.

Wright, Q. (1926) "The Government in Iraq," *American Political Science Review*, 20: 743–69.

Yaphe, J.S. (2000) "Tribalism in Iraq: the old and the new," *Middle East Policy*, 7: 51–8.

—— (2003) "War and occupation in Iraq: what went right? what could go wrong?" *Middle East Journal*, 57: 381–99.

Yergin, D. (1991) *The Prize: the epic quest for oil, money and power*, New York: Free Press.

Index

Lightning Source UK Ltd.
Milton Keynes UK
29 March 2010

152051UK00001B/41/P